**Entrepreneur** MAGAZINE'S

# ULTIMATE
## GUIDE TO

# eBay
## FOR BUSINESS

- Launch an ecommerce powerhouse with little to no investment while growing a following of delighted customers

- Streamline processes, avoid common mistakes, and establish sustainable, reliable, and profitable product sources

- Scale your way from a small business to global ecommerce success with time-tested, cross-border trading practices

# CHRISTOPHER MATTHEW SPENCER

Entrepreneur Press®

Entrepreneur Press, Publisher
Cover Design: Andrew Welyczko
Production and Composition: Eliot House Productions

This publication is designed to provide accurate and authoritative information in regard to the
subject matter covered. It is sold with the understanding that the publisher is not engaged in
rendering legal, accounting, or other professional services. If legal advice or other expert assistance is
required, the services of a competent professional person should be sought.

Entrepreneur Press® is a registered trademark of Entrepreneur Media, Inc.

**Library of Congress Cataloging-in-Publication Data**
    Names: Spencer, Christopher Matthew, author.
    Title: Ultimate guide to eBay for business / by Christopher Matthew Spencer.
    Description: Irvine, CA : Entrepreneur Press, [2021] | Summary: "A master class on the entire
        process of setting up an eBay store and increasing sales reach for both new and existing
        businesses. Features poven tips and techniques for planning, starting, and executing a
        successful, profitable eBay business"-- Provided by publisher.
    Identifiers: LCCN 2021037923 (print) | LCCN 2021037924 (ebook) | ISBN 978-1-64201-144-9
        (trade paperback) | ISBN 978-1-61308-457-1 (epub)
    Subjects: LCSH: eBay (Firm) | Internet auctions. | Electronic commerce.
    Classification: LCC HF5478 .S644 2021 (print) | LCC HF5478 (ebook) | DDC 658.8/777--dc23
    LC record available at https://lccn.loc.gov/2021037923
    LC ebook record available at https://lccn.loc.gov/2021037924

Printed in the United States of America

25  24  23  22                                                    10 9 8 7 6 5 4 3 2 1

# Contents

# What's Under the Hood?

This book is dedicated to every entrepreneur who has the courage to walk over hot coals, and who's far too committed to notice they did. We live in a time when geography no longer limits our business opportunities—the most exceptional world that has ever existed. eBay has been around just about as long as ecommerce, so they know a thing or two about selling online. My eBay experience dates back to 1999, so I can boast about as many things I've done wrong as I've done right. You don't need this book but you should have it because you'll quickly step over all the puddles that I naively stepped into over the years.

I wrote this book to provide actionable ideas to amplify your success when using eBay as a platform for both product sourcing and selling. Not everyone will be successful in business, but when you follow proven techniques, your probability for success will be nearly certain. Your persistence, patience, and tolerance for risk carry you forward with poise in the business world. While I never endorse get-rich-quick ideas, I am passionately convinced you will grow rich at a steady clip—and I am confident this book will help propel you forward.

This book is my collection of ideas for doing business on eBay and beyond, curated from many very smart people. Every impressive automobile should have a mighty engine under the hood, and this book has all the horsepower you'll need to win the eBay race. This is the *Ultimate Guide to eBay for Business.* Everything you've accomplished thus far in your professional life has made you ready for this. Let's crush it together because the sky is the limit on eBay!

May the odds be ever in your favor!

## THIS BOOK HAS LOTS OF RAM

A reference guide such as this one is intended for flipping. I refer to the content as random access material, or RAM. This buffet of advice works well if read in a linear fashion, but it is equally helpful if you choose to go straight to whichever section you're most interested in. If you love reading books cover to cover, by all means, please do so here. Otherwise, flip to the Contents and explore whatever interests you without regretting skipping over the things you've already mastered.

## WHAT'S IN THIS BOOK

Remember that this is not exclusively a book on how to sell on eBay. This is a business guide to using eBay. In my humble opinion, learning to score great deals when sourcing merchandise has peer importance to learning how to sell. Both are moneymaking business opportunities. Savvy corporate purchasing agents cut costs every day by sourcing on eBay, tradespersons locate scarce parts to repair older equipment, and eBay sellers buy pallets of goods to resell using both eBay and other channels.

Here are the key points of what I'll be discussing:

- An introduction to eBay and all the wonderful things and people that make eBay great!
- The basics of how to use eBay

- How to search eBay like a pro and filter out the clutter so you'll uncover the gem merchandise you're looking for
- Selling essentials that support onboarding as an eBay merchant
- Advanced selling concepts that will substantially enhance your sales results and propel your eBay business forward
- Sourcing and "Power Buyer" tips that are guaranteed to expand your expertise and ensure that all your trades are safe and successful
- All sorts of clever ways to help you sell your stuff with ideas that I've collected along my eBay journey
- Layering in some extra income via the eBay Partner Network, eBay's very own affiliate program
- All sorts of important back-office stuff that will keep you on the right path at work and with the government

## SILLY SUPPOSITIONS

I hate to assume things about you, but I'll make a few silly suppositions, beyond the fact that you'd love to earn enough money on eBay to fill a bank vault. I'm going to assume that you:

- Own a computer
- Have an internet connection
- Have a bank account
- Are proficient with email
- Have a way to capture photos, such as your phone, a tablet, or a camera (Your mobile phone is all you really need to photograph items)
- Have a backdrop or background to place behind your items for photography
- Have good, indirect natural light or lighting equipment

After the sale you'll need a few more tools:

- A cheap flexible tape measure
- Packing supplies, such as boxes, tape, a tape dispenser, bubble wrap, or other packing materials
- A way to print shipping labels, such as an ordinary printer or a dedicated label printer
- A postal-compliant shipping scale with a capacity large enough to weigh your biggest item and the ability to weigh as little as one ounce (I paid less than $20 for mine)

By no means is my list going to predict every possibility. You've probably also been around business long enough to realize that persistence and determination are worth their weight in diamonds. You'll need those, too. Curiosity, passion, and consistency will also help you thrive. If you have those in spades, you will be both successful and triumphant in your eBay business.

# Chapter 1

# Why eBay Is the Most Powerful Global Marketplace

With an incredible array of products from new to nostalgic, eBay offers a robust and delightful marketplace for buyers to source their needs and passions. As of 2020, eBay was the third-largest online marketplace, with 1.6 billion visits per month. In the U.S., it was the second largest, beaten only by Amazon. And, unlike Amazon, it has never competed with its third-party sellers. Consider the broad array of Amazon Basics products sold at lower prices than the third-party vendors can match—because they have to pay seller fees to trade on the site. There is no "eBay Basics" discount product line to seduce price-conscious customers away from eBay marketplace sellers.

Amazon's enormous growth may also have led to staffing challenges. CNBC reporter Eugene Kim identified Amazon marketplace sellers who faced problems trying to reinstate their suspended accounts after Amazon's machine learning system purportedly closed them erroneously. The sellers' attempts were met with "a dark hole of unresponsiveness." It's nice to be the biggest, but there are advantages to being just a little smaller. I've always found eBay approachable, reachable, and responsive.

I also find eBay's culture more handcrafted, personal, and far more fun than other marketplaces I've sold on. While eBay still maintains the garage-sale feel for secondhand goods, new items with a UPC or ISBN bar code are well-organized into structured shopping experiences and presented intuitively so that buyers can easily conduct price comparisons from multiple sellers.

## ONLINE IS THE NEW NORMAL

The SBA maintains oodles of data on the U.S. economy and small businesses comprise 99.9 percent of all American companies, so it's the little guys like you and me who are the economic engine of the country. *eMarketer* tracks U.S. ecommerce spending and to my delight, online shopping reached a record high in 2020, with worldwide retail sales of more than $4 trillion. The record is twofold—ecommerce made up the greatest historical percentage of retail sales as well as the highest gross merchandise volume.

The internet allows brick-and-mortar businesses to enjoy a dramatically expanded customer base that can reach every corner of the globe. Startups can launch online and avoid the headwinds experienced by stores with public front doors. Online retailers rarely offer consumer credit to customers (meaning no write-offs and no bad debts), and they conduct business with far less friction than the stores of yesteryear. Customers enjoy the convenience of online shopping, there are far fewer hassles than brick-and-mortar retailers endure, and opening a business is accomplished with minimal investment. Setup and operational expenses for online sellers are leaner, and rapid growth rarely means an address change. Pick, pack, and ship warehouses permit unlimited expansion for entrepreneurs with zero infrastructure investment when scaling. Digital merchandising is robust and dramatically less expensive than window dressing.

Ecommerce isn't just increasing as a result of the 2020 global pandemic—it's been snowballing for a very long time. Online shopping offers advantages like:

- Greater variety and deeper availability
- Convenient delivery
- Access to hard-to-find goods
- The availability of popular brands while providing emerging brands a level playing field

- A user-friendly experience for anyone regardless of location, mobility, and schedule
- Stores that never close with sales potential around the clock
- The convenience of mobile shopping
- Lower prices as a result of efficiencies and less shrinkage
- AI-powered individualized shopping experiences

For shoppers who love to see the product in person before buying, the browsing experience of a physical shop will always remain attractive, but internet merchants that offer free or liberal returns are slowly beginning to attract those touchy-feely buyers into their orbit. If the shoes don't fit, press one button and return them. The post office even offers free parcel pickup.

I don't give the COVID-19 pandemic all the credit for reshaping people's buying habits, but it did press the gas pedal to the floor, and the inevitable occurred sooner rather than later. According to the U.S. Census Bureau, ecommerce sales grew 13.8 percent year-over-year when comparing the first quarter of 2020 to the first quarter of 2019. Ecommerce sales in the second quarter of 2020 accounted for 14.7 percent of total retail sales, and there is still plenty of room to grow.

This means there is no better time to accelerate sales with eBay than today. If you're worried that you're starting too late and eBay has already matured—nothing could be further from the truth. Online retailing is still growing impressively, and you're seizing this opportunity at the perfect time. If you think of the internet as the auto industry, we are still in the Model T years. There is plenty of business out there for you.

## eBAY'S OFFERINGS FOR BUYERS AND SELLERS

I'll be focusing on the use case for business and breezing past the Pez dispensers, Hummels, and Beanie Babies—even that wonderful old treasure found at last. Sellers (and buyers) of those items have already discovered the joys of eBay. This book is a reference guide for companies that want to use eBay as a serious business tool. While it is certainly not a prerequisite, I recommend expanding your reading list with another book, *Start Your Own eBay Business, 3rd Edition* (Entrepreneur Press, 2020). The *Start Your Own* book is a more freshman view of eBay as opposed to this book, which I consider a master class.

Let's talk candidly about the big players for a moment. Mega retailers aren't going to disappear any time soon. As a clever seller, you'll need to trade the merchandise they don't sell, so you aren't competing against them directly. But there are huge opportunities for everyone (see Figure 1-1 on page 4).

**FIGURE 1–1.** Here are some of the epic sales made on eBay.
Are you green with envy yet? Don't be, just go get 'em!

## AUTHENTICALLY CHANGING

The following is a quote from a recent eBay's *Annual Report*:

> "Our strategy is to drive the best choice, the most relevance, and the most powerful selling platform for our buyers and sellers. We focus on connecting buyers and sellers through simplified experiences to make it easier for users to list, buy, and sell items, and we are working to serve our customers in an authentically eBay way."

I am quite fond of the phrase "authentically eBay." It speaks to how I feel about the eBay community, a tool that was forged with a different kind of metal. Early on, the eBay platform allowed collectibles sellers to command stratospheric prices for very rare items while the value of more common items crashed due to supply substantially exceeding demand. Many of the earliest eBay users transitioned from viewing eBay as a panacea for collectors to a serious business tool. In addition, eBay's business unit of the mid-2000s spent years wooing businesses into the fold.

I speak from firsthand experience when I say that eBay's managers in those early years worked from intuition rather than metrics and analytical data. I'm not judging—I was one of the rainmakers at eBay back then, and hindsight offers 20/20 clarity. But big data decision making and revenue optimization algorithms are now the norm for eBay and its competitors. I have seen a recent uptick in sales conversion rates in my own business—something that had gradually declined over the years. I attribute it to eBay's improved use of data and machine learning tools.

The use case for businesses selling on eBay is very strong, so long as the numbers make sense. Because eBay sellers pay an *insertion fee*, a *final value fee*, and a fee for payment processing, the profit margin must be sufficient to more than cover these expenses, or what's the point? The businesses that trade on eBay can be quite large, such as Adidas and Dell. They sell direct-to-consumer, and they have their own eBay Stores. That said, most business sellers are small—like you and me.

eBay was founded in 1995 and was successful from Day One. It's among the oldest internet businesses. If you have never used the site, you may not immediately understand what loyal eBayers see in it. But after you get a few deals under your belt, both buying and selling, you'll start to get a feel for the unique vibe and camaraderie that eBay brings to the table. There's always someone ready to help, whether it's a kind eBay employee assisting you over the phone or by chat, or a fellow eBayer hanging out on the discussion boards who is ready to lend a hand.

Sellers have the option to select from a variety of listing formats. Hummel dealers agonize over pricing their precious figurines, while a fashionista knows Banana Republic pricing like the back of their hand. Collectibles have uncertain prices, while commodities have predictable values. Selling formats need to accommodate both the type of item a seller is offering and the urgency of the transaction. A rare car warrants a carefully planned auction-style listing, but a buyer of AA batteries needs them as soon as possible, so eBay offers both auction-style and fixed price listings; there are also some special format variants for certain categories. I'll refer to the auction-style listing as simply an *auction* for the remainder of the book. An eBay auction, while less dramatic than a true live auction with its fast-talking auctioneer, offers the same opportunity to generate excitement and heighten buyer interest. An auction can be great for the buyer, the seller, or both, depending on many factors.

Here are a few key points to know about eBay:

- It's a marketplace for buyers and sellers that never competes with its own sellers.
- Buyers shop without fees or subscriptions.

> **TIP**
>
> Here's a trivia tidbit: way back on Labor Day in 1995, 28-year-old Pierre Omidyar launched AuctionWeb, a person-to-person auction site for collectible items, and the site that would eventually be renamed eBay. Electrical engineer Mark Fraser purchased the first item that Omidyar listed for sale on the site: a broken laser pointer.

---

### AUCTION OR FIXED PRICE?

I'm often asked when to use an auction and when to list at a fixed price. Very rare collectibles should always hit the auction block first. However, what about everyday items? My view on this is plastic, and I like to study the numbers, so I searched the word "blouse" on eBay and turned up more than 2 million listings. I discovered that sellers list blouses in the auction format only 3.5 percent of the time. But when I checked the listings that actually converted into sales, 18.8 percent were auctions. The data reinforces that auctions are still a strong tool for sellers of ordinary items.

- Sellers can sell at any time without subscriptions; however, a subscription will extend discounts on selling fees and offer enhanced selling opportunities.
- Sellers are charged an insertion fee for listing and advertising an item and a final value fee when that item sells.
- Every trade on eBay is person-to-person and eBay facilitates the deal.
- Fraud, forgeries, and intellectual property infringement on eBay mirror the internet retail environment in general; however, eBay offers a *Money Back Guarantee* to buyers and *seller protections* to merchants to help boost marketplace confidence.

According to their annual reports, eBay stumbled and saw lower revenue after peaking in 2013. Fortunately, former rock star eBay executive Jamie Iannone returned to the company in 2020 after an absence of more than a decade and now helms the organization as CEO. He and I had the good fortune to interact on business development projects when I served as an eBay University "professor" from 2001 to 2008. Back then, he was an essential asset to eBay, and I am glad he returned. Iannone is among the sharpest tools in the shed. Competitive forces have attenuated eBay's position in the world of ecommerce; I believe the management change will turn the tide moving forward. I am optimistic for eBay's future.

## A CULTURE OF ENTREPRENEURSHIP

Pierre Omidyar, eBay's founder, believes that all people are inherently good and capable, and this belief has shaped the company's culture. Workers at eBay are not merely cubicle jockeys. Its employees trade passionately on the site. Senior product manager Maunish Shah, for instance, is one of the thousands of company executives who is an avid buyer and seller on eBay. In addition to helping eBayers, Shah collects and deals in coins of exceptional rarity and quality. And he's not alone—there's a deeply ingrained culture of entrepreneurship at eBay.

eBay sellers inspire other people to become successful, so the company encourages their employees to become sellers, too. A remarkable energy is unleashed when eBay merchants put their heads together to share ideas. Entrepreneurs admire other entrepreneurs, so even fierce competitors love to get together for a spirited debate over business practices or to boast about their latest achievements.

Sellers on eBay are a community of learners, and the site offers the opportunity boost that they need. eBay is not particularly simple, but it's not overly complicated either—it's somewhere in between. You don't need to understand high-tech mumbo-jumbo to thrive on the site. There are no lines of code to learn. You don't even need to lay out any additional money to start selling on eBay, because it offers all sellers a nice handful of zero insertion fee listings each month. This allows anyone in the embryonic stage of ecommerce to gain an immediate benefit from the eBay audition process. And you can head out for a vacation, family emergency, or just take a quick break at any time. Your eBay business will still be there when you get back.

## eBAY INVESTS FOR THE FUTURE

Like all technology companies, eBay has made a substantial investment in equipment and code, but it also invests tremendously in people. That's essential because it's driven by the energy of human beings. High-tech tools facilitate success, but the buyers and sellers remain the bedrock that keeps eBay going. The site is constantly taking measures to improve conditions for buyers, sellers, and their own workers.

Buyers enjoy a faster, smoother, and more entertaining shopping experience than in the past and have access to more payment methods, increasing interest in and adoption of the shopping experience. They can buy from multiple sellers or combine items from the same seller and check out in a single, convenient step. While the auction experience offers a fun, nostalgic format for die-hard eBayers, the site continues to build on its product catalog, offering a simplified buying experience with greater price transparency. It has reduced focus on third-party ads that tend to draw customers off the site and expanded its *Promoted Listing* program. These are eBay marketplace ads, paid for by sellers, that are conducive to growth in the core marketplace. Buyers see more relevant advertising and less visual distraction.

Customer support for both buyers and sellers is faster and nimbler than ever before, engaging users by intuitive AI chat, live chat, inbound and outbound call center support, and email. Response times are snappy.

Meanwhile, top sellers are rewarded for their loyalty with discounts, freebies, and favorable listing placement. Exceptional eBay sellers qualify for the *Top Rated Seller* program. Because eBay only succeeds when its sellers do, it continuously invests in programs and tools to expand the seller environment. Listing on eBay is easier than ever with a more intuitive selling form, and the site allows sellers to list up to 200 items for free each month—paying only when those items sell. Moreover, because eBay is one of the largest online marketplaces, quality and in-demand merchandise will certainly sell.

The company also takes good care of its workers; its equity incentive plan grants performance-based restricted stock units, stock payment awards, and performance share units to its management and employees. And in turn, eBay's workers take great care of the company and its customers.

## BUYER AND SELLER PROTECTIONS

Even though all goods are sold by individual sellers who operate their own businesses, the eBay marketplace is no Wild West of ecommerce. There are protections for both sides of each transaction. The site builds buyer trust by offering a Money Back Guarantee, which allows buyers to get their money back when they receive damaged or faulty goods, or when the order never arrives. The *eBay Authenticate* service further enhances buyer confidence by allowing sellers to have high-end handbags, jewelry, and luxury timepieces authenticated. In fact, all timepieces sold on eBay for $2,000 or more must now be shipped to an eBay authenticator for inspection before being delivered to the new owner.

Most people use seller ratings and product reviews when shopping online, and eBay is no different. Buyers recognize reputable eBay sellers by looking at the number of products they've sold, their feedback score, and their seller rating. eBay uses star icons to denote feedback scores. *Detailed seller ratings (DSR)* offer prospective buyers insights left by former customers into key seller metrics, such as item description, seller communication, shipping time, and shipping and handling charges. The eBay marketplace is generally self-regulating, but when a situation does go off the rails, eBay will moderate the dispute through the *Resolution Center*.

Sellers are well protected, too. When an item is returned used or damaged, or if a buyer demands something that wasn't offered, eBay will step in; they can also assist in nearly any other issue that may arise. Of course, eBay wants buyers to have an exceptional experience, but the company is looking out for the sellers too because they are equally as important to the health of the eBay marketplace.

# Chapter 2

# The Essentials of eBay Trading

I f you're one of those business owners who delegates everything, I'd recommend handing this book to your company's ecommerce manager. This guide works best if you actually put your hands on the product—in this case, eBay. While anyone can buy and sell on eBay with relative ease, even if you eventually delegate the work (and I do), you'll want a front-row seat at the start of this show. You'll be in great company—with 187 million active buyers and 20 million sellers around the world.

As far as technology goes, you'll need more than your phone. Running a serious eBay enterprise will require a nice, big computer screen, a generous amount of memory, a fair amount of hard disk space for all your photos, a printer for shipping labels, and a snappy internet connection.

You'll want the fastest internet connection you can reasonably afford, but connections that are great for streaming and downloading content aren't always as fast when uploading pictures onto an ecommerce site such as eBay. You need to make sure that your upload speed is fast. Fiber-optic networks offer synchronous, or symmetric, internet connections (meaning they have the same upload and download speeds) as part of Dedicated Internet Access (DIA) circuits. Most of us can only get DSL, wifi, or cable modems, which are asynchronous or asymmetric connections, where the download speed is usually much faster than the upload speed. Try typing "speed test" into Google and run a test on your connection (see Figure 2-1 below). Hopefully everyone will soon have access to much faster synchronous fiber-optic connections as internet service providers (ISPs) upgrade their networks.

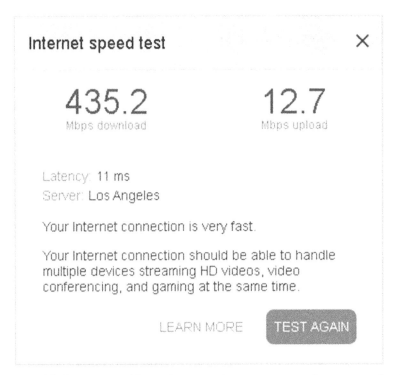

**FIGURE 2-1.** My Spectrum cable modem asynchronous connection test results. Note that the download speed is more than 34 times faster than the upload speed.

## IT'S TIME FOR ASSIMILATION

Yes, it's time to be absorbed into the Google collective. I'm a big fan of using Google products to operate my eBay business. Gmail is an incredible productivity tool that comes with a collection of products, and I use them every day in my eBay business. In addition to email, a Google account comes with a free calendar app, Google Drive cloud file storage, Google Meet videoconferencing, Google Photos cloud storage, and an expanding list of other free products to help a business. While most of Google's cool stuff is free to use, if you prefer to have everything branded and ad-free, Google Workspace adds enterprise features such as additional tools for admins, branded email (yourname@yourdomain.com), and 24/7 support for a nominal fee.

If you're already married to another company's email and cloud services platform, consider getting a divorce and falling in love all over again with Google. I have yet to find a better provider. Ignore the panic peddlers that claim leaving your current email provider for Gmail will result in losing everything in your inbox—that's never been true. Google provides email migration guides, or you can learn from watching a good video on YouTube. So when you switch to Google, you can bring all your emails with you.

While I'm on the subject of Google, I'd encourage you to use Google's free Chrome browser as well. Figure 2–2 on page 14 shows the spooky fall version of eBay's homepage as viewed in Chrome. Chrome is super-fast, highly capable, and it integrates with your login to synchronize settings, passwords, and bookmarks. This is essential when working on multiple devices. To find out more about Google apps, go to https://www.Google.com and click on the nine-dots icon in the top-right corner of the page.

## EXPLORING eBAY'S HOMEPAGE: THE NEVER-ENDING JOURNEY

Before you begin selling on eBay, you should check out the buying experience. This serves the dual purpose of putting yourself in the shoes of your future customers and building your eBay reputation. Every eBayer relies on their feedback score to build trust within the eBay community, and buying and selling both help build that score. It's easier to sell when a potential buyer believes that you'll complete the transaction reliably, and a solid feedback profile is a little like an eBay credit score that signals you're a great person to trade with.

Your eBay journey starts at the homepage seen in Figure 2–2 on page 14. When you start getting more familiar with the site, you'll notice that the homepage is a chameleon that changes constantly—predicting and promoting what's hot according to customer trends and the global retail calendar. But there's a method to eBay's madness, and by this point they have many years of experience building and sustaining strong retail excitement.

While the basic structure of eBay's homepage remains predictable, what's displayed changes every day. When you sign into eBay with your user ID, the homepage adapts

**FIGURE 2-2.** eBay's homepage displayed in the Google Chrome browser.

based on your preferences and actions that you've taken in the past. Take a closer look at Figure 2–2 on page 14 and you'll notice these sections:

- A top menu for accessing your account, help, and selling and buying links (you'll be using the My eBay link a lot)
- A search box that says "Search for anything"
- A list of links to popular eBay categories, along with a pull-down menu that includes all the categories
- Sections promoting seasonal and popular items
- A bottom menu that allows access to every corner of the site

## Top Menu

The top menu looks simple, but it offers access to most of the key features you'll be using on eBay. Once you create an account, you'll need to sign in before you can use many of eBay's features, such as account details, buying, watching, selling, managing activities, viewing notifications, and accessing your shopping cart. Here are some of the links you'll find up top:

- *Account.* When you're signed in, hovering over this link (which appears on the page as "Hi [Name]!") reveals further links to your user and feedback profiles, account settings, and the sign-out link.
- *Daily Deals.* This tempts you with spotlight and featured deals, trending products, sales, and special events—with category links to uncover promotions by product type.
- *Brand Outlet.* Discover retail trends and the latest styles and brands you love—all at a discount (hence "outlet").
- *Help & Contact.* This is your gateway to a library of help pages that you can search by keyword or browse. If you have a free eBay account, you can chat with its automated assistant or a live person. If you have an eBay Store, you'll see expanded options to call live support or have them call you. There's even an email option. These features aren't always available, and eBay gives priority to its Store subscribers.
- *Sell.* This sends you straight to where all the selling action is. From here, you'll find what you need to create and manage your eBay listings.
- *Watchlist.* For power buyers, every eBay listing has a button that lets you add the item to your *Watchlist.* I've provided an example in Figure 2–3 on page 16. This link takes you to the list of items you're currently watching.
- *My eBay.* What is *My eBay*? Access to everything! Well, almost everything. By hovering over My eBay, you'll see the following links:
  - *Summary.* Just what it says—a summary and a handy reminder of your eBay activities.

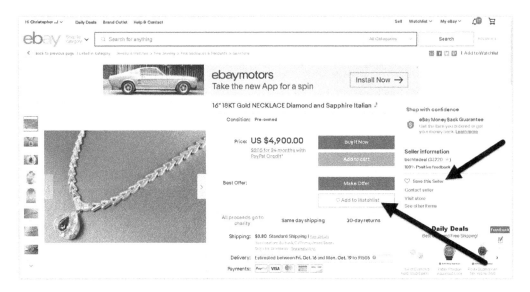

**FIGURE 2–3.** Here's an item listing page showing the Save This Seller link (top arrow) and Add to Watchlist button (bottom arrow).

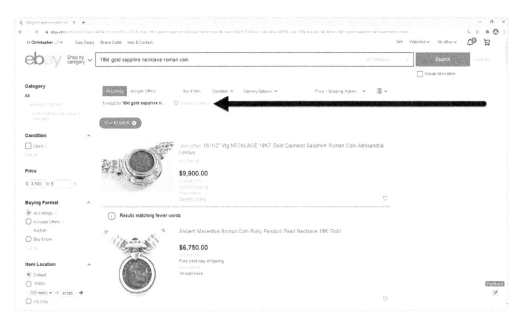

**FIGURE 2–4.** After you conduct a keyword search, click on this link to save the search and later access it from My eBay > Saved Searches.

- *Recently Viewed.* A visual digest of your recently viewed eBay items.
- *Bids/Offers.* A list of items you're currently bidding on, pending offers you've made, and a 60-day view of items you bid on but didn't win.
- *Watchlist.* The list of items you're currently watching.

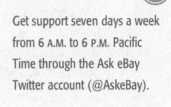

- *Purchase History.* Your most recent eBay purchases, with links to return an item, buy again, leave feedback, check on delivery tracking, contact the seller, and other links relating to your purchases. You can look at your purchases going back as far as three years ago.
- *Buy Again.* A gallery of your recent purchases, in case you need to buy any items again.
- *Selling.* A link to eBay's Seller Hub.
- *Saved Searches.* A link to your saved searches—see Figure 2-4 on page 16 to see how it works.
- *Saved Sellers.* Quick access to your favorite eBay sellers. Figure 2-3 on page 16 shows you which link to click on if you want to save a seller.
- *Messages.* A link to your secure eBay inbox, where you'll receive official communications from eBay and exchange messages with other users.

I'll spend more time discussing the "Search for anything" box and browsing categories in Chapter 3, and keep in mind that the sections promoting seasonal and popular items change regularly. If you have the money and the time, keep coming back for a nonstop stream of shopping excitement. Stock up on what you need, grab what you love, or simply gather intelligence for your own eBay selling strategy.

## Bottom Menu

The eBay homepage has oodles of links in the bottom menu, grouped into sections to help you sleuth out where to go for what you need. Here is a quick overview:

- *Buy.* These links allow you to register, learn about eBay's Money Back Guarantee, obtain help with buying items, and gain access to millions of eBay Stores. You can also learn about eBay for Charity (and shop for items benefiting charities).
- *Sell.* From here you can start selling, learn the basics of selling for yourself or your company, and sign up for the eBay Partner Network (which allows you to earn commissions for driving traffic and encouraging sales on eBay).

- *Tools & Apps.* While app developers will definitely want to visit this area, the rest of us should also drop by periodically to learn about the latest security and safe trading advice. You can also check eBay official time here—useful when checking the ending time of an eBay auction, which is based on eBay's official time, which is Pacific Time Zone. In my opinion, the most important link in this section is the one to eBay's site map—a guide to every nook and cranny on eBay.

- *eBay Companies.* This is a link to the current list of all the companies eBay owns and operates across the globe. This would be useful, for example, if you wanted to trade on eBay's other country sites.

- *Stay Connected.* Links to eBay's blogs and social media profiles. Share your success stories and big-money ideas, and get feedback on your posts from eBay employees.

- *About eBay.* A real grab bag—learn the inner workings of eBay, apply for jobs, and read about its global impact and policies. There's also a link to its Verified Rights Owner (VeRO) program, which allows intellectual property (IP) owners and their authorized representatives to report eBay listings that may infringe on those rights—one of the many tools eBay uses to fight fraud and fakes.

- *Help & Contact.* Links to the help you need, whether you're buying or selling. The Resolution Center is eBay's venue for resolving disputes between members, and eBay will step in if members can't work it out themselves. You'll also find contact information for eBay.

---

## READING (NOT RUNNING) A 10K

I love to keep pace with eBay's annual 10-K. No, that's not a yearly charity race: Form 10-K is the annual report that all publicly traded companies have to file with the SEC. It's as long as a book. Among many other things, eBay's 10-K provides details on its global businesses and some meaningful industry scuttlebutt. Every serious businessperson should read eBay's 10-K. It's a master class on ecommerce—not just the rosy stuff, but gritty, in-depth discussions about the company, its competition, and a wealth of fascinating details on how eBay is leveraging AI, working to improve the customer experience, and even designing share repurchase programs to prop up its stock price. From the bottom menu on the homepage, go to About eBay and click on Investors. If you're going to commit to selling on eBay, you'd benefit greatly from reading these reports.

---

- *Community*. Find the latest announcements, dip into eBay's knowledge base of user-generated content and FAQs, dive into one of its many discussion boards and join or start an open or private eBay group within the eBay Community.
- *eBay Sites*. Try taking a virtual trip around the world and visit some of the many eBay sites operated in other countries by using this pull-down menu.

## BECOMING AN eBAYER

If analysis paralysis has kept you on the sidelines, but you're nonetheless excited about the prospect of finally taking the eBay plunge—just *go for it!* The internet—and eBay—are still relatively young, and the chance to join the online gold rush is still bright and shiny. Trading on eBay—buying *and* selling—is fun and can be incredibly lucrative. You can kick the tires on eBay all you want without creating an account—you can even buy items as a guest, sort of an eBay dating ritual—but you'll be limited to purchasing using *Buy It Now*. If you want to bid on an auction or send a *Best Offer* (i.e., haggle over price), you'll need an account. The truth is that you can't do much without one, so I recommend registering today.

An email address is all you need to sign up for eBay. Once you've become a member, you can:

- buy and sell
- use My eBay to track your buying and selling activity
- send secure messages to other members
- contact eBay for support by chat, phone, or email
- watch up to 300 items you're considering buying

Do you just want to buy things for yourself? Then a personal account is for you. Are you planning to sell on eBay? If you can't see the back of your garage, and your closets and the space under your bed have become museums of well-meaning but unwanted gifts (or shopping sprees), then a personal account is still fine, as long as you plan to sell casually. While you can always convert a personal account to a business account later, if you plan to buy merchandise on eBay for resale, or if you're creating or buying large quantities of items, go ahead and register as a business account.

> **TIP**
>
> Never reuse passwords across different websites. Use a password manager such as LastPass or Apple's Keychain to generate and recall safe, secure passwords. With a password manager, you can store and quickly recall passwords without having to remember them or write them down. LastPass (which I use) is available as a website, as a mobile app, or through a browser extension, which will automatically fill in site passwords.

### How to Register

At the top of the homepage, click on Register. The default choice is to register a personal account, but you will also see the link to create a business account.

First, use your social login or fill in the first page of the registration form.

1. Enter your name, email, and desired password, or
2. Register with your Google account, or
3. Register with your Facebook account, or
4. Register with your Apple ID.

Before you can start trading, you'll be required to verify your account. eBay sends an email containing the required steps to complete your account verification.

Next, provide your contact information.

1. Using the pull-down menu, select your country.
2. Enter your street address.
3. Enter your mobile number (or select the landline link, for those few people who still have landlines).
4. Click Continue and you'll be signed into eBay and automatically taken to the Activity tab on the My eBay page.

### Changing Your User ID

Once you register, you'll receive a friendly email welcoming you to the site that includes a preassigned username (eBay also refers to this as your user ID; the terms are interchangeable). This initial user ID will make you turn up your nose—eBay assigned me the unappealing "chrisspe_8942," for instance. Yuck!

Don't let this tarnish your brand's image. There's a handy link in that welcome email that permits you to immediately change your user ID. Give this some careful thought and don't put yourself into a box that's too narrow. The user ID "glassbycms" is too limiting. A better choice would be "curiositiesbycms." Don't pick something embarrassing or offensive, even if eBay doesn't put the kibosh on it. Your user ID should be relevant, trustworthy, simple, and memorable (and G-rated).

As your business changes, so can your user ID. You can change your ID once every 30 days; a change icon will appear next to your ID for 30 days after you rename it. But you should think twice before changing your user ID once you've established your eBay reputation. Once you've invested time and energy in promoting your brand as an eBay power buyer, power seller, or both, people will remember you. Can you imagine Coke changing their name?

Here are a few of the rules you must follow when choosing a user ID:

- It must be at least six characters long.
- It cannot contain spaces or these symbols: @, &, ', (, ), <, or >.
- No profane or obscene language is permitted (eBay gets to decide what is inappropriate).
- You cannot use any third-party trademarks (i.e., trademarks you *don't* own).
- You cannot include any email addresses or web addresses.
- The word "eBay" can't be part of the user ID.

To read eBay's full policy, click on Help & Contact and type "username" in the search box, then select the Username Policy help page from the list of results.

### Opening Multiple Accounts

You can open more than one eBay account. There's a simple use case for this: groupings of similar and complementary merchandise sell better than a hodgepodge of different items, and eBay cross-promotes seller listings when buyers view items and make purchases.

Each eBay account is blessed with 250 zero insertion fee listings per month (even more if you subscribe to an eBay Store). The downside is that each new account you set up requires its own expenditure of time, focus, and energy. If you're an administration guru and plan to sell many items, then managing multiple accounts will be no problem. If you're buying wholesale to resell on eBay, it's wise to have two accounts—one for buying and one for selling. Some sellers become bitter when they realize you're reselling their items at a much higher price, and a separate account for reselling will avoid acrimony.

If, for some reason, you never receive your eBay welcome email, it's not cause for alarm. You may have simply mistyped your email address, in which case you'll need to restart the registration process. While it's very unlikely eBay's emails will get caught in your spam filter, be sure to check your junk mail folder before registering a second time.

## LEARNING THE RULES

It may be true that it's human nature to question authority, but the moment you registered for an eBay account, you had to agree to abide by their policies and follow their *User Agreement*. Perhaps in all the excitement you missed the fine print.

To view eBay's policies, scroll down to the bottom of the homepage. Under About eBay, click the Policies link. There's also a link to the User Agreement at the bottom of nearly every page on the site.

eBay has been around for a long time and has pretty much seen everything—so they know how to detect and stop fraudsters or trading activity that breaks its rules. Its members are expected to trade fairly, honestly, and legally. If you *are* a rebel, trying to get your fellow eBayers to operate by your rules is like trying to maneuver a cruise ship with one finger. You'll just have to play nicely with all the other kids in the sandbox.

The site's AI scouts can detect many illicit activities and policy violations, but the community also benefits when members police one another. When other eBayers don't follow the rules, you can (and should) report them. I'm not talking about minor infractions but truly egregious violations—eBay becomes a better place to trade for everyone when you do.

Here are some prohibited selling practices:

- *Fee avoidance.* An eBayer asks you to engage in prohibited activities such as trading off eBay or canceling a sale to avoid paying transaction fees to eBay.
- *Bid manipulation and invalid bid retraction.* When a bid is made on an auction then retracted, the bidder could gain an unfair advantage, such as discovering the reserve price or where another bidder's maximum bid stands. eBay only permits bids to be retracted in two circumstances. A bid may be retracted if the wrong amount was entered, but eBay requires that you enter the correct amount immediately after retracting your bid. A bid can also be retracted when the listing changed significantly after the bid was placed.
- *Shill bidders.* While it's OK to buy an item on eBay from someone you know, you may never artificially increase its price or desirability. Shill bidding involves collusion and manipulation of the bid process to ensure that an unsuspecting bidder

**TIP**

While *feedback manipulation* is never allowed on eBay, asking a buyer to revise their original feedback rating and comment is completely legit. Before you go atomic over negative or neutral feedback, try reaching out to the buyer to resolve whatever issue prompted them to leave the unfavorable review in the first place. Once the problem has been taken care of, politely ask if they would be willing to revise their feedback. If the buyer consents, you can request a revision for feedback that is less than 30 days old, and you are allowed up to five revision requests per calendar year. To initiate a revision request, go to the menu at the bottom of most eBay pages and click on the Site Map link. On the Site Map, press Ctrl + F (or ⌘ + F on a Mac) to open a search box and search for "feedback." Then click on the Request Feedback Revision link and follow the instructions.

---

## SAY GOODBYE TO THE GADFLY!

If you sell on eBay for any length of time, you'll encounter painful people who expect you to grade, certify, and guarantee your $1 item—or ask endless questions and request tons of additional pictures for a super-cheap or as-is product. While it's not against eBay policy to be annoying, if someone is rude or otherwise an undesirable trading partner, you can block them. To block unwanted buyers, go to the menu at the bottom of most eBay pages and click Site Map. Then press Ctrl + F (or ⌘ + F on a Mac) to open a search box and search for "block." Then click on Block Bidder/Buyer List to access the Buyer Management system. Buyer Management has tools that allow you to block undesirable buyers and set buyer requirements, thus preventing those annoying buyers from taking up any more of your time.

---

pays top dollar. The seller conspires with others to place fake bids in order to create the illusion of high demand—or to determine a real bidder's top bid amount. Once they figure out the legitimate maximum bid, the fraudsters retract their inflated bids and immediately place a lower bid to keep the real one elevated without outbidding it. With fixed price listings, the seller arranges for other eBayers to make phony purchases to give the perception that the item is selling like hotcakes. Most people check sales history before buying, and these phony transactions mislead them. Report a provable case of shill bidding to eBay and law enforcement.

- *Sale cancellation.* This typically occurs when a seller fails to achieve their desired price at the conclusion of an auction and without warning cancels the sale, falsely claiming that the item is out of stock or damaged, the buyer asked to cancel, or something is wrong with the shipping address. The seller may then lie low for a while and relist the item at a higher price.
- *Feedback limitations in seller's terms and conditions.* Some sellers include language in their listings to limit or restrict the buyer from leaving negative feedback—this is a big no-no. A seller's listing cannot attempt to stop a buyer from leaving feedback, whether good or bad.
- *Feedback manipulation.* In this scheme, an unscrupulous seller artificially elevates their feedback score by using multiple accounts or working with others to exchange positive—but phony—feedback. It's against eBay's rules to buy, sell, trade, or give away feedback.

Here are some prohibited buying practices:

- *Underage buyers.* Minors are not allowed to use eBay unless an adult over the age of 18 permits their account to be used and accepts responsibility for all activities.
- *Deadbeats.* Occasionally, buyers fail to pay. An eBay seller may cancel an order if the buyer has not paid within four calendar days. Order cancellation results in a refund of the final value fee. An eBayer who is a chronic flake will end up indefinitely suspended by the site; however, a one-time failure to pay could be explained by lack of internet access, illness or other misfortune, or simply forgetfulness. In most product categories, bids are considered binding; however, bids for motor vehicles and real estate are considered nonbinding because these high priced sales are usually complex and subject to a variety of laws, and they may require an exchange of additional information before the deal is finalized.
- *Duty dodgers.* Sometimes a cross-border customer may ask you to undervalue their shipment so they can save money on customs duties and taxes. But remember: if the parcel is lost or damaged, you'll end up eating it and the financial loss will be all yours—eBay won't cover the seller for damage in transit on uninsured or underinsured shipments.
- *Bid manipulation.* A bidder places an exorbitant bid amount to determine the next highest bid, then later retracts their bid and places a new one just above the current high bidder. This unscrupulous bidder times the retraction to occur at the last possible moment to discourage others from placing bids while the auction is running. eBay prohibits this practice as it allows the bidder to gain an unfair advantage.
- *Bid shielding.* Two bidders work together, with the first one bidding what he wants to pay for the item and the second one placing a very high bid that he retracts just prior to the 12-hour cancellation deadline. This *bid shielding* discourages others from placing bids and leaves the first bidder's lower bid in position to win the auction.
- *Improper bid retraction.* A bidder places a high bid and immediately retracts it simply to discover the auction's reserve price, or does so to find out how high another buyer bid, or because they changed their mind about buying the item, or because they bid on the same item offered by multiple sellers—but only intended to buy one. Bids are only allowed to be retracted on eBay if the buyer accidentally keys in the wrong amount, the seller changes the listing significantly, or the seller can't be reached for questions.
- *Malicious feedback.* A buyer leaves a nasty, irrelevant feedback comment. You can ask eBay to remove feedback if it's unrelated to the transaction or violates eBay's

feedback policy. Contact eBay customer support if you're unsure whether the negative feedback qualifies for removal.

- *Feedback extortion.* A dissatisfied buyer threatens to leave negative feedback if you don't agree to terms you never offered in the listing or demands a discount rather than simply returning the product. Ask eBay to remove provable cases of feedback extortion.
- *Threats or stalking.* An eBayer engages in other threats, stalking, discrimination, or other illegal behavior. Report the incident to eBay and, if appropriate, the authorities.
- *Misusing returns.* A buyer returns a different item, returns an item they used or damaged, or returns an item falsely claiming that it was not as described.
- *Abusing buyer protection programs.* A buyer opens duplicate requests using other buyer protection programs (e.g., filing a dispute both on eBay and with their card company, harasses the seller about an item not received while still within their delivery date window, or opens an eBay Money Back Guarantee request after having already received a refund from the seller or their payment provider, or does so in retaliation for a previous transaction dispute.
- *Offers to trade outside eBay.* For the protection of both parties, eBay doesn't permit any action with a user on the site designed to complete or facilitate a transaction outside eBay. Buyers and sellers also can't share contact information before completing a transaction on eBay. Only *official* deals that occur on the site benefit from eBay protections and its Money Back Guarantee.

Promptly report and block offenders, and contact eBay at through the Help & Contact link at the top of most eBay pages. You can use Buyer Requirements to deflect many types of undesirable buyers. To access Buyer Requirements, go to My eBay > Account > Selling Preferences > Blocked Buyer List.

Safe eBay trading starts with common sense and following the site's policies—they will protect you from most fraudsters and rule breakers.

## CONNECTING WITH THE eBAY COMMUNITY

This section is a condensed version of Chapter 15 from my book *Start Your Own eBay Business, 3rd Ed.* (Entrepreneur Press, 2020). While not a prerequisite, I believe that book is also essential reading and a key partner to this book for serious eBayers. I've curated key highlights from that chapter for this section.

Developing a talent for connecting with other eBay users will return guaranteed dividends for your business. When people engage in conversation, great things happen.

You can network with other users and eBay employees through the Community, found in the bottom menu of the homepage.

The eBay Community functions as a peer-to-peer support network and is mostly self-managed, with eBay staff moderating and contributing content. Scan the QR code in Figure 2–5 below for eBay's time-tested tips for making the most of the Community, the rules of the road, and a list of eBay employees who make up the Community team. You might get to join in on engaging and surprising conversations—or even discover the love of your life, like Monique and Adrian Frankel, who found lasting romance after Monique bought some books from Adrian and they began messaging on the site. (Of course, eBay offers no warranty of postnuptial success.)

**FIGURE 2–5.** This handy QR code will take you to eBay's About the Community help page.

While visiting the Community, you can:

- Find out what's going on with other sellers and buyers on eBay
- Discuss topics that interest you
- Learn from successful eBayers
- Check eBay's system status to learn about problems affecting the site

You should primp your Community profile before diving in. Here's how:

1. Scroll to the bottom of the homepage.
2. Click Community.
3. Click your Avatar (top right).
4. Click My Settings.
5. Click the Personal tab.
6. Click Personal Information.
7. Fill in everything you want people to know about you (the signature field allows HTML code, permitting you to add optional graphics and fancy formatting).
8. Click Save.

There are a plethora of Community profile settings you can adjust, so click the Preferences tab and explore to your heart's content. Note that the Home Page tab allows you to show only the discussion boards that interest you. Depending on your preferences, the Privacy tab allows you to hide your Community profile information, email address, and online status (the default option), display them to eBay Community friends only, or make them visible to everyone.

Whether you're a big-time CEO or a small-business owner, social networks can easily consume your life if you don't self-moderate your usage. Like a crop farmer, I want to generate the maximum yield for the smallest investment of time. While the Community is social, there are plenty of sellers who leverage it to:

- promote themselves (posts include backlinks to your listings)
- seek help with item identification and pricing
- engage in scuttlebutt (i.e., intel) with other sellers

Imagine being able to post a question about one of your listings on a discussion board and receive responses in minutes from other eBayers who share your passion! Figure 2-6 on page 28 is eBay's list of discussion boards, which has a little something for everyone.

You'll get the most out of the eBay Community by following these simple rules:

- Have a specific purpose in mind.
- Be polite and professional.
- Avoid trolls who spew doom and gloom—these are people who couldn't find happiness even if they were holding a winning lottery ticket.
- Use visual aids—pictures often say it best and the discussion boards allow you to post text, images, and graphics.
- Enable alerts so that you'll know when someone answers your questions.
- Get in and get out—don't become consumed by endless browsing.
- If someone is mean to you, don't return the favor. Remember that no response is also a response.

**TIP**

Suffering from email overload? If you want to stop eBay from sending you email alerts related to your Community activity, simply tick the check box under the Email section of My Settings on your Community profile.

**TIP**

The *eBay for Business Podcast* is a weekly podcast featuring eBay employees and sellers offering advice to other sellers. You'll find the link to this official eBay podcast on the main Community page. You can join the fun—and become a famous eBay seller—by calling and becoming a guest. Email the podcast team at podcast@ebay.com or call (888) 723-4630.

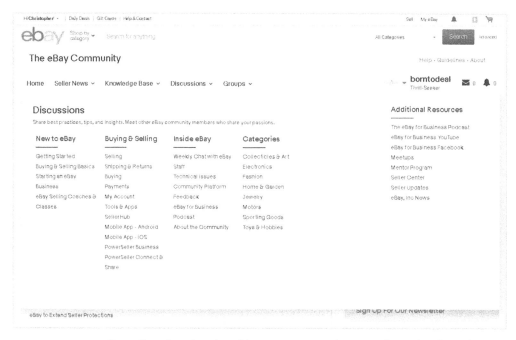

**FIGURE 2–6.** One of my favorite virtual hangout spots, the eBay discussion boards.

In the Community, you'll find great information and wonderful ideas from official eBay staff and fellow eBayers. You can enhance and elevate your eBay sales by sharing ideas there.

In the next chapter, we'll look at the other side of the eBay equation: the buyers.

# Chapter 3

# Buying Like an eBay MVP

Before you start building your eBay business, you'll want to get to know the buying process inside and out. This is important for two reasons: One, you want to get in the mindset of the eBay customer so you know how best to sell to them (and delight them!). Second, eBay has the potential to be your number-one source for merchandise to resell.

Landing a fantastic deal on eBay doesn't require a degree in haggling—but knowing how to navigate the site expertly will garner you the best products at great prices from reputable sellers. Merchants who sell on eBay create listings that include images, product details, and varying payment and shipping options. Some listings allow you to buy immediately, while others offer a thrilling (and fiercely competitive) auction format. Let's jump right in and see how this all works.

## BROWSING CATEGORIES

What I didn't know before I first started browsing eBay is that doing so is the ultimate treasure hunt. Power buyers who are also power sellers flip their purchases fast—and turn a pretty penny. I've made a mint over the years doing this. Meanwhile, less experienced sellers' mistakes can be a bargain hunter's paradise.

Just like the aisles of enticing goodies at retail stores, eBay organizes its products in categories. Buyers who have a specific product they're looking for use the search box at the top of most eBay pages, but there's a recreational aspect to shopping. Whether you only have a couple of bucks left on your debit card or you've been blessed with an American Express Centurion Card, eBay is your very own slice of shopping heaven.

At any given moment, there are usually more than one billion active eBay listings. Without the categories, browsing for bargains would be like trying to find the Ark of the Covenant in that warehouse at the end of the film *Raiders of the Lost Ark*.

You may have noticed when I showed you the homepage earlier (in Figure 2-2 on page 14) that eBay displays its most popular categories just below the search box, to encourage you to peruse its bestselling merchandise. For people who love to shop, that's a good sort of pressure—like when you come across the Girl Scout cookie table at the entrance of the supermarket. But if you glance to the left of the Search for Anything box, you'll see the Shop by Category link. Click it, and a layer with eBay's most popular categories will appear. At the bottom of the new layer is a link to all categories. That list is massive—after all, you can buy practically anything on eBay.

The site continually updates its categories to create a more intuitive user experience, pruning out sleepy categories with sparse inventory and merging them with others that are brimming with more products. New categories spring up when something novel arrives on the scene and maintains sufficient buyer interest to warrant its own category. The browsing experience offers context and purchase guidance, with the ability to narrow down by brand, popularity, item attributes, and more. You'll find reviews and guides along the way for popular products. All this has been developed by eBay to tailor the experience to the way people shop—helping buyers locate what they want, but also helping them discover what they didn't know they wanted.

As you browse, you'll notice the category structure's hierarchy. There's the top-level category, the branch category or categories (these can extend for many levels), and the leaf category. The leaf category is the one sellers use to list items, but it belongs to a family of other categories in the category tree structure.

Now let's go for a test drive.

Let's say you're looking for a kitchen faucet. You want something with an old world look and an oil-rubbed antique bronze finish but don't care about brand. Here's how it works:

Home & Garden > Kitchen Fixtures > Kitchen Faucets

1. *Home & Garden* is the top-level category.
2. *Kitchen Fixtures* is the branch category.
3. *Kitchen Faucets* is the leaf category.

Figure 3–1 on page 32 is a browse page for the Kitchen Faucets category. Notice all the nicely organized buttons, links, and check boxes that help make it easier to find inventory. Browsing lets buyers see what's widely available, and the context and purchasing guidance provide the information they need to move from deliberation to purchase. This is part of what's authentically eBay about the shopping experience.

When you've found what looks like the perfect kitchen faucet, click the listing title or image (eBay calls it the *gallery* photo), and the expanded listing page appears.

## CLAIMING A SALES TAX EXEMPTION FOR YOUR eBAY RESALE PURCHASES

A huge rookie mistake many new eBay entrepreneurs make is to pay sales tax on their resale purchases. Most states require resellers and retailers to have an active, valid *resale license*, and you'll want to get one. In fact, you are probably legally required to have one if you are purchasing merchandise for resale in a state that collects sales tax. With a resale license, you can purchase wholesale without having to pay sales tax. You're then required to collect sales tax from your customers when you resell the items; eBay does this for its sellers automatically. Once you've secured your resale license (contact your state's department of revenue to find out how), click on Help & Contact at the top of the homepage or most eBay pages, type "tax" in the Search eBay Help box, and then select Paying Tax on eBay Purchases. Scroll down until you find the section titled "eBay's Buyer Exemption program for sales tax," and follow the instructions to get started.

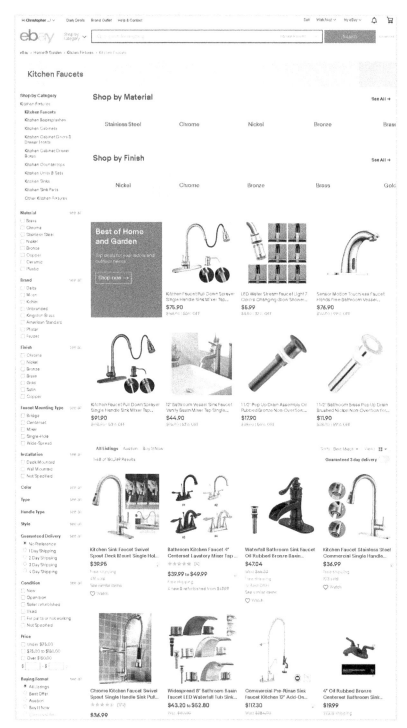

**FIGURE 3-1.** Here's a browse page for the leaf category Kitchen Faucets—notice the buttons and check boxes (aka filters) that help buyers narrow their results.

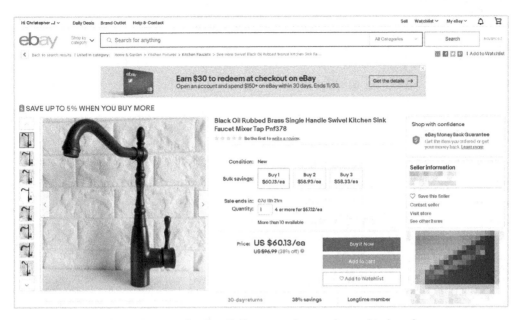

**FIGURE 3–2.** A sample eBay listing page for my dream kitchen faucet.

Figure 3–2 above displays the fruits of my browsing adventure—a brand-new oil-rubbed kitchen faucet. It's brass and I really wanted bronze, but I love this design.

Here are a few key points I'd like to share that are true of all listing pages:

- Clicking the colorful eBay logo at the top left takes you to the homepage.
- Next to the words Listed in Category, you'll see its entire category structure, including the top-level category, branch category or categories, and leaf category.
- Item condition (new, used, refurbished, etc.) is displayed.
- The seller's user ID and feedback score are shown.
- Photos can be enlarged and scrolled when the seller has uploaded more than one image.
- The seller's returns policy is explained.
- Seller-provided details about the item are included (these are usually visible below the fold, i.e., after scrolling down).

Browsing is how many people begin shopping at eBay, and savvy eBayers often reap huge rewards when they discover valuable merchandise listed in the wrong category. These are typically auctions where the bids remain low due to poor titles and mediocre images, making them more difficult to find through search and less attractive to buyers who rapidly scan pictures. I've landed many deals by browsing eBay categories and profiting from other sellers' mistakes (their goof is my gain!). You too can unearth these treasures by patiently browsing through high-potential eBay categories. What is high potential? That's for you to decide. Personally, I gravitate to what I know best—antiques, collectibles, jewelry, porcelain, pottery, timepieces, and vintage film cameras. I trade in everything, but these have the highest potential for profit because I know them so well.

## SEARCHING FOR DEALS

The extraordinary thing about eBay is that you can collect what you love, buy what you need, discover things you realize you probably should *never* have laid eyes on, and purchase them anyway. At any given time, eBay can have more than one billion active listings, so becoming a search guru will improve your chances of scoring extraordinary deals. In this section, I'll cover power buyer tips that will hone your search skills and empower you to become a master eBay sleuth.

Go ahead and choose something to search for—eBay searches are *case insensitive*, so don't worry about capitalization—and you'll notice that in my examples, I won't worry about it either. Use keywords rather than grammatically correct phrases—eBay is a search engine, not an English teacher. Figure 3–3 on page 35 shows the search results that eBay returned when I typed in "air pods." Psst! The actual name is AirPods. Will Apple get cranky about the misspelling? Well, people are typing incorrect spellings into search engines all the time and I'm being realistic here. Here are some of the key elements of the search results page:

- *Related.* At the top of the page are a series of links to related keywords; click any of them and eBay will search for that. In this case, some of the suggestions are "airpods," "air pods pro," and "air jordans."
- *Include Description.* Check this box, and eBay will expand the search to include item descriptions instead of only searching titles. Adding descriptions can return a mind-boggling number of results. Some sellers (including me) add hashtags to their listing descriptions to facilitate discoverability. With so many eBay accounts, it's not easy to link buyers to all of them at once, but a hashtag is quite easy to find.
- *Category.* These links appear on the left-hand side of the search results and allow you to drill down into the category structure to limit your search returns to only the items that interest you.
- *All Listings.* This and the buttons next to it permit you to filter search results by listing format—you can view everything or limit the results to show listings that allow offers (if you love to haggle), display only auctions, or show only listings with Buy It Now enabled.
- *Save This Search.* This allows you to store and redo this search from your My eBay page—and even receive alerts of newly listed items that match your search criteria.

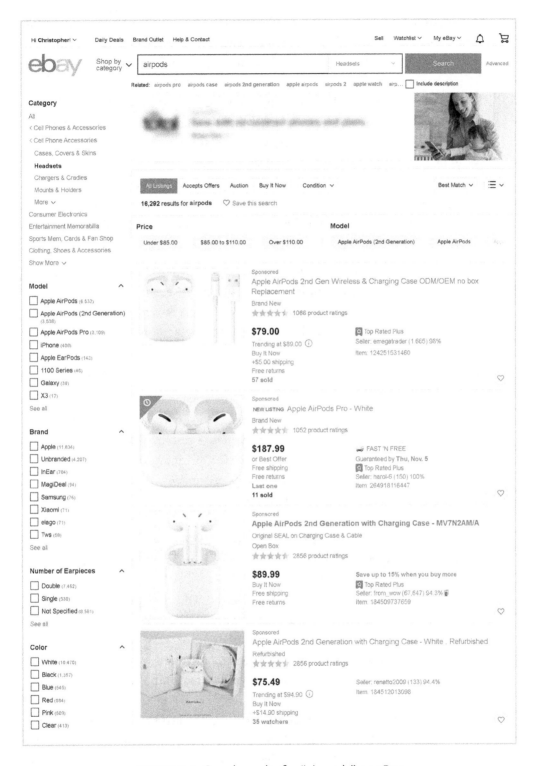

**FIGURE 3–3.** Search results for "air pods" on eBay.

▨ *Filters.* Additional filters appear on the left-hand side of the page, below the categories. These allow further refinements based on specific details in the listing, which may include brand, size, length, width, height, type, color, style, price, location, and many more.

▨ *Views.* On the far right side at the top of the search results is a button with three lines on it (in list view; in gallery view it has four small squares on it). You can switch between list view and gallery view; the gallery view showcases larger pictures in a tiled array for a more visual shopping experience.

▨ *Pagination.* A search that returns more than 25 results will have an option at the bottom of the page (not seen in Figure 3-3 on page 35 due to space limitations) to adjust the number of visible items per page to 25, 50, 100, or 200 and arrows (◀ and ▶) for navigating the results.

When searching for a unique product name, you typically won't need to add the brand name—you'll notice that I didn't include "Apple," because AirPods can stand on its own in a search. There are many instances when fewer keywords provide a perfectly good result—e.g., "Duracell AAA" will be just as good as "Duracell AAA batteries."

As you experiment with your searches, you'll notice some clever as well as peculiar traits of eBay's search engine. Here are a few nuances:

▨ *Words such as* and, a, an, or, *and* the. Database and search experts refer to these as *noise words.* They will be omitted by many sellers. A search for "platinum diamond bracelet" will yield better results than a search for "platinum *and* diamond bracelet."

▨ *Plurals.* The search engine treats the plurals of some words as equivalent to the singular, so searching for "football helmet" and "football helmets" will return the same results.

▨ *Search intuition.* You'll notice that eBay's AI is clever—a search for "the birthstone for may" will display emerald jewelry and other listings with the word "emerald" in the title.

▨ *Spellcheck.* If you type *schlumburger*, eBay will ask, "Did you mean: schlumberger?" (And either way you'll need some serious cash to afford Tiffany's Jean Schlumberger jewelry—it's top-notch and luxurious!)

▨ *Start broadly and add focus.* Being too specific out of the gate may lead to lost opportunities. Many sellers' listings have too few important keywords, and searching "2002 BMW 530i wheels," for example, will turn up way too many irrelevant results. BMW wheels (aka rims) were designed to fit many different years and models. The 525i, 528i, and 530i rims are interchangeable. BMW produced the E39 cars (the line under which the 2002 530i was made) from 1995 to 2004,

## BOOLEAN SEARCH OPERATORS

Boolean is a type of database search strategy named in honor of 19th-century English mathematician George Boole. A Boolean search allows you to combine your search terms with search operators (such as AND, OR, and NOT) for more powerful and precise searches. Here are a few little-known eBay search tricks using Boolean search operators:

- *The minus sign.* Placing a minus sign before a word acts as the NOT operator, excluding that word. The search "-faux pearl necklace" will omit any results containing the word "faux" and help limit the results to genuine pearl necklaces.

- *Parentheses.* Parentheses around words act as the OR operator. The search "sterling (pin,brooch,necklace,pendant) -gold" will return all listings that have the word "sterling" and any of the words inside the parentheses, but not the word "gold" because I excluded it using the minus sign.

- *Minus sign with parentheses.* Placing the minus sign in front of the parentheses, such as "necklace -(platinum,gold)," will act like two separate searches—for necklaces without platinum OR for necklaces without gold.

- *Quotation marks.* Keywords within quotation marks will search for the exact phrase in the listing title. For example, *floor mat* will search listings with these words in any order ("floor mat," "mat for wood floors," etc.), while *"floor mat"* will only return listings with these words in this specific order. eBay may expand its searches to include a plural version or alternate spelling of your search word. If you want to prevent this, enclose just that one word within quotes. Try searching for *notebook DVD* and then *"notebook" DVD* and see the difference!

- *The asterisk.* Enter a sequence of letters followed by an asterisk to return any items whose titles contain words starting with that sequence. You can combine this technique with other Boolean search tactics for amazing results! Are you looking for genuine megalodon shark's teeth but aren't quite sure how to spell it? Try searching for "meg* (shark,sharks,shark's) -replica."

so a search for "E39 rim" will produce much more relevant search results, even though it is less specific.

You can also add focus to a broad search by drilling down into the category structure; arranging the results; and filtering by buying format, condition, item specifics (e.g., brand, size, type, color, style, etc.), price range, seller location, shipping options, and other listing features such as free returns.

Under the hood, eBay's search technology narrows the gap between wanting and finding. Inside the company, the search engine is called Cassini, and the default order of search results is known as Best Match—eBay's proprietary way of presenting listings. It's no secret that sellers need to know how to optimize their listings for Best Match. According to eBay, here's the list of factors that the site considers when ranking listings:

- How closely the listing matches the buyer's search terms
- How popular the item is
- The price of the item
- The quality of the listing (description, photos, etc.)
- How complete the listing is
- The listing terms of service, such as the seller's returns policy and handling time
- The seller's track record

So what if you're unhappy with the results even after drilling down into the category structure and applying a few filters? Catching the best deals will require you to separate yourself from the pack and become a different kind of bargain hunter. You'll notice in Figure 3–3 on page 35 that at the top of the listings on the right, there is also a button labeled "Best Match." This gives you even more options for sorting the listings.

Here are your choices:

- *Best Match.* This is the default option, ranked by the criteria in the key points above.
- *Time: Ending Soonest.* This is helpful if you like to snipe auctions at the very last moment—a technique used by the savviest bidders.
- *Time: Newly Listed.* This is useful when browsing for bargains. Clever buyers patrol for seller mistakes 24/7, and you'll have to act quickly to snap up an item that's undervalued or poorly titled. Keep in mind other buyers may have saved searches to be alerted to these listings, so it pays to be decisive!
- *Price + Shipping: Lowest First.* This search is often paired with the Buy It Now filter to hide the auction listings (unless they also offer a Buy It Now option). You wouldn't want to see the auctions if you're looking for the best price on goods available for immediate purchase.

- *Price + Shipping: Highest First.* This may not have as many applications as sorting by the lowest first simply because you're probably looking for bargains, right? But you may find it useful for scoping out wholesale lots, where the listing is likely to have a higher price.
- *Distance: Nearest First.* This helps you find nearby items, which is helpful if the seller offers free local pickup. (You can filter for that on the left-hand side.) This is also useful if you're in a hurry and on a budget—closer merchandise arrives faster and costs less to ship.

Now imagine all the clever ways you can sort your search results. The most obvious one is to search your keywords and then sort by Price + Shipping: Lowest First paired with Buy It Now. Then you could try sorting by Time: Ending Soonest and refreshing the view to see which listings are about to end so you can snipe a bid in at the last moment—hopefully outwitting your competition. (You need a really fast and reliable internet connection for this strategy.)

If an item piques your interest, click the gallery image or the listing title to view the full listing page. You'll remember I showed this to you earlier in Figure 3-2 on page 33 (the kitchen faucet). Now let's check out the buying process and how to complete the sale.

You'll come across two main types of listings—some are auctions where bidders battle each other in a tug of war until the highest bidder wins, while others have a Buy It Now option so you can purchase and pay for the item immediately at the listed price, with no bidding required.

Here are key points to consider when bidding on eBay auctions:

- *You can place the absolute maximum bid you are willing to pay.* Then eBay will automatically bid in increments on your behalf to maintain your position as high bidder, but only up to your maximum bid price. The *bid increment* is smaller for lower-priced items and becomes larger as the price escalates, which discourages silly bidding wars on expensive items (e.g., you can't just bid one penny higher than the current high bid).
- *Research before bidding.* Typos are common and provide opportunities for savvy buyers who know which spelling mistakes occur often. While eBay may correct the most common misspellings automatically, it won't save every seller from a typo. Fewer people will find these listings. This is especially useful on auctions, which will receive fewer bids when the seller goofs. Be sure to use quotes when searching words or terms that you don't want eBay to automatically correct, e.g., "air pods."
- *Remove emotions from your bidding strategy.* Know the precise value of the item you want to buy, and bid only as much as you must to get a bargain. If the bidding

goes too high, let the item go. It may take you longer to earn these deals, but you will find them. Remember to always account for shipping cost and sales tax (unless the item is for resale) when determining how much you should pay.

- *Note what time the auction ends and use this to your advantage.* Most (but not all) items are in healthy supply on eBay. Items that end Sunday afternoon or evening tend to get more competition, while you're less likely to be outbid late on weeknights.
- *Bid up reserve price auctions early.* That way other bidders won't be attracted by the low starting price. But only do this if the reserve, once met, is still below the price you're willing to pay—remember that you'll be placing an additional bid at the last minute. Not very many sellers use reserves because eBay discourages them by charging the seller an extra fee, but use this clever trick when you do run into them.
- *Bid uneven amounts because most bidders use even amounts.* When someone bids $22.50, outdo them by bidding $22.53. Make cents?
- *Snipe your highest bid in the closing seconds.* The next bidder will be caught off guard and won't have time to place another bid. You can automate your sniping with third-party software. My favorite is AuctionStealer (http://www.auctionstealer.com), which automatically places bids at the time you specify. AuctionStealer offers free and premium subscriptions depending on your bid volume.
- *Retract a bid if you've made an error.* You can also retract your bid if the seller made significant changes to the listing or you can't reach them—and there are 12 hours or more left before the listing ends. If the listing ends in less than 12 hours, you can retract your most recent bid if it's been less than an hour since you placed it.

Here are key points to consider when purchasing Buy It Now listings:

- *Guest shopping allows you to shop without an account.* However, you'll miss some important benefits of being a member. As a member, you can:
  - View full order details
  - Bid on auctions
  - Leave and receive feedback

**TIP**

If the shipping on an item seems excessive, it's usually not because the seller is trying to pad their profits—often they're just inexperienced and don't know about the wide variety of shipping services eBay supports. It couldn't hurt to ask if the seller is willing to add other shipping options to their listing for a more favorable rate. If you're buying multiple items, another option is to ask about a combined shipping discount. Not all sellers know how to automatically extend shipping discounts to buyers. Use the Contact Seller link on the listing page to inquire about shipping options.

- Use the eBay message system to contact other members
- Track and manage purchases
- Post on discussion boards and access other member resources

■ *With eBay's shopping cart, you can add multiple items from one or more sellers and check out in one convenient step.* But beware: items can magically disappear from your cart before you pay if the listings expire or another buyer purchases them before you finalize your order.

■ *When the seller has enabled Best Offer on a listing, you should always haggle.* Why pay full price if you don't have to? The Best Offer option is a signal that the seller is willing to negotiate. The seller can always accept, counter your offer, or reject it entirely.

■ *Watch items you're interested in by clicking the Add to Watchlist link.* This link is in the upper-right corner of all listing pages. Sellers can send offers to watchers (a little-known secret that's used by savvy sellers). If a seller decides to drop the price on an item you're watching, eBay will alert you. You can also quickly view the status of items on your Watchlist by going to My eBay > Watchlist.

■ *Message the seller before buying to ask for a discount if the listing lacks the Make Offer button.* Another lesser-known seller feature is the Reply with Offer button that is visible to the seller when they receive a message from an interested customer. See Figure 3–4 on page 42.

■ *Need to cancel?* Go to My eBay > Purchase History, and select the More Actions drop-down menu, select Cancel This Order, and then select Submit. Don't do this too frequently, or eBay may limit your buying privileges. Asking to cancel if you made the purchase within the past hour will be automatically approved so long as the seller has not shipped the item yet. After that, the seller will need to approve the request. You'll receive a refund if the cancellation is approved and you've already paid for the item.

> **TIP**
>
> Don't fret too much if a seller doesn't allow returns—most do, but not all. If a purchase fails to arrive, suffers from major undisclosed defects—or you receive an empty box—eBay's Money Back Guarantee will provide you a full refund. (Buyer's remorse is not covered.) You can learn more about this coverage by clicking the Learn More link under the section titled "eBay Money Back Guarantee," displayed on the right-hand side of every listing.

## THINGS YOU MUST DO BEFORE YOU BUY

Before you bid, haggle, or Buy It Now, here's what you must do:

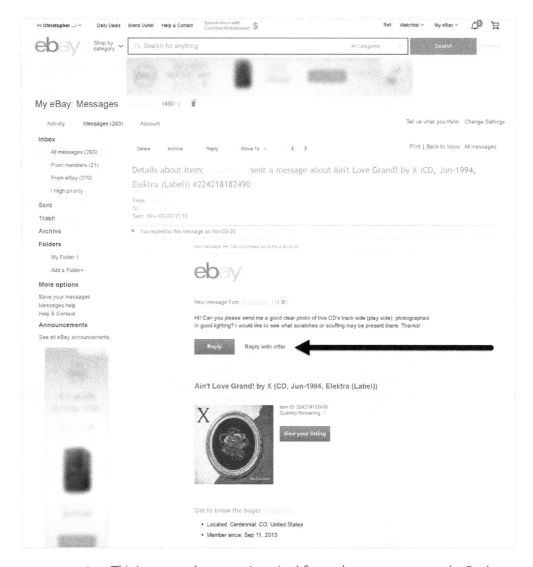

**FIGURE 3–4.** This is an actual message I received from a buyer; you can see the Reply With Offer feature on the message. I clicked the button and sent the buyer an attractive offer—a healthy percentage of these offers result in sales. I replied to this man, and he immediately purchased this CD.

1. *Don't buy the first item shown in your search results.* Sellers who pay for premium placement appear at the top of eBay search results, and you will see the word "Sponsored" just above the item title in these listings. Sellers must pay extra for this placement, and they pass that cost along to you in the form of a higher purchase price—remember that there's no such thing as a free lunch!

## ARE YOU NEW TO eBAY? HERE'S HOW TO AVOID BUYING LIMITS!

From time to time, eBay will place a buying limit on a member's account. These limits protect the eBay community and ensure responsible trading—keeping the marketplace safe for everyone.

You can expect eBay to put the brakes on your purchase activity under the following circumstances:

- You're a total newbie and have been racking up a tab on a bunch of purchases or buying high-ticket items.

- Your current trading habits deviate substantially from your past behavior.

- You've failed to pay for past winnings or canceled too many orders—sellers value their time and eBay does, too. Being a deadbeat or suffering chronic buyer's remorse isn't good for business.

- You're currently the high bidder on a bunch of auctions, but you haven't completed payment yet. Pay up and the restriction will go away.

Buying limits are rare, and you can avoid them by following a few simple rules. Do the following to stay in the good graces of eBay management:

- Verify your identity by adding a credit card to your eBay account—after you sign in, hover over your name on the top-left corner of the site and click Account Settings, then click Payments, and then click Add Payment Option. There are some circumstances where a credit card is required to bid:

  - You must add a card before placing bids for $15,000 or more (except when trading on eBay Motors).

  - You must add a credit card before bidding $25,000 or more on eBay Motors.

- Pay quickly whenever you win a listing.

- Encourage positive seller feedback—thereby improving your feedback reputation—by leaving nice feedback (or by contacting your seller before leaving adverse feedback and giving them a chance to correct the problem).

If you have multiple eBay accounts and one or more of them receives a buying limit, you'll need to resolve whatever caused the issue—eBay cross-references

---

**ARE YOU NEW TO eBAY? HERE'S HOW TO AVOID BUYING LIMITS!, cont.**

accounts based on who owns them, but it may also determine which accounts are related if they were accessed from the same network or computer.

If eBay restricts your buying, you'll receive an email as well as a message in My eBay explaining their reasons, as well as what you need to do to have the restriction removed. All your accounts will be limited until you've complied with eBay's conditions for reinstatement.

---

2. *Read every word on the listing page.* Did you become giddy when no one outbid you on a listing for a $10 toolshed? A closer look reveals that what you'll win is not a shed at all—merely written plans and instructions for building your own shed. Read beyond the listing title and review the complete description as well as the seller's terms (e.g., their returns policy).

3. *Read the Seller Information section.* See Figure 3–5 below to view mine. This information appears on the top right of every listing page and shines light on the seller's reputation.

4. *Review the seller's profile.* Click the user ID under the Seller Information section, review the DSR, and find out how long they've been an eBay member.

5. *Read the seller's feedback.* Click the feedback number located next to the seller's user ID, and read the feedback comments about prior transactions. You can filter the

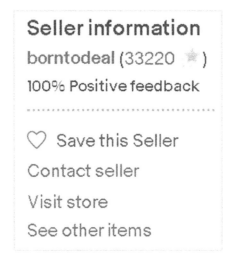

**FIGURE 3–5.** Here's my Seller Information, which shows my user ID and my feedback score.

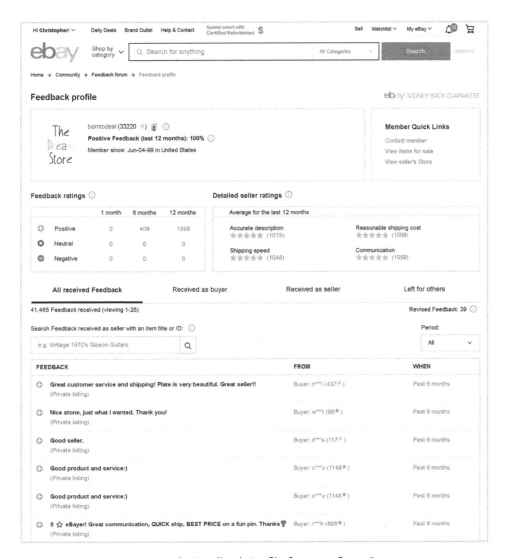

**FIGURE 3–6.** Here's the Feedback Profile for one of my eBay accounts.

comments to display the member's feedback received as a buyer, as a seller, or left for others. Feedback is also searchable. Figure 3-6 above is the feedback profile for my oldest eBay account—opened on June 4, 1999!

6. *Review the shipping costs.* An attractive price can quickly turn into a nightmare deal when you realize that the freight cost to deliver the pallet of wholesale dictionaries you're looking at will cost three times what you're paying for the merchandise itself. You'll also want to ensure the seller delivers to your location—which eBay will tell you when you're signed into your account. Figure 3-7 on page 46 is the shipping, payment, and returns information for a lawn mower that costs only $200 but adds another $100 in shipping—and the seller doesn't allow returns. When searching

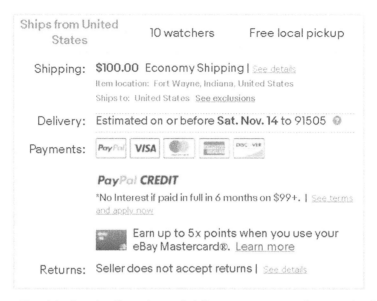

**FIGURE 3–7.** The shipping details, estimated delivery, payment options, and seller returns policy on a listing for a lawn mower. A $100 shipping cost and no returns allowed—both make me a bit uncomfortable.

for heavy items, try narrowing your search to items within your community and filter for listings that allow pickup. Go to the Item Location section on the left-hand side of the search results and check Within, and then use the pull-down menu to select a comfortable driving distance from your zip code. You should also tick the Free Local Pickup check box on the left-hand side of the search results under the Delivery Options section and then pick it up in person. Figure 3-8 on page 47 offers an example of how the Item Location and Free Local Pickup options work to display nearby local pickup items.

7. *Check if the seller allows returns.* The best sellers on eBay offer returns—some even pay return shipping. A listing can be configured in the following ways:

> **TIP**
>
> I'm making the assumption you're in the U.S.—shame on me if you aren't, and in that case, thanks for taking an interest in my book nonetheless (all are welcome). By default, eBay displays everything from everyone. You'll see items in London, England, right next to items that will ship from London, Ohio. You can filter your searches to display only items in the U.S.; under Item Location, tick the US Only check box. You'll save on postage, avoid customs duties and fees, and receive what you're buying faster.

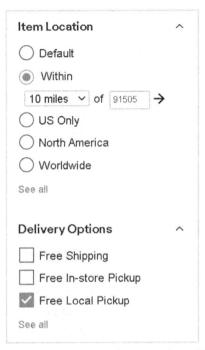

**FIGURE 3–8.** The Item Location and Delivery Options filters appear on the left-hand side of every eBay search results page.

- No returns allowed
- Domestic returns, but no returns from international buyers
- Both domestic and international returns

The grace period—the time limit within which a buyer must initiate the return—can be set to 14, 30, or 60 days. The listing must indicate who will pay for the return shipping, the buyer or the seller. As a convenience, eBay will automatically generate seller-approved prepaid return labels. If the buyer and seller come to a mutual agreement, the seller can offer a replacement or exchange in lieu of a refund for returned items.

8. *Check the estimated delivery date.* Shipping time varies based on the carrier, type of service used, distance, weather, and other factors. Cross-border shipments take longer because they travel farther and require a customs inspection. FedEx, UPS, and USPS offer different shipping services that move packages at different speeds (e.g., cheap Media Mail takes much longer than the pricier Priority Mail). You will find the estimated delivery date on every eBay listing (see Figure 3-7 on page 46). The delivery estimate includes the seller's handling time as well as how long the shipping method normally takes. In

a hurry? Ask the seller if they'd be willing to use a faster shipping method before you buy.

9. *Ignore temptation.* The site's first-party advertising business is a listing enhancement service known as Promoted Listings. On every listing page (as well as all over eBay), you'll see Promoted Listings from the same seller as well as other sellers. You can easily become sidetracked from your mission with all the distracting shopping opportunities. Move forward with focus and purpose to buy the item you need for your business. Mental focus is the perfect tonic for excessive and needless spending.

## COMPLETING THE SALE

Now that you've found the perfect Ming dynasty blue and white dragon vase offered by a seller with 100 percent positive feedback and you're ready to go for it, what's next? If you're the high bidder on an auction, use the Contact Seller link on the right-hand side of the listing to ask for an invoice that includes shipping. Don't be surprised to see sales tax added to your invoice if you haven't uploaded a resale license to your eBay account. This is also your chance to share any special concerns or expectations. If what you're acquiring is highly collectible, ask the seller to explain their packing protocol and ask that special care be taken in packing and insuring the precious cargo. While it is the seller's responsibility to deliver your purchase in the same condition shown on eBay, a broken Ming vase is irreplaceable.

For fixed price purchases, use the Buy It Now button if you're buying a single item or the Add to Cart button if you're buying multiple items from one or more sellers. When you view your cart, you'll need to decide how you'll be paying for your purchases.

Sellers aren't allowed to require you to mail cash or use point-to-point cash transfer services such as Western Union or MoneyGram. Site policy also states that direct contact information can only be exchanged after checkout is complete. This includes asking buyers to get in touch with details of alternative payment methods. Be cautious and avoid scams by completing your trades on eBay.

Here's a list of eBay-approved payment methods:

- Apple Pay
- Credit card or debit card
- Google Pay
- PayPal
- PayPal Credit
- Payment upon pickup

## MAKING GUEST PURCHASES

If you'd still like to try out the eBay buying experience without registering for an account, you can do so as a guest. Once you've found an item you'd like to buy, you can go to checkout to complete your purchase. Here's how:

1. Select Buy It Now on the listing.

2. Select Check Out as Guest.

3. Fill in your shipping address, email address, and payment information.

4. Select Confirm and Pay.

You can buy without an eBay account if:

- The item costs less than $5,000.

- The item can be purchased using Buy It Now. If you want to bid on an auction or send a Best Offer to a seller, you'll need an eBay account.

- You pay for the item using PayPal, a credit or debit card, Apple Pay, or Google Pay.

Some of eBay's categories permit sellers to also accept payment by the following methods:

- Bank-to-bank transfers
- Checks
- Money orders
- Online payment services (e.g., Allpay, CertaPay, Fiserv, Nochex, Xoom)

Double-check your delivery address before completing your eBay purchase. Many sellers won't agree to ship to an address that's different from the one you entered—eBay's seller protections require that the shipment be sent to the address that was entered. You won't be able to file a Money Back Guarantee claim for nondelivery if the item tracking shows it was delivered to the address you provided during checkout—so make sure it's correct. A signature is required for purchases totaling $750 or more—so be sure you're around to sign for the parcel when it arrives. A failed delivery attempt will void your ability to make a nondelivery claim.

## KEEPING TRACK OF PURCHASES

When you start making many purchases on eBay (like I do), you'll want to be able to track and manage things efficiently. You'll be using your My eBay section frequently as a buyer and seller. The link to My eBay is found at the top right of most eBay pages. Hover over My eBay and then click Purchase History (see Figure 3–9 on page 51) to pull up your recent buying activity. The default display shows the last 60 days of purchases, and you can view up to three years of purchases by changing the pull-down menu located under See Orders From: at the top of the page. You can use the Filter By: option to show shipped items and those that are ready for feedback.

You'll find these sections and options under Purchase History:

- *Orders.* This includes purchases you've made within the past 60 days, with the option to view up to three years' worth of purchase history. From this section you can see the following information:
  - Order date
  - Order number: A unique number automatically assigned by eBay that can have one or more items associated with it—think of this like an invoice number
  - Sold by: The eBay user ID of the seller
  - Item title
  - eBay item number: The unique number that eBay assigns to the listing
  - Shipment tracking number: Also, if applicable, the delivery date
  - Order total: The total of all items if there are two or more in the order
  - Item price
  - Action buttons that let you initiate a return, purchase again, and leave feedback
  - More actions: A pull-down menu with links, some of which are only accessible at certain phases of the order process. The list will change after the seller ships your order and subsequently uploads the tracking number. Here are the links:
    · Write a review
    · View order details
    · Contact seller
    · Ask to cancel order: Only visible during the grace period, within which you are allowed to cancel the order
    · Report late delivery
    · View seller's other items
    · View similar items
    · Sell this item: A useful way to prefill the selling form if you are reselling the purchase back on eBay

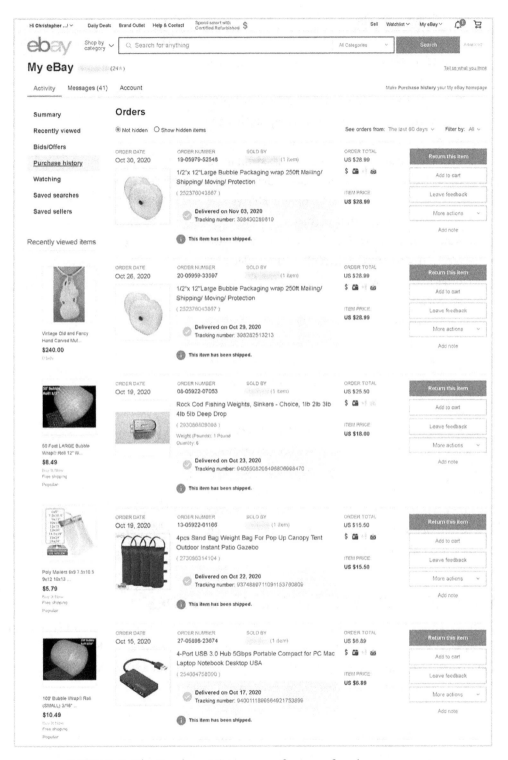

**FIGURE 3–9.** The Purchase History page for one of my buyer accounts.

- · Save this seller
- · Hide order
- – Add note: A handy spot to store private notes

- Canceled Items. Here you'll see recent purchases that you made and subsequently canceled.
- Canceled Invoices. This section is similar to Canceled Items, only here the seller emailed you an invoice for one or more purchases and you later canceled that invoice.
- Returns and Canceled Orders. Orders that you received and later returned to the seller and orders that you canceled before the seller shipped appear here.
- Unpaid Items. Items appear here when you've failed to pay for them.
- Unpaid Invoices. This section is similar to Unpaid Items, but it displays orders where the seller invoiced you and you didn't pay.

Now you've paid for your perfect prize and you're anxiously awaiting the delivery. Everything usually goes smoothly on eBay—even more so when you've mastered all the buying tips I've shared with you. In the next section, I'll show you how to get back to smooth sailing on those rare occasions when you run into choppy waters.

**TIP**

If you paid for your eBay purchase with a credit card—whether that was on eBay directly or through your PayPal, Apple Pay, or Google Pay account—do not file an eBay Money Back Guarantee case and simultaneously dispute the payment through your credit card company. Opening duplicate buyer protection requests violates eBay's abusive buyer policy. They won't have an issue if you decide to seek help from your credit card company, but by doing so you'll waive your right to file a Money Back Guarantee claim. I personally prefer eBay's protection program because its employees understand the nuances of eBay buying and do a great job helping to work things out.

## AVOIDING (AND RESOLVING) BUYING ISSUES

I hope all your eBay purchases go well. If you've taken my tips to heart, you shouldn't run into seller- or order-related challenges. Sellers with fantastic feedback are the best eBay has to offer, and trading with the best means they'll take great care of you.

Here are some common issues and how to deal with them:

- Nothing arrives. Deliveries can be delayed for a number of reasons—address mix-ups, weather, a torn address label, the box was left with a neighbor (rare nowadays), and so on. Before you panic, go back to your Purchase History (Figure

3-9 on page 51) and review the estimated delivery date range. If you made the purchase from an overseas seller, the delivery would typically take much longer, not so much due to distance (parcels are usually sent by plane), but because customs must inspect the parcel before it can continue its journey. Click the tracking number and review the details. If the tracking doesn't show delivery and the shipment is overdue based on eBay's estimate for delivery, open a case. Go to the Orders section in your Purchase History and click More Actions. Select Report Late Delivery from the pull-down menu and follow the instructions. This opens a case that requires action from the seller—either to refund your money or to provide a replacement for the lost merchandise.

- *The item doesn't match the listing.* The Money Back Guarantee is your first line of defense when there are problems with your order. Resist the temptation to dispute the charge with your credit card company or PayPal—this could create unnecessary hassle and work. The process has been streamlined and automated, and an eBay representative will mediate if necessary. Before you do that, though, try contacting the seller for assistance with whatever problem you're having. From your Purchase History, click More Actions, and from the pull-down menu, select Contact Seller. A screen will pop up with a variety of contact options (shown in Figure 3-10 below). When you select the topic describing the problem with your order, eBay will automatically open a case for you. You can

**FIGURE 3-10.** Here's the Contact Seller form that you can access from your Purchase History.

view and manage your open cases by clicking the Resolution Center link at the bottom of the homepage, under the Help & Contact section. You will also see the Resolution Center link at the bottom of most eBay pages.

- *Damage in transit.* Some products are harder to protect from normal handling in transit. Antique 78 RPM record albums (a product I've sold a lot of) are so fragile that they are like glass and require extra special care in packing. Many products can be broken inside the box even if there's no outward damage. Parcel contents can be ruined if the carrier leaves it exposed to weather on your porch. If there are visible problems with the box, take pictures before and after opening it to send to the seller. It's ultimately the seller's responsibility to ensure safe delivery, and you have every right to open a Money Back Guarantee claim when an order arrives in poor condition.

- *Porch theft.* This is not covered by the Money Back Guarantee. In fairness to the seller, it's unkind to open a case for a refund when porch theft occurs. Once the seller's tracking shows the parcel has been delivered to your address, their responsibility has been fulfilled. I receive high-value parcels securely through a P.O. box to avoid this problem. The postal service rents low-cost P.O. boxes for receiving mail, including USPS parcels and deliveries through private carriers, such as Amazon, UPS, and FedEx. If you do fall victim to porch thieves, you should report it to the police.

- *Buying limits and restrictions.* It's important to understand the difference between buying limits and buying restrictions. A buying limit protects sellers from unpaid items and ensures that buyers don't bid or buy more than they are comfortable with. Buying restrictions occur when eBay's policies are violated. Scan the QR code in Figure 3–11 below to learn more about how eBay limits and restricts buyer activities.

- *Account takeovers.* It's extremely rare, but it does happen. Unexplained purchases on your eBay account and an inability to log in are signs that a fraudster has hijacked your account. You should never share your passwords with other

**FIGURE 3–11.** This QR code leads to eBay's full policy page
that explains how buying activity is sometimes limited and restricted.

people. It's also a bad idea to use public and shared computers. Malicious keylogging software can covertly track what you type on these machines and send it back to the cybercriminal who planted it—and now they have your password. Phishing emails can trick you into thinking they are from a legitimate source and ask you to click a link using the ruse of an account limitation or other problem to motivate you to act. Phishing emails also often contain attachments that will infect your computer with malware. To avoid these problems, here's what you should do:

- Don't use eBay while connected to public wifi—use your mobile data and mobile device, tether your laptop to your mobile device, or use your secure home or office networks. That hotel courtesy network is fine if you're searching for a local restaurant, but don't access your eBay account with it (or any accounts involving sensitive information).

- Avoid revealing birthdays and other personal information on social media and elsewhere online.

- Never click on attachments unless you know you can trust the source, and never click links in emails even if they look official. I make sure to type "https://www.ebay.com" into your browser and sign in from there.

- Keep your devices up-to-date. Many software updates include enhanced security protections and bug fixes to protect you from hackers. Turn on automatic updates on all your devices to receive the newest fixes as they become available.

- Use a password manager to store and recall your passwords. I prefer *and* use LastPass. This allows you to use very complex passwords that are hard for anyone to guess or hack. A colleague recommends two-factor authentication which eBay refers to as *2 step verification*. eBay 2 step verification protects your privacy by adding an extra layer of security. This can be accomplished one of two ways: 1) by installing the eBay app on your mobile device and using the app to acknowledge when you sign into your computer or 2) allowing eBay to send a security code to your phone so that you can confirm your identity.

**TIP**

Use the following steps to enable eBay 2 step verification:

1. Sign into your account from a laptop or desktop computer.

2. Hover over your name in the upper-left-hand corner of the eBay homepage.

3. Click Account Settings.

4. Click Sign In and Security.

5. Click Edit in the section titled "2 step verification."

6. Click Get Started next to your preferred 2 step verification method.

---

### DON'T LET THE CLOCK RUN OUT—FILE CLAIMS PROMPTLY

You can open a case under eBay's Money Back Guarantee protection program up to 30 days after you received (or should have received) your purchase. You can confirm the delivery date or estimated delivery date for your order by hovering over My eBay at the top of the homepage or on most eBay pages and then clicking Purchase History. If more than 30 days have elapsed, and if you used PayPal to pay for the item, you can still file for PayPal Purchase Protection. PayPal offers a 180-day window for items that are not as described or not received. If you didn't use PayPal and it's more than 30 days after the delivery date, your credit or debit card company may have other options for you—contact them for help.

---

A simple and effective way to avoid most problems when buying on eBay is to read the listing carefully, look at all the photos provided, check the seller's feedback, and ask questions before you bid or buy. Caveat emptor!

That said, sellers who offer returns expect a certain percentage of buyers to send items back, and you may request to return an item in the condition it was received if you simply change your mind.

When you do experience a problem, contact the seller first. If that doesn't resolve the issue, reach out to eBay using the Help & Contact link at the top of the homepage or most eBay pages.

## FOREIGN SOURCING—YOUR RESPONSIBILITIES AND LIABILITIES (AND A WARNING FOR DUTY DODGERS)

The internet has made the earth a much smaller place; it's now easy to find and purchase goods from virtually anywhere around the world. While it is entirely possible to become rich buying, importing, and reselling goods, like every business that has a low barrier to entry, it is teeming with competitors who will be snapping at your profits and trying to reverse-engineer your success.

There are YouTube gurus who say "Do the math. I'm reselling this $1 item for $10, and so can you." Many of these prophets promise drop-ship riches where you never have to pack a single order. But at the end of each of these get-rich-quick self-help videos is a pitch to join an insiders club or pay dues to unlock a list of secret import products that will purportedly yield a cornucopia of profits. Before you fall for one of these pipe dreams, know that most overseas factories already sell direct-to-consumer on eBay themselves. It is possible (but very unlikely) to score a contract with a foreign manufacturer to act as their exclusive eBay reseller—good luck landing that opportunity.

I'm not being negative—just candid. The pitfalls of foreign sourcing for resale include:

- The high cost of postage
- Unforeseen delays and costs related to import inspection, taxes, and customs fees
- Language barriers
- Poor-quality items with high defect rates
- The high cost of return freight if things go wrong
- A lack of buying power as a result of being a small business
- The difficulty of finding niche products that haven't already been overexposed on eBay (remember fidget spinners?)
- Low barriers to entry—by the time you receive your wholesale shipment of the latest hot product, a hundred other sellers are listing them on eBay

Importing is not for the faint of heart. Before you fall in love with the idea of becoming a large-scale importer who makes money while sipping a mai tai at Nassau's Cable Beach, understand that importing products comes with a tangle of rules and regulations, and becoming a successful importer requires a lot of hard work and skills developed from experience. Selling on eBay will protect you in a lot of ways, many of which I have already discussed, but eBay cannot inoculate you against the loss of capital or missed opportunities due to poor judgment or dead inventory caused by rapidly changing consumer tastes.

If you're buying for personal use, in most cases you'll be just fine. I've ordered goods from cross-border sellers since the 1980s and have never been assessed an import duty for small orders. When you move goods from any foreign country to the U.S., they are being imported. When importing for resale (or commercial purposes), you are subject to U.S. government regulations.

U.S. Customs and Border Protection (CBP), a division of the U.S. Department of Homeland Security, has a number of roles within the federal government, two of which are overseeing commercial trade regulations and collecting import duties. See https://www.cbp.gov/trade/basic-import-export/internet-purchases.

When you become an importer, you'll need to consider these key points:

- Legally, are you allowed to import the product?
- Are there any unique restrictions by the CBP on the importation of the product, e.g., is it regulated food or made from an endangered species animal?
- Are special forms required by the CBP?

- Is the purchase being imported for resale or personal use?
- The cost of shipping plus any import taxes might be more than the purchase cost. Who pays for shipping?
- Not all shippers offer the same quality care. Is the freight company considered to be reliable?
- Is the shipment a large or small one? Small packages are usually sent through the postal service to be delivered directly to the customer. If the seller does not make arrangements for postal or door-to-door delivery, it may be necessary to hire a customs broker in order to clear your goods. They can then be forwarded on or arrangements made to pick up the purchase at the port of entry.
- Does the seller have experience with cross-border trades? Giving misleading or inaccurate information about an item and its value is illegal. The importer could face legal action and fines for this violation.

> **TIP**
>
> Parcels sent through the postal service (as opposed to a private carrier such as DHL, FedEx, or UPS) with a declared value below $800 ($100 if being sent as a gift to someone other than the purchaser) will generally be cleared by customs without any additional paperwork or duty. See https://www.cbp.gov/trade/basic-import-export/internet-purchases for more advice from U.S. Customs and Border Protection.

The buyer in a cross-border trade is normally responsible for taxes and import charges. It's illegal to ask the seller to undervalue the goods to lower these costs. Getting caught may result in criminal prosecution. In 2020, a German company and its U.S. subsidiary paid a $22.2 million fine to resolve allegations that they violated the False Claims Act (also called the "Lincoln Law") for knowingly making false statements on customs declarations to avoid paying import duties. To enter goods into the U.S., an importer must use reasonable care when reporting the origin and value of what's being imported. If you manage a petite operation, a fine for fibbing won't be in the millions, but it is great to sleep soundly, so run your business with integrity.

You've learned a lot about buying on eBay already. In the next chapter I'll show you some tips for sourcing merchandise that will turn you into an absolute eBay expert.

# Chapter 4

# On the Prowl for Epic Merchandise

I f eBay will be your first business venture, then start by putting your toe in the water. Avoid diving into the deep end of the pool on your first day. There's a learning curve, especially when it comes to product sourcing, and to make a living selling on eBay, you'll need to have a steady stream of merchandise coming in. But finding products to sell isn't hard if you learn how to source and negotiate good deals. In the previous chapter, you learned about buying on eBay so you can not only get into the mind of the eBay customer, but also so you can resell those items. In this chapter, I'll teach you how to apply my techniques for finding products outside of the eBay ecosystem and help you become inspired to think up new ways to source products yourself.

## START WITH WHAT YOU HAVE

Because eBay feedback reinforces buyer trust, the first thing to do is build up a bit of feedback and develop a good reputation. Before you head to a wholesaler and start stocking up, start by selling high-quality items that you no longer want or need from around your home. Don't sell your old junk. No one wants a mass-market paperback you left out in the rain or a pile of dead batteries. Listing your unbranded tees is a waste of time. Used socks should become rags or trash. However, sometimes what you think is trash turns out to be treasure. As you will discover in Chapter 8, even seemingly worthless old software can turn huge profits. I was surprised to discover very recently that certain albums on CD, which sold for $5 to $10 when new, are now routinely selling for $25 to $35 each. While many artists and music labels have digitized their music, there are thousands of albums sitting in collections that are not available online, and collectors will pay good money for them.

I live in Burbank, California, where I have a long reputation for my consignment success and for being Burbank's "eBay guy." A man from the neighboring city of North Hollywood brought me 69 mint condition G.I. Joe action figures and toys that he had found while cleaning out his family's garage. They had been stored away at his home since the early 1980s, undisturbed for decades. From my research, I thought the collection had a high probability of doing very well, but there were zero comparable sales for vintage G.I. Joe toys in such pristine condition. As usual, I listed them at auction with high starting prices that I felt represented the top range of fair market value. Why leave money on the table?

After the auctions ended, the collection had sold for $28,921.14. The 1982 Snake Eyes commando action figure alone sold for $2,950.51 (see Figure 4–1 on page 61). The consignor had actually considered tossing them out or donating them before he heard about me. Trash to treasure indeed. In candor, I had no idea what the toy collection was going to bring because their condition was exceptional and most had never been opened. The results were a pleasant surprise.

You never know what you'll find in the closet, attic, or garage. Is that footlocker under the bed brimming with treasure? While those G.I. Joes did extremely well, the owner had to share a healthy cut of the profits with me. I encourage you to start in your own home and make it an exhilarating treasure hunt. Challenge yourself—go to Chapter 3 to discover the advanced techniques and tips and determine the value of what you already own. Are those baubles worth a bunch? Your research will reveal their true value.

Figure 4–2 on pages 62 to 64 is a chart showing the items most commonly found in homes, along with my comments and a rating of one to five stars next to each—with one being the least viable for selling on eBay and five being the most.

**FIGURE 4–1.** I sold this super mint condition garage-found 1982 Snake Eyes commando action figure for $2,950.51. One of the best places to source merchandise can be right in your own home or the homes of family and friends.

If you've never sold an item on eBay, start by clearing out your household clutter. Once you've gone through your own home, dive into the forgotten treasure in the homes of your family and friends, and then venture into the world of consignment sales.

## CONSIGN FOR BIG PROFITS

In a consignment sale, the supplier of the merchandise is the *consignor*. They retain ownership (referred to as *title*) of the goods until they are sold. The *consignee* is

| Product Category | Comments | Viability |
|---|---|---|
| Clothing, shoes, and accessories | Pros: there's always an endless supply of these items out there. Cons: there's an endless supply of these! Stick to top brand names when selling individual items and make bulk lots for less popular brands. You must clean garments before selling them. | ★★★ |
| Mobile phones and accessories | Pros: phones that are light and newer models are easy to sell. Brands matter in this category. Cell phones of some kind are now owned by 96 percent of Americans. Cons: accessories are very cheap, so bundle them with a phone rather than selling them separately. | ★★★★ |
| Computers and peripherals | Pros: there's always demand, and shipping is usually affordable. Virtually every home has some forgotten computer gear tucked away. Cons: value declines rapidly with age (until they become really old, and then value rises); desktop computers usually hold less value than laptops. | ★★★ |
| Consumer electronics | Pros: shipping is usually cheap (for most small electronics) and there's always a demand for games, gadgets, and accessories. If the gear was quality when new and has been stored properly, eBay is a great place to sell—and most homes have some items tucked away. Cons: the market is very flooded, and only timely brand-name or unique merchandise sells well. | ★★★ |
| Jewelry and timepieces | Pros: easy to pack and easy to ship. There's always someone looking for jewelry and timepieces, especially men's timepieces. The sweet spot is in high-quality antique and vintage items, which are found in many homes. Cons: the market is flooded with imported, low-priced jewelry and timepieces, requiring sellers to offer timely and unique designs, fair prices, and high-quality workmanship. Cheap overseas labor makes it hard to compete with offshore sellers, and commercial jewelry is often worth much less than people imagine. Be sure you've secured permission before listing Grandma's jewels! | ★★★★★ (for top brands, antique, and vintage goods only) |
| Home and garden | Pros: pretty much everyone has unwanted items of this genre around the house. Brand-name, high-quality goods are the best choice. Interesting, high-quality bar and kitchen gadgets do well. The older the item or better the brand (or both), the more likely it will sell for good money. | ★★ |

**FIGURE 4–2.** This table shows the sales viability on eBay of common household items. I've provided the pros and cons and a viability score using a one through five-star ranking system.

| Product Category | Comments | Viability |
|---|---|---|
| Home and garden, cont. | Cons: it's often hard to tell what will sell. Used linens probably won't do well unless they're high-end brands. There's so much of this stuff sold at mass retail stores that you'll need to acquire a nose for what moves. Sometimes it gets difficult when you bought the item and are being pressed to let it go for a fraction of what it originally cost. But if you're not using it, take any amount of money you can score for it. | ★★ |
| Art and collectibles | Pros: virtually everyone is a potential customer. Everyone I know owns art and collectibles of some kind. I sold a winsome Falstaff figurine to renowned actor John Rhys-Davies, who played the character on stage. Unwanted art and collectibles sit in storage in most homes. Cons: unknown artists are a hard sell. Big art is expensive to ship and can be easily damaged in transit (offer local pickup). Collectibles come in all sorts of genres, but scarce merchandise always sells best. | ★★★★ |
| Travel-related items | Pros: every home has luggage, backpacks, or some form of travel merchandise. Branded items always do best. Cons: cheap and bulky items don't do well on eBay. | ★★ |
| Mothers and babies | Pros: quality products are easy to rehome. Feeding equipment, training merchandise, and souvenirs do well. Cons: due to mass production and cheap imports, only brands sell well (am I sounding like a broken record yet?). | ★★★ |
| Sporting goods | Pros: people love activities, sports, and the outdoors, and there's always tremendous interest in quality, brand-name sporting goods. There's huge money in virtually every subcategory, and almost everyone has merchandise in this category at home. Cons: larger items such as skis, bikes, etc. aren't easy to ship, and eBay is awash in no-brand products made overseas. | ★★★ |
| Beauty and health | Pros: everyone uses products in this category. Shaving and grooming, anti-aging, makeup, and many other subcategories are all multibillion-dollar industries. You'll find something around the house to sell in this category. Cons: not everything is easily sold, and used cosmetics or other items that come in contact with the body may be restricted or prohibited on eBay. | ★★ |
| Hobbies and toys | Pros: well-cared-for toys sell well, and these items are found in most homes. Vintage and rare examples can generate big money (as we saw with the G.I. Joe auctions). Dolls are an interesting category with a huge audience. Cons: condition is vital, and well-used toys lose much of their worth. Unbranded merchandise holds very little value. | ★★ |

**FIGURE 4–2.** continued

| Product Category | Comments | Viability |
|---|---|---|
| Home improvement | Pros: tools are found in every home, and there's always a need for them. Project leftovers move easily on eBay (e.g., fasteners, wire, blades, adhesives, etc.). Cons: there are not too many downsides to this category. Larger items will need to be sold for local pickup only, such as leftover timber, unused roofing, etc.; and because that could be more of a hassle, I'm giving this four stars. | ★★★★ |
| Wedding and events | Pros: brides on a budget are always on the prowl for discounts on dresses, men's formalwear, and everything else related to weddings. There are also folks looking for discount clothing for other formal occasions, such as prom, homecoming, cocktail parties, quinceañera, and so on. Buyers love deals and unique items. Another plus? People are likely to have many of these items in their household. Cons: selling outfits requires careful measuring to avoid returns. | ★★★ |
| Motors | Pros: vehicle accessories and replacement parts are in most homes. When you're ready to sell a car, eBay is a great venue for advertising it—even for local pickup. Vintage and rare items sell very well. Cons: the market is flooded with aftermarket replacement merchandise (i.e., generic). Prices for the most common items are soft. | Antique and vintage: ★★★★★ Vehicles: ★★★★ Parts and accessories: ★★ |
| Furniture | Pros: antique and high-quality furniture sells well on eBay. Everyone has furniture at home. Cons: unless it's very valuable, furniture is generally local pickup only, which substantially limits the audience. | ★★ |

**FIGURE 4–2.** continued

allowed to sell the goods and is only required to pay the consignor if and when a sale occurs. This arrangement allows the consignor to sell something they no longer want and the consignee a chance to source goods with zero investment—a match made in heaven!

Some consignees charge their consignors a flat fee for their services, while others take a commission based on the final selling price. If the consignee chooses the commission model, they should disclose that they are selling the goods on eBay and share their user ID with the consignor, so the selling prices are transparent. Consignors who are familiar with eBay's auction format may opt to pay a commission and ask for confirmation of the final sales price by getting the eBay item number from the consignee and looking up the sold listing. (In case you don't know, looking up an eBay listing using the item number is as simple as typing "https://www.ebay.com/itm/number" [replace "number" with the actual item number].) Either arrangement can be mutually fair and profitable, but a successful sale will require realistic pricing by the consignor—whether that is a fixed price or an auction starting price. The commission model would be more profitable on higher-ticket items and I use the commission model. Commission-based selling means that the interests of the consignor and consignee are in alignment and both parties profit from successful sales.

When I sell consigned merchandise on eBay, I require physical possession so that I can rapidly ship the item to the buyer once it sells. I provide same-day shipping as one of my customer-satisfaction techniques. I previously allowed my consignors to pack and ship the goods, and for the most part, it worked fine. The problem occurred when seller's remorse set in. Occasionally a consignor would change their mind, and that affected my reputation on eBay, because the buyers would leave poor feedback for my failure to follow through on the transaction. As a result, I no longer consign any item unless I control the inventory at my place of business, unless the consignor is a factory that produces those goods on a daily basis, thus guaranteeing a steady and available supply. My excellent reputation in the field of eBay consignment has ensured a ready supply of goods without having to drop-ship through my consignors.

## WARNING! AVOID BECOMING YOUR CLIENTS' FREE STORAGE FACILITY

Storage in urban areas is expensive, and these very same areas are likely to have an endless supply of consignment goods. Be cautious when accepting consignments if you live in one of these communities. You must develop a clear understanding of what sells easily and what does not sell well on eBay.

People living in densely populated cities will gladly part with bags of worthless old clothes and cheap household goods. Some may already be eBay sellers who cream the good stuff off the top to sell themselves and then want you to take their clutter. Learn the art of the polite decline. Take it slowly and research items before accepting them. The last thing you want is to become a free storage facility for your clients—with piles of deadstock collecting dust in your place, not theirs.

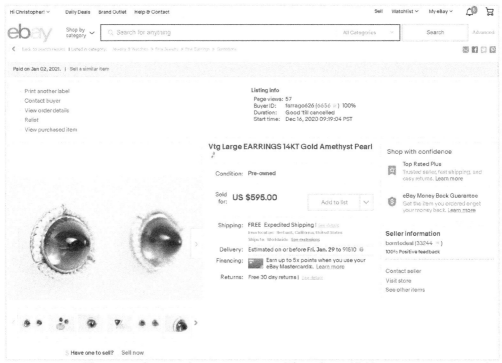

**FIGURE 4–3.** These amethyst earrings are stunners. These beautiful images were captured by Hannah Yonce. I consigned these for $175 and sold them for $595. I did not take advantage of the consignor—I set my starting price high and was fortunate enough to do *very* well.

Figure 4–3 above shows one of my listings for a pair of amethyst earrings. The starting price for the auction was $175, which was the amount the consignor asked for, regardless of the final sales price. They ended up selling for $595, which resulted in $420 in gross profit. The consignor was still very happy to receive their $175.

I have been coaching eBay sellers on the finer points of eBay consignment for a very long time. Consignment has been my core eBay sourcing strategy since 1999. With eBay consignment, you can make huge profits with zero investment.

As a small business owner, you'll never have the buying power of the big guys, so why try to compete directly with them? I would never in a million years discourage you from pursuing your dreams, but be realistic and start with a plan that is likely to return an immediate profit. Buying and reselling readily available goods is hard to do profitably unless you score a super-secret deal like no other. That's about as rare as a unicorn. Many companies intentionally sell their goods below cost to weaken their competition and eventually put them out of business. That strategy requires a lot of capital—and these days that means billions of dollars. I'd prefer to focus on something more achievable, like consignment.

Start by asking friends and family if you can consign items they no longer want. Perhaps you're worried about doing business with people close to you. It is true that if something goes wrong with the business relationship, you could lose a friend or a family member could hold onto hurt feelings for a long time. So make sure that whatever you consign holds no sentimental value for the consignor, no matter who they are. The transaction should be pragmatic, not emotional.

If you're still concerned that emotions with family and friends might override good business sense, look for consignment opportunities elsewhere. Who could use your service? Here are a few other possible sources of consignment goods, in no particular order:

- People who are moving or downsizing
- Estates of deceased individuals—a situation that often leaves relatives with homes filled with unwanted items
- Wealthy individuals who enjoy buying new things and want to rehome their past purchases
- Bankruptcy, divorce, and probate attorneys who can refer you to their clients so that you can assist them in converting unwanted assets into money
- Pawn shops
- Dissolved businesses or partnerships
- Nonprofits that have donated items and eager donors but lack the staff to sell them
- Local government agencies with surplus property
- Auctioneers with unsold items
- Businesses with excess inventory
- Banks and finance companies with repossessed merchandise
- Leasing companies with off-lease inventory
- Rental companies that need to retire their assets
- Insurance companies with damaged (but salable) goods for which they have already paid out claims
- Manufacturers with overruns, canceled orders, and factory seconds
- Custom imprinting companies with misprinted items
- Installers and movers who routinely come across unwanted client items
- Public storage unit operators
- Hotels and motels that are renovating
- Antique stores and antique malls, many of which are struggling to adjust to a new way of doing business online
- Members of the local chamber of commerce—you may have to join to attend their mixers, but almost all chambers post their member directories online

I have done business with all these types of people and businesses. Members of the chamber of commerce will be a bit friendlier than most, because they understand that you're simply networking the same way they do. You'll also find a warmer reception if you take the time to learn a little about their businesses and offer to network for them with others when you see an opportunity.

You should also learn how to toot your own horn. Before you spend a dollar from your advertising budget, grab your business cards and hit the pavement. Business cards are very cheap. You can print them for as little as two cents each. It will take time for people to get to know you, but trust and awareness will build—and business opportunities will gradually snowball until there's an avalanche of consignments.

Just remember that everyone has unwanted items suitable for selling on eBay. But prospecting requires some common sense. Networking events are a great place to discuss your services, but going door-to-door in a residential neighborhood is far too aggressive and intrusive. Dropping off door hangers in those neighborhoods is fine. YouTube ads are very cheap, but as with all technology, there's a learning curve that may discourage you. YouTube is currently my favorite advertising platform for reaching new clients, but something else will probably become the advertising method of choice soon. I realize that TikTok is all the rage as I write this, and I may be showing my age when I say I have never used it in my eBay business, but I encourage you to try anything you believe will benefit your business. You should use any means of promotion that you can understand and from which you see profitable results. If it works, keep doing it. Stop when it doesn't.

There is no better day than today to start selling on eBay. Just go for it. If you sold on eBay in the past but stopped, give it a try again. It's a very different and better marketplace than in the past, with far more buyers than ever before.

## DROP-SHIPPING FOR HASSLE-FREE SELLING

Drop-shipping is a supply method in which you don't hold physical inventory. You send transfer orders to the wholesaler or supplier, who then ships the products directly to the customer. It's elegant when it works well and uncomplicated because you don't maintain and manage inventory. This lack of inventory comes with a number of benefits, including:

- No investment in the inventory
- No merchandise storage costs from rent or a mortgage
- No warehouse shelving or equipment to buy
- No warehouse staffing labor costs

- No losses from accidents, *force majeure* (acts of God), employee theft, or break-ins
- No shipping carrier accounts to manage
- No packing supplies to order

The essence of the drop-shipping relationship boils down to allowing someone else to cope with all the headaches associated with sourcing and managing the goods and fulfilling orders. On eBay, drop-shipping is referred to as *product sourcing*.

On the surface, drop-shipping sounds awesome. Someone else buys high-demand, high-quality, brand-name goods and delivers them directly to your customer. The trouble is that everyone else is trying to do the same thing, and the drop-shipper has already incorporated a tidy profit for their own

**TIP**

Drop-shipping is allowed on eBay as long as the product is shipped from a wholesale supplier. You are always responsible for the safe, timely delivery of the items you sell on eBay even if they are drop-shipped. Listing an item on eBay and then buying the item from another retailer or website that ships directly to your customer is not allowed.

company in the price tag. Don't forget to factor in the costs of selling, such as eBay's insertion and final value fees. In the end, there may be little or no profit left for you. My advice is to test and explore the process before you spend a lot of time listing someone else's inventory until you're sure it makes financial sense. Be certain that your drop-ship partner hasn't oversaturated eBay by working with too many sellers. When this occurs, it typically results in a race to the bottom.

Don't confuse drop-shipping with consignment. I am skeptical about the former and very fond of the latter. Consignors usually hand you the goods they want you to sell, while a drop-shipper sends goods from their warehouse or business location. Consignors lend you their item and you only pay them when that product sells. Drop-shippers require payment before they send the merchandise. Proceed with caution. Be careful about tall tales and wild claims from drop-ship suppliers. Never under any circumstances should you pay a monthly subscription fee to gain access to a drop-shipper's inventory. Those offers are always a bad deal.

Don't be seduced by the guy standing in front of his red Ferrari on YouTube, offering to allow you to enter his circle of special friends by granting you access to his drop-shipping system. Instead, run the other direction when you're asked for a credit card number. Hard work and knowledge beat systems every time. While you're busy learning someone else's expensive drop-shipping system, your competition is busy taking photos, writing descriptions, packing and shipping, and counting dollars.

Here are some common claims you'll hear about drop-shipping:

- You'll get rich quick.
- It's easy to become successful at it.
- Drop-shipping is new.

None of those statements is true. Drop-shipping is a process, not an industry, that has been around for a very long time. I believe making money with drop-shipping is harder than making money with consignment, but if you're working with conscientious, fair drop-ship partners, you stand a good chance of actually making a profit. You don't need to reveal where you make your sales because doing so may prompt the drop shipper to sell on eBay themselves.

Now that you've heard the good, the bad, and the ugly about drop-shipping, I'll share some tips for finding good drop-shipping suppliers. Skip the ads for companies offering to drop-ship for you—you'll see a ton of them in your Google search results. Instead, look for trusted brands from smaller manufacturers in your local retail stores. Pick ones you love that you feel would do well on eBay, and make sure eBay isn't already oversaturated in those products. Reach out to the factory's wholesale department, and find out if the company will drop-ship individual orders. Don't expect this process to be easy. It is hard work to find an exclusive, profitable drop-ship partnership, but the harder it is, the bigger your eventual reward.

Another potential source for drop-shipping opportunities is to contact third-party logistics companies, sometimes referred to as 3PL. These firms operate independent warehouses, where they store, pick, pack, and ship goods for other firms. Factories of all sizes use 3PL companies to avoid the high cost and complexity of outfitting and managing their own warehouses. According to IBISWorld, an industry research company, in 2020, 3PLs represented $225 billion in gross merchandise volume, shipped by more than 22,000 companies in the U.S. Known, proven, and mature 3PL firms are very attractive to factories, distributors, and dealers. Introduce yourself to 3PL companies and ask if they would be willing to share information about your services with their clients. You never know—the 3PLs themselves may stock goods that they would be willing to drop-ship for you.

## SECOND-QUALITY GOODS FOR FIRST-RATE RETURNS

*Factory seconds*, also referred to as *factory rejects* (a horrible term) or simply *seconds*, are items that weren't quite up to par and are therefore sold to the public for a reduced price rather than being discarded. Here in the Los Angeles area where I live, seconds from the apparel, footwear, accessories, and fabrics industries are sold for very low prices in the downtown Los Angeles Fashion District. Most issues are so minor that you would never notice them if you weren't already aware they are seconds: a crooked seam, a stain, or some other insignificant flaw. Most of the goods sold within the Fashion District are manufactured locally.

Finding high-profit seconds that would do well on eBay takes skill, so stick to products you know well. The Fashion District seconds would be excellent for a fashionista with the skill to spot current trends and products that are in vogue. Ask factories in your town how they handle seconds. Many companies sell seconds locally to avoid cannibalizing their channels of distribution, so looking in your area makes good sense. You can also go on buying trips to shopping districts that specialize in selling seconds, such as outlet malls. Be careful about slick outlet malls that have become popular because buyers assume they are scoring a bargain. Some are now simply selling first-quality goods without a discount.

For years, I visited better off-price stores to source seconds. You can make money this way, but it's not a slam-dunk proposition. You'll have to practice this technique. There's been a lot of discussion about this sourcing method on YouTube, so you'll face some competition finding sources of supply. You'll make mistakes along the way, so start slowly to lessen the financial sting when you do make errors. As your confidence grows, you can increase the volume and average price of your purchases.

I am fond of sourcing seconds. While retail store buyers are usually quite particular about getting top-quality merchandise, eBay buyers represent a broad spectrum of customers with a variety of tastes. Bargain lovers will be happy to buy a slightly irregular product or one that's missing an accessory they don't care about anyway. A very famous perfume manufacturer once consigned to me 300 bottles of a fragrance that normally retails for $200. This company, which shall remain nameless (because I don't want you hustling them for the same deal!), had decided not to sell the bottles at retail because the printing on the bottle was off-center by a fraction of an inch. The company founder and CEO decided to sell them on eBay and gave me access to the inventory. Buyers didn't care about the (disclosed) printing defect because the fragrance smelled just as wonderful, and they paid less than half the usual price.

Every factory puts out seconds. A cookie factory can easily sell broken cookies to ice cream shops in bulk to use as a topping. But moving other product seconds is sometimes a bit more complex. Brands don't want to damage their reputation by allowing these seconds to enter their normal channels of distribution, but they still want to find a way to sell them. Reach out to the sales departments of your favorite brands, ask if they have a program to sell seconds, and find out how to become a wholesale customer.

Trade shows allow you to rapidly connect with many vendors in one place. One such example is the ASD Market Week, held twice a year in Las Vegas, Nevada, (https://www.asdonline.com). You can discover information about regional shows through your local or state economic development departments.

## HANDLING CUSTOMER RETURNS

Many websites sell case lots or entire pallets of customer returns. Most of these product aggregators are official liquidators for retail stores, and the goods are generally uninspected returns. Buying returned merchandise is always a gamble, but with a careful eye and a bit of common sense, there's money to be made. You can find these firms by googling "customer returns." As with all business opportunities, you'll face substantial competition. Uninspected returns involve some risk because you don't know why the products were returned. Wholesale lots also involve substantial freight charges, which can cost nearly as much as the merchandise itself, so be sure to factor in the freight as part of your cost of goods sold. New, retail clearance merchandise won't carry the same uncertainty associated with customer returns.

Make the rounds at your local independent retailers, and speak with the owner or general manager. Ask if they'll sell you deadstock and customer returns at a steep discount or, even better, offer to consign the items and sell them for a fee, so you have zero investment and no risk. Most big chains have existing relationships and won't change their returns process management, but local, family-owned businesses may appreciate the opportunity to cash in on their idle inventory. Companies in high-rent districts must manage their inventory aggressively because storage costs are high and space is typically limited.

According to eBay, the reseller business is booming, representing at least $42 billion in gross merchandise volume. Their exclusive partnership with BULQ (https://www.ebay.com/str/bulq) makes retail clearance and returned inventory sourcing available on eBay (see Figure 4-4 on page 73). BULQ is eBay's trusted wholesale liquidation source that works with retailers to grant sellers access to excess and returned inventory. Here's how it works:

- Browse lots on BULQ's eBay Store by category and condition.
- Place your order and have it shipped right to your door.
- List and resell the individual items on eBay.
- Save time with generated listings with prefilled data.

You'll find an endless supply of goods from liquidators specializing in both clearance and returned merchandise. Proceed with caution, but don't pass up an obviously great deal!

## MENDING BROKEN STUFF

We've been conditioned to seek perfection in our everyday lives, and that attitude extends to our possessions. Because of this, people tend to immediately discard or store

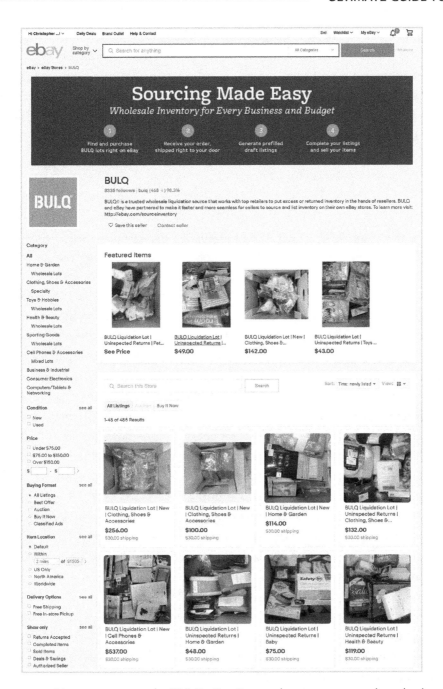

**FIGURE 4–4.** Here you can see the BULQ eBay Store, where you can purchase both new, wholesale goods (retail clearance) and uninspected returns. BULQ Store purchases are delivered to your home or business, with the added bonus of having eBay create drafts of listings based on the lot you purchased. You can then complete, refine, and launch these listings to sell the BULQ items individually.

imperfect and broken items. Yard sales, estate sales, and public auctions all yield an abundance of broken stuff that you can mend and resell for huge profits.

Surprisingly few people have the vision or experience to turn trash into treasure. A bespoke business suit made from the most expensive fabric money can buy will be tossed because of a few tiny moth holes that can be easily mended with the invisible reweaving technique. I rescued one such suit, paid a reweaving expert $100 to fix it, and immediately sold it for more than $900. The rescue suit was a consignment and on clothing I charge 50 percent commission!

There are so many eBay-friendly items that can be mended for instant profits. Worn-out but expensive shoes will look brand-new once a cobbler replaces the heels and soles and adds a flawless shine. A high-end blazer with one missing button is revived by cutting off all the old buttons and sewing on a new set (sourced on, you guessed it, eBay)—you can sell the old buttons separately so nothing is wasted. Many earrings are lost, so convert the surviving earring into a pendant by adding an inexpensive chain. Use a two-part epoxy to marry old-world coins to the top of a worn-out trinket box to create an exotic conversation piece. Use the same epoxy to repair the broken handle on an antique decorative teacup. Learn how to replace depleted watch batteries and watchbands yourself to generate huge profits from bulk used-watch lots. Buy a complete set of chess pieces to make an interesting chessboard more attractive to a prospective customer. I regularly buy broken jewelry, and my friend and colleague Carmelita Burns assembles the loose components into fantastic new creations. If you're highly ambitious, you can even buy nonoperational vehicles, fix them up, and sell them.

If you lack the time to go treasure hunting in person, eBay has endless buying opportunities. Countless untested electronics and toys are available for next to nothing. Buy them and see if you can fix them yourself. Leaky, old alkaline batteries often cause battery terminals to corrode, preventing proper operation—you can clean them off with a cotton swab dipped in vinegar.

When I met Hannah Yonce, she was unemployed and paying her rent with the money she had saved from her last job. She would ride around Burbank on her mountain bike, picking up broken stuff sitting on the parkway in front of homes, and see what she could salvage from it. She developed a lucrative business dismantling discarded vacuum cleaners and reselling the parts on eBay. In her case, she was parting out broken stuff to other eBay members, who could use the parts to mend *their* items.

See "Preparing Your Products Before Listing" in Chapter 8 for my guide to preparing your merchandise for sale. Items that are simply broken may require additional tools. For example, if you're routinely working with watches, you'll need a watch back-opening knife, an adjustable case opener, and a set of itsy-bitsy screwdrivers to remove the batteries. I have lots of tools that I've used just once, and I made a profit even after buying them. And, yes: I buy the tools on eBay.

Can't fix it? Repurpose it! I took shop class way back when at Glasgow Middle School (they called it Glasgow Junior High back then). There I learned the transformative art of making new stuff from recycled materials: lamps from car parts, old bottles, even Coke cans. Part of the curriculum included the ritual of selling our creations to the faculty and staff, who loved every handmade lamp, trinket box, and toy.

My sister Mariam discovered a local artist near the family farm in Catlett, Virginia, who weaves baskets with pieces of broken deer antler incorporated into the designs. (Deer are plentiful in Virginia, and shed antlers are easy to find.) Mariam is a loyal customer, and the baskets are all over the farmhouse. My sister won't part with any of her cherished baskets, but I bet they'd do very well on eBay.

Some of the more popular categories on eBay that work well for the buy-fix-resell business model are:

- Antiques and collectibles
- Clothing, shoes, and accessories
- Computers
- Dolls and bears
- Electronics
- Sporting goods
- Tools
- Toys

No doubt you'll discover other categories that will yield a pretty penny as well.

If you're particularly busy and prefer to delegate repairs to someone else, you can still make a nice profit. Track how much you spend and remember to include eBay's fees when tallying your profits.

While buying items to fix for resale can be hit-or-miss, the trick is to pay virtually nothing, or even score the item for free, and then learn to fix it yourself. YouTube can be your greatest asset here.

## THE ROADS LESS TRAVELED

America abounds with buying opportunities. While you must research commodified items carefully to ensure a reasonable profit, there's no rule requiring you to find comparable sold listings for every item you wish to sell. You will seldom find comps for rare antiques, if at all, but they will occasionally surprise you with stratospheric sales prices. With caution and ingenuity, you'll find even more fortuitous moments by taking the roads less traveled.

I'll wrap up this chapter by giving you a few more ways to develop your product sourcing process. This section is somewhat of a grab bag, but it may give you a few new ideas to explore.

Consider these opportunities for profits that others may not have been willing to pursue:

- *Junkyards.* Self-service salvage yards have many hidden treasures. The obvious one is auto salvage, and there's enough opportunity there to grow into a full-time business. Look for places that let you pick your own parts, and bring a well-appointed tool bag. I've seen salvage businesses in other genres, too, such as the incredibly lucrative industry of reclaimed restoration hardware.

- *Personal and business organization.* The problem of hoarding fascinated Americans so much that it engaged audiences for a remarkable 11 seasons as a reality TV series. It also established organization as a virtue and propelled the business of professional organizers forward. Start an organization firm and offer eBay consignment services as a complement to your core business. Stuffed hall closets and storage spaces will become beautiful again, plus you'll help your clients profit from decluttering.

- *Free local trade shows.* I've attended and staffed booths at hundreds of trade shows. Exhibiting at these events is expensive and many exhibitors simply throw valuable items away because it's cheaper than shipping them back home. Attend low-cost and free trade shows within driving distance. Go toward the very end when the show closes and see what freebies you can take away with you. Bring a folding, rolling shopping cart (purchased on eBay, of course) to make carrying items back to your vehicle easier.

- *Auctions.* Many valuable items never receive bids at live auctions, so attend local auctions and see what's left over at the end. Ask the auctioneer if you can consign or purchase these remainders for a low price. Of course, you can also attend the auction and place bids, but I've found that you really need to know values to be a regular at auctions. It's competitive, but there are always slow days and sleeper items, and that's when you can pick up some bargains.

- *Curb discards and dumpster diving.* America is a very wealthy country, and people throw perfectly good stuff away. While you should never go diving into a restaurant's dumpster, the trash in high-end commercial and residential areas can be quite lucrative. I've also picked up quite a few items sitting on the parkway in front of homes, cleaned them up, and made a tidy profit reselling them. Be sure that what you are doing is legal in your community; and don't trespass on private property!

- *Social media groups.* My team and I have sourced mountains of free items through social media. Many groups exist for the purpose of finding new homes for free items. I have yet to come across any group that asks the receiver why they want the item—whether it's to keep or to resell. These groups are about the spirit of giving and generosity and are a wonderful place to source valuable merchandise to sell on eBay.

- *General wheeling and dealing.* Even if your core business model revolves around consigning goods, never pass up a great opportunity. Proactively and frequently pursue deals. Work your contacts and relationships. If someone owns something interesting that you think would do well for you on eBay, ask if it's for sale. While you may strike out 99 times out of 100, or even 199 times out of 200, each new connection you activate will create a steady stream of repeat opportunity. My longtime housekeeper Erica, who knows my business well, once received a gift from another client. Erica said she ordinarily would have declined it—a box of 25 vintage perfumes—but knowing my expertise with eBay, she welcomed the kindness and gave them to me. The 25 bottles, most of which were still sealed, sold on eBay for a total of $1,920.77. While Erica gifted them to me, I promptly cut her a check for 50 percent of the sales, which is the customary commission I charge on items such as perfumes.

I'll close with one final reminder: look for opportunity everywhere. Before you can spot opportunities, you have to be looking for them. There's a reason people like me continue to succeed, and that's because we prospect for success.

Everyone wants to become a millionaire, but many won't risk the discomfort of asking and being turned down. Everyone hopes for an opportunity to be the boss but won't take the chance. The great thing about eBay is that you can begin with just one item and grow at your own pace. As I write these words, I have 15,565 items listed on eBay and many thousands more in my pipeline.

There's fantastic merchandise to be found everywhere, and I invite you to look for those opportunities today.

# Chapter 5

# Boosting Opportunity—
# Advanced Techniques and Tips

There are a few advanced techniques you need to know to be a truly expert user of eBay and to get the absolute most you can out of the site. I'm blurring the lines slightly here because we have not yet gone too far down the path of discussing selling even though the techniques and tips in this chapter are great for both buyers and sellers. I'll go ahead and cover these now with the understanding that the "aha" moments for you may come later after you read the selling content in this guide.

## TWO QUICK TIPS

Here are two cool tips that will help you become the eBay guru you aspire to be. (You can even show off a little to your friends by revealing your eBay savvy!)

1. *Find a user profile.* A friend tells you that they've been listing items for sale on eBay, and you'd like to check out their listings. They mention their user ID—so how do you find their profile and see what they're up to? You can't simply type their user ID in the Search for Anything box. Sure, they can send you a link, but finding a specific user on eBay is easy when you know how. Open a browser window and type the URL https://www.ebay.com/usr/(user ID) and insert the user ID that your friend gave you. Here are a few things you'll find on an eBay profile (see Figure 5–1 below for an example):

   - The detailed seller rating (if the member is a seller), which are ratings that buyers leave sellers along with their feedback

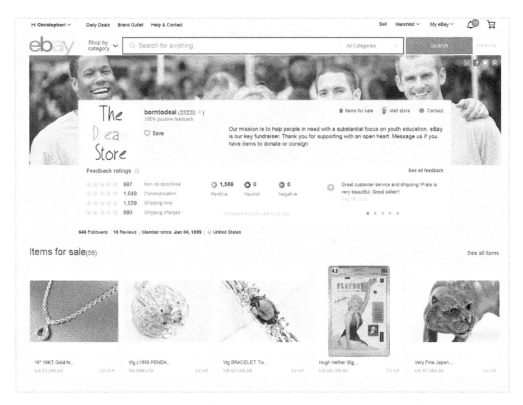

**FIGURE 5–1.** Here's my very first eBay account, which you can find by typing "https://www.ebay.com/usr/borntodeal" into a browser window.

- The number of followers, which includes people who clicked the Save link on the member's profile or the Save This Seller link on any of the seller's listing pages, if the member is a seller
- The number of product reviews the member has contributed to the eBay community
- The date the user became a member
- The member's country
- Feedback counts from the past 12 months
- Recent feedback comments and a link to view all their feedback
- A few of the member's items for sale and a link to see all their eBay listings
- The Visit Store link, if the member has subscribed to and operates an eBay Store
- A Contact link to message the member

2. *Find a listing using the eBay item number.* If you know the item number for a listing, you can simply type it into the Search for Anything box on the homepage or most eBay pages. Another way is to open a browser window and type "https://www.ebay.com/itm/itemnumber"—replacing "itemnumber" with the eBay item number you're looking for.

## WHEN eBAY GOES ON A DATE WITH GOOGLE

The search engine on eBay is mighty fine, but it won't surprise you to know that Google has mastered search like no one else. Fortunately, you can leverage that Google magic when searching eBay, and I'll explain how.

Let's say I'm on the prowl for a vintage Longines watch, and I google "Longines watch" to see what I can find. Google says, "About 41,000,000 results . . ." That's useless. That's like searching for a needle in a haystack the size of Texas.

Let's try using an incredibly powerful feature in Google that allows you to search results on a specific site by putting "site:" in front of a site or domain. For example, type "site:ebay.com" and then key in your search term. Let's search for "site:ebay.com longines watch" (Google's search engine, like eBay's, is case insensitive). Check out the results in Figure 5–2 on page 82.

While it's a fun hack, it still yields far too many results—about 498,000—to be truly useful. Let's try searching for something a bit more obscure and specific.

Are you a numismatic nut? Do you obsess about ancient Roman coins? Licinius was a Roman emperor from 308 to 324 AD and his likeness lives on, immortalized on a plethora of Roman coins. Some of them have been fashioned into jewelry. Let's try

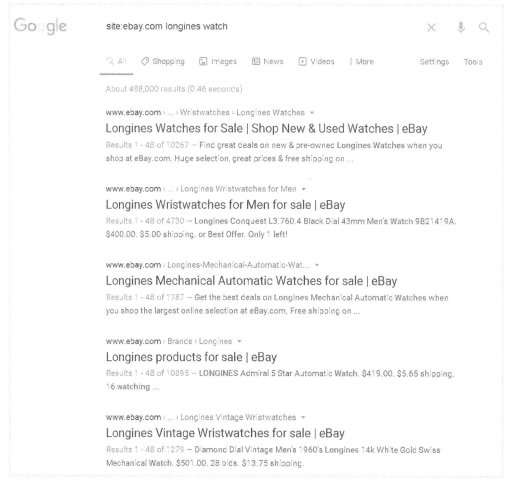

**FIGURE 5–2.** Here's what Google displayd when I searched "site:ebay.com longines watch."

finding some of that jewelry on eBay using Google. Figure 5-3 on page 83 shows the Google search results for "site:ebay.com licinius pendant."

You can also bring more precision to your Google searches with symbols and words. Here are some other common techniques you can use to search eBay via Google:

1. *Search for a price.* Put "$" in front of a number. For example: "site:ebay.com DVD $5"
2. *Combine searches.* Put "OR" between each search query. For example: "site:ebay.com jeans OR slacks"
3. *Search for an exact match.* Put a word or phrase inside quotes. For example: site:ebay.com "blocking a buyer"

Even if you don't use the site:ebay.com trick limiting Google searches to eBay, you'll notice that searching on Google will display eBay listings in two ways. You'll see

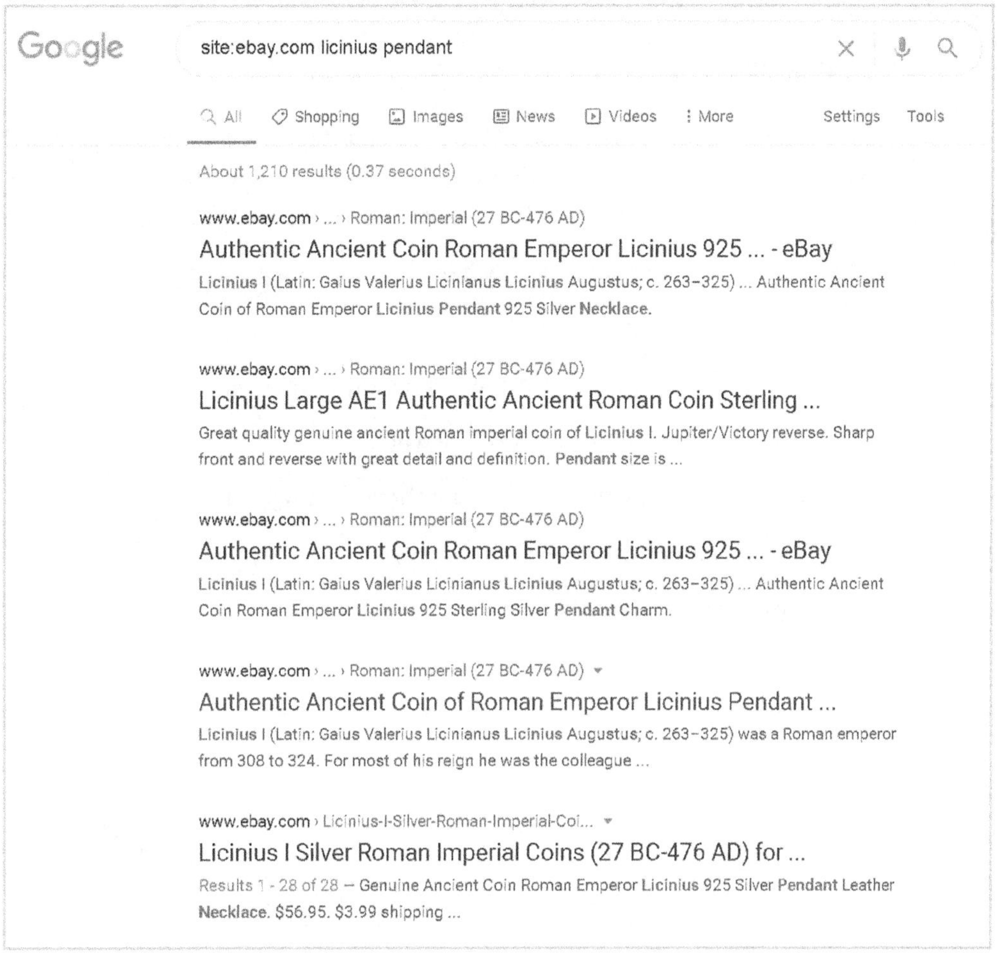

**FIGURE 5–3.** Here's my Google search for "site:ebay.com licinius pendant" that came back with in 1,210 results. When I clicked one of the links, I discovered an intriguing necklace made from one of these ancient coins.

products at the top of relevant Google searches and in the Google Shopping tab. Getting eBay listings to show up in Google Shopping isn't free, but eBay invests a lot of money into paid-search marketing for the benefit of buyers and sellers.

## ADVANCED SEARCH

The Advanced Search is the greatest unsung hero for eBay buyers *and* sellers. By adding this incredible and oft unknown instrument to your gig bag, you'll become an eBay rock star for the ages. That's not hyperbole. I'm dead serious.

You'll find this innocuous-looking link at the top right of the eBay homepage and most eBay pages. See Figure 5–4 on page 84.

## COVER YOUR BEHIND

When you use Google's sites, apps, and services, your activity is saved in your Google account. If you're shopping for a gift and you share your computer with the recipient, you'll want to keep your search activity private.

Follow these steps to delete your history when signed into your Google account:

1. Go to https://myaccount.google.com.

2. In the left-hand column, click Data & Personalization.

3. Under Activity and Timeline, click My Activity.

4. At the Search Your Activity box, click the three dots icon: ⋮

5. In the pop-up menu, click Delete Activity By.

6. Below Delete Activity, click All Time.

7. Click Delete.

**FIGURE 5–4.** The Advanced Search link is hidden in plain sight on most eBay pages, including the homepage.

Clicking the Advanced Search link opens a page that offers multiple variants for advanced searches, which you can choose through links on the left-hand side of the page (see Figure 5-5 on page 85). They are:

- *Find Items.* This is where most of your advanced searching will take place. Here, you'll find a seemingly endless array of options for tweaking and tuning your eBay search experience.

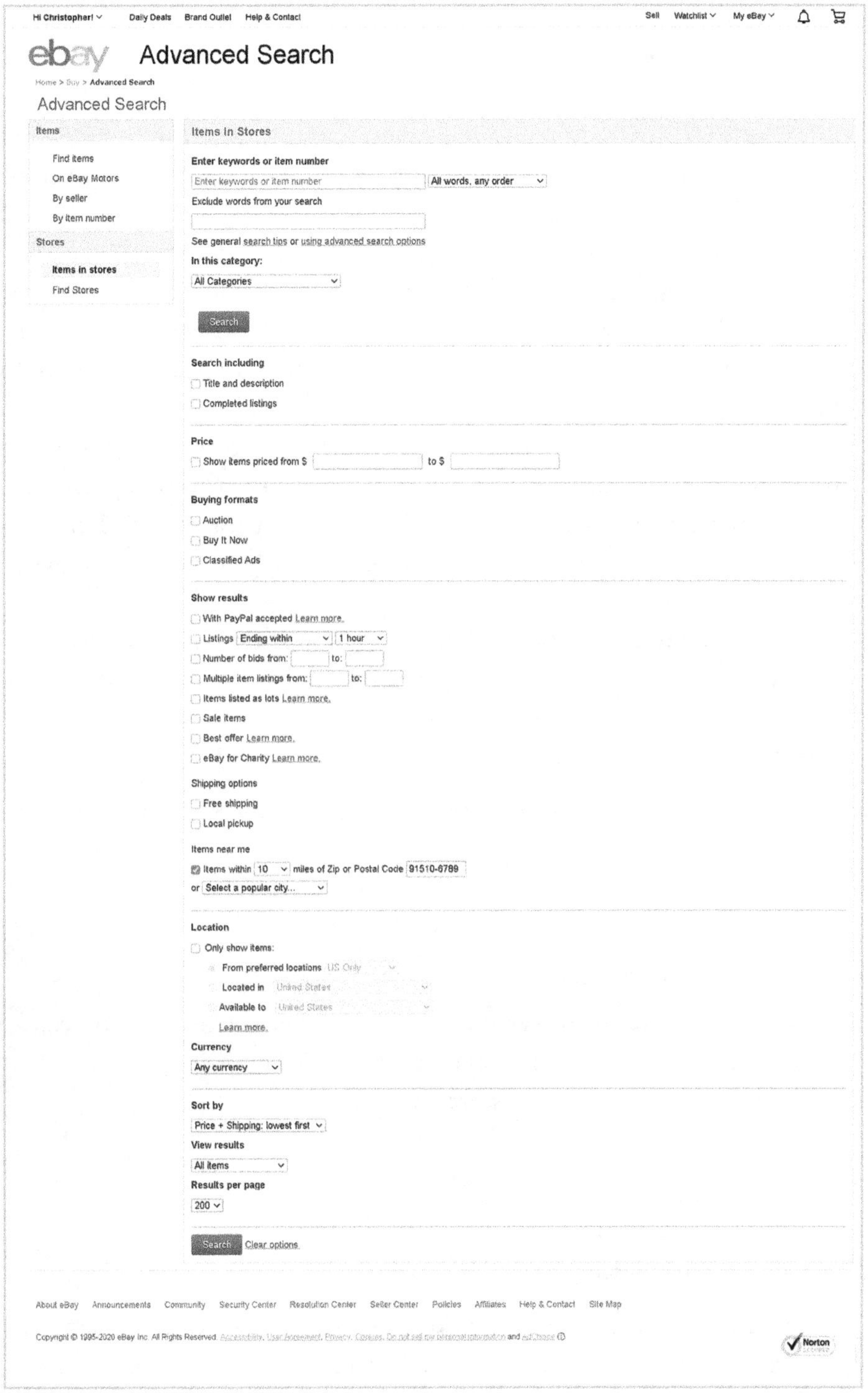

**FIGURE 5–5.** Here's what pops up after clicking the Advanced Search link—this is actually multiple pages that are enabled using the navigation links on the left.

▨ *On eBay Motors.* This is the place to conduct advanced searches for cars, trucks, motorcycles, powersports, boats, RVs, campers, parts and accessories, and even aircraft.

▨ *By Seller.* This is not a separate page, but clicking this link scrolls to the Find Items page for you to a section where you can key in one or more eBay user IDs from which to limit your search.

▨ *By Item Number.* This option exists more for nostalgia than for any useful purpose. It's a Jurassic holdover from the early days when you could only do this type of search through the Advanced Search option. It allows you to key in the eBay item number to locate a listing—which is something you can now do from the homepage search box.

▨ *Items in Stores.* This closely mirrors the Find Items page in terms of search functionality; however, it only searches for items within eBay Stores operated by sellers who have a Store subscription. This is also a legacy search tool—long ago eBay Store items weren't presented along with everything else when using the Search for Anything box.

▨ *Find Stores.* Not to be confused with Items in Stores. This feature will search across the names of eBay Stores or the keywords in their Store descriptions. The next time someone gives you their eBay Store name, this is how to quickly look up what they're selling.

Now let's look at some of the neat tricks you can accomplish with the Advanced Search tools. While the possibilities are endless, I'll cover most of the essentials. These search tools can be used a la carte, or you can combine options to increase focus.

### Enter Keywords or Item Number

This subsection allows keyword searches or item number searches, so you can key in what you're looking for as a starting point. See Figure 5–6 on page 87.

The pull-down menu allows four search iterations:

1. All words, any order
2. Any words, any order
3. Exact words, exact order
4. Exact words, any order

Use the Exclude Words from Your Search box to omit words—for example, when you want a ruby necklace that does not have the word "synthetic" in the listing title or if you're looking for *Thriller* in vinyl and want to exclude "cd" and "cassette" from the search. Remember that eBay searches are always case insensitive.

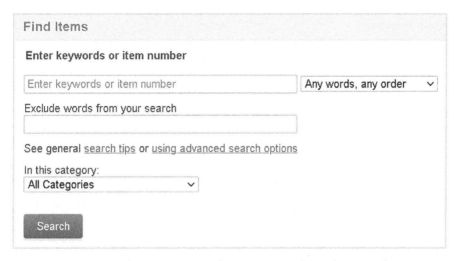

**FIGURE 5–6.** The Enter Keywords or Item Number subsection from
the Find Items section of eBay's Advanced Search page.

The pull-down menu In This Category limits results to a top-level category, but expert eBay buyers know that improperly categorized items are an opportunity to potentially score bargains. If the items are in the wrong category, people who browse by category may miss them.

### Search Including

The Search Including subsection (see Figure 5–7 on page 88) may look modest, but it's *really* powerful. Here's what you can do with it:

- *Title and Description.* Expand the search to include both the title and the description. Titles are limited to just 80 characters, so sellers have to be judicious with their keywords. Expanding the search to the descriptions will pull in a lot more listings.
- *Completed Listings.* Limit the search to listings that have ended and the results will include *both* sold and unsold items.
- *Sold Listings.* Limit the search to only sold items to gain visibility on potential comparable sales to use when pricing your merchandise.

### Price

The Price subsection (Figure 5–7 on page 88) offers a few advantages:

- When searching for a new phone, for example, you can enter a price range that will help weed out the zillions of "phone earbuds," "phone cases," and other

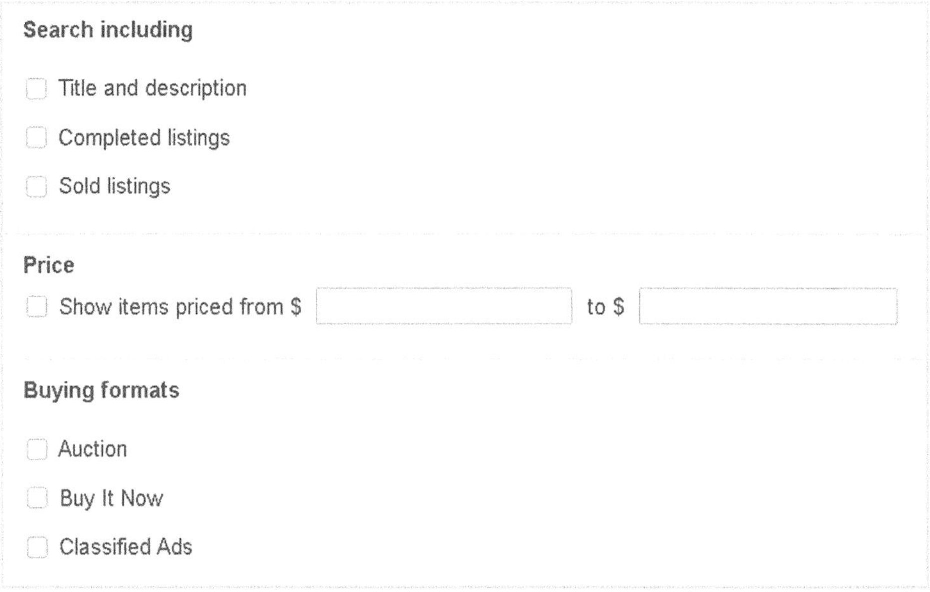

**Search including**

☐ Title and description

☐ Completed listings

☐ Sold listings

**Price**

☐ Show items priced from $ [          ] to $ [          ]

**Buying formats**

☐ Auction

☐ Buy It Now

☐ Classified Ads

**FIGURE 5–7.** The Search Including, Price, and Buying Formats subsections from the Find Items section of eBay's Advanced Search page.

accessories, but is also low enough to deliver value *and* prune out higher-priced wholesale lots.

- Set a price limit by leaving the first price box blank and entering the highest price you're willing to pay.
- Look for incredible bargains by entering a penny in the first box and a buck in the second. Sort the results to show items near you and buy—then pick up your winnings!

## Buying Formats

The Buying Formats subsection (Figure 5-7 above) has the following three options:

1. *Auction.* This is useful when you're looking to snipe auctions and score great deals. Use AuctionStealer or a similar app to automate this—it's free for occasional use and very affordable for professionals. It's what I use.
2. *Buy It Now.* Need AA batteries immediately? Looking for parts for your 530i to buy and pick up locally today? Maybe auctions just aren't your thing? Check this box to display only Buy It Now listings.
3. *Classified Ads.* In July 2020, international classified ads company Adevinta signed an agreement to acquire eBay Classifieds Group, so I'm not sure whether this box will remain, but it's there as I write this. It allows you to view

eBay's classified ad format listings, in which the seller and buyer complete the transaction off the site.

One thing you should know—you can select each option on its own or select both Auction and Buy It Now, but you cannot select all three or combine Auction or Buy It Now with Classified Ads. Also remember that you can filter by Auction and Buy It Now on your regular search results pages.

## Condition

The Condition subsection (Figure 5–8 on page 90) has the following three check boxes:

1. *New.* Selecting New limits searches to items that the sellers have indicated are brand spanking new.

2. *Used.* Selecting Used will limit searches to pre-owned items with the very important caveat that the condition of used items is subjective. Cautious buyers will read (and reread) the description and review the item photos to ensure that they will receive a product that's satisfactory to them. Sellers of used items should offer returns, but not all do. After conducting your search, you can further refine the search results page (using the filters on the left-hand side) to show only items where the seller accepts returns (or even better, free returns).

3. *Not Specified.* Certain eBay categories don't require the seller to specify the item's condition, such as antique or vintage products, where the condition would be "used" nearly 100 percent of the time. Rare exceptions would be when the product is "new old stock," referring to obsolete and discontinued items that were never actually opened and used. Selecting Not Specified pulls up items where eBay doesn't require the condition to be included in those listings.

## Show Results

The Show Results subsection (Figure 5–8 on page 90) has the following seven check boxes and features:

1. *Listings.* This filter allows you to limit searches to items that will be ending within a specific time, ending in more than a certain time, or have been started within a certain time. The pull-down options span between one hour and seven days. This is a useful tool when looking for fixed price listings that just went live (use the Started Within option) or for filtering auctions that are about to end (use the Ending Within option).

2. *Number of Bids From [x to y].* A high number of bids signal that the item has captured strong buyer interest. You could also combine this with the Auction

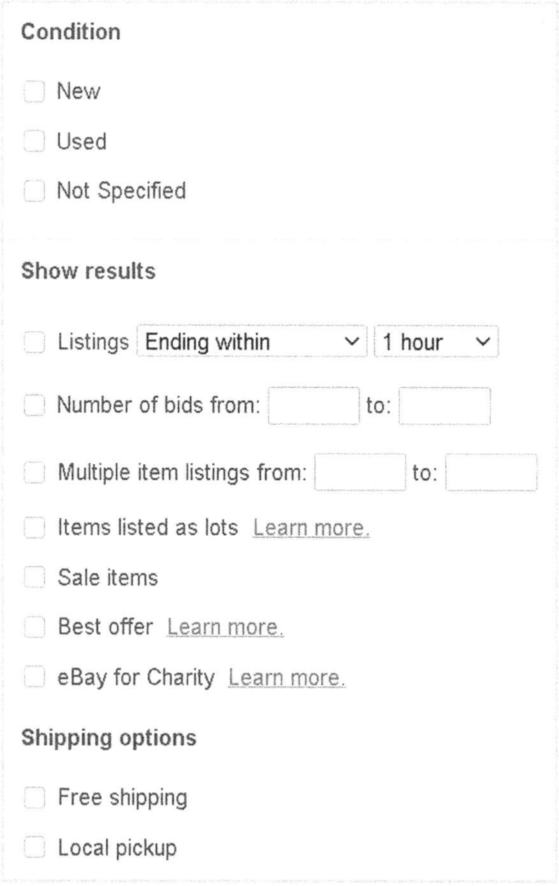

**FIGURE 5–8.** The Condition, Show Results, and Shipping Options subsections from the Find Items section of eBay's Advanced Search page.

and Listings Ending Within filters to display auctions with no bids that are about to end; they might be a chance for you to seize some neglected but valuable goodies.

3. *Multiple Item Listings from [x to y].* Need a bunch of CR2032 lithium watch batteries? Are all four of your tires bald and need replacing? Use this option to identify listings that have more than one of the same item for sale (as opposed to selling them together as a lot—see the next item in the list).

4. *Items Listed as Lots.* You can filter for eBay listings where the seller has indicated that they are selling a group of similar or identical items together to one buyer (a dozen Christmas bows, a case of 100 tea lights, a carton of 500 face masks, etc.).

5. *Sale Items.* Sellers have special tools available to promote their listings and they sometimes hold sale events—like a virtual "Everything Must Go!" sign on their

eBay listings. Use this to find only listings where the fixed price has been lowered in connection with a seller-initiated sales promotion.

6. *Best Offer.* This is your eBay truffle hog. It helps you identify those valuable listings where the seller has signaled they're open to wheeling and dealing by enabling the Best Offer feature. If a seller is in a particularly good mood, they'll accept your aggressive (but fair) offer to buy what they're selling below their asking price. Make enough offers, and someone will accept one of them. Then you're the instant winner—no waiting!

7. *eBay for Charity.* If you become a seller, support the causes you love by donating a portion of the proceeds from your eBay sales by enabling eBay for Charity on the listing. As a buyer, you can filter only those listings where the seller has agreed to donate. eBay has vetted and approved every nonprofit organization within their system, and it collects and conveys all donations directly to the nonprofits, taking no fees for the service. If the nonprofit you love isn't already listed, urge them to sign up at https://charity.ebay.com/. Sellers can choose to give as little as 10 percent (1 percent for eBay Motors) or as much as 100 percent.

### Shipping Options

The Shipping Options subsection (Figure 5–8 on page 90) has the following two check boxes:

1. *Free Shipping.* Many eBay sellers offer free shipping (and some offer free returns as well). This search option lets you filter only the sellers who offer this perk—but remember that someone has to pay for shipping, and items with free shipping are marked up by the seller to cover the cost. Savvy buyers understand this and are more likely to use the Price + Shipping: Lowest First sort option in their search results to identify the best value in what they're looking for. But it's there in case you want to use it. I contend that you will often find a better price from fair sellers even if they don't offer free shipping. Experiment with these search options and see if you agree with me.

2. *Local Pickup.* This is a tool that really smiles at you if you're willing to get out and meet people. Many eBay sellers love local pickup, and a whole lot of buyers love it, too. You must still complete the purchase on the site—after all, eBay charges the seller a final value fee on all successful listings, and they deserve to get their cut. There are two excellent ways to identify goods that are close enough to grab in person. After filtering for items that offer Local Pickup, you can sort the search results using the Distance: Nearest First pull-down menu or you can combine the

Local Pickup filter with the Located filter option, which I'll discuss in the next section. Here are a few reasons buyers and sellers love local pickup:

- Merchandise can be inspected in person before taking it home.
- Delicate items won't break in transit.
- Heavy items won't break the bank with expensive shipping costs.
- There's no cost to either party for shipping.
- Time-consuming packing and expensive packing supplies are avoided.
- Meeting is safe—eBay has everyone's information and feedback lets you size up the other person in advance.

After you purchase an item that's available for local pickup, use the Contact Seller link on the listing to make the necessary arrangements. The eBay mobile app has a code scan function that confirms the exchange occurred and displays a *picked up* tracking event on the listing.

### Location

The Location subsection (see Figure 5–9 on page 93) has the following three check boxes:

1. *Located.* This genius filter lets you see what's within 2 to 2,000 miles of the zip code of your choice—with eBay prefilling the zip code you provided when you registered for an account. Two great use cases for this:
   - Use it to find items you'd like to pick up (combine this with the Local Pickup option in Figure 5–8 on page 90 to identify sellers who allow pickups).
   - Buy from closer sellers to receive your merchandise faster, because the shorter the distance, the less time it takes a shipment to arrive.
2. *From Preferred Locations.* This tool includes a pull-down menu that allows you to limit your advanced searches to the most popular areas for eBay trading, such as Worldwide, US Only, North America, Europe, and Asia.
3. *Located In.* Ideally, eBay wants you to fall in love with all its sellers, but I tend to prefer sellers in the U.S. unless what I want can't be found stateside. I also normally don't have a lot of lead time when purchasing essentials like batteries, office supplies, and shipping needs like bubble wrap and boxes. The Located In option has a pull-down menu that lets you view only sellers in a selected country. Just be sure to order your fancy chocolate from Lausanne, Switzerland, in the winter months to avoid receiving them melted!

### Sellers

The Sellers subsection (Figure 5–9 on page 93) has the following three ways to Only Show Items from specific sellers:

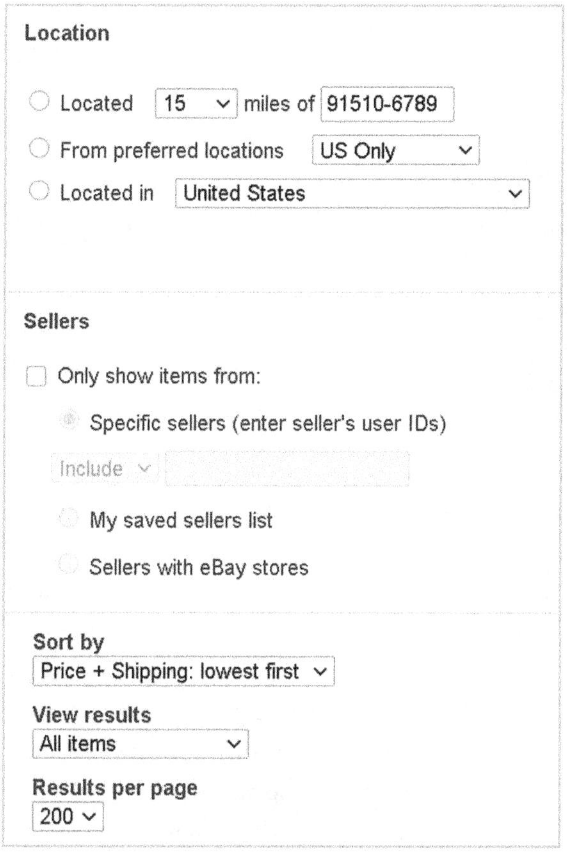

**FIGURE 5–9.** The Location, Sellers, Sort By, View Results, and Results Per Page subsections from the Find Items section of eBay's Advanced Search page.

1. *Specific Sellers.* If you'd like to use keywords to search within the listings for one or more eBay sellers, use the Specific Sellers option and the pull-down Include or Exclude (I haven't actually found a use case for Exclude yet) and enter one or more sellers' user IDs, separating multiple user IDs with a comma and no spaces. For example: "userid1,userid2,userid3." This offers buyers tremendous focus and flexibility in searching for listings from only the sellers they love. As a seller, I've leveraged this Advanced Search tool as part of my concierge service to potential and current buyers. I use it to search all my eBay IDs simultaneously for whatever my customer is looking for and then send them a link to the search results. This yields increased customer loyalty and converts lookers into buyers.

2. *My Saved Sellers List.* So you've spent untold hours scouring what eBay has to offer and you've curated the best of the absolute best sellers—make sure you click the Save This Seller link on one of their listings (see Figure 5-10 on page 94) so you

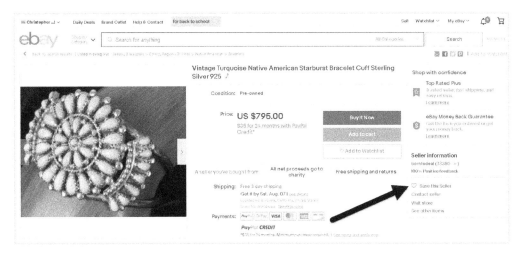

**FIGURE 5-10.** Here's the Save This Seller link on one of my eBay listings.

can use the My Saved Sellers List feature to search only their listings. What do you do after you're no longer in love (or one of your saved sellers is no longer listing items)? That's easy—from the homepage or most eBay pages, hover over My eBay, click Saved Sellers, and click Delete under the seller's user ID.

3. *Sellers with eBay Stores.* There was a time long ago when eBay kept the Store listings in a separate part of the site, but those days are long gone. All eBay Store listings now appear alongside listings from other sellers, so I feel like this tool falls into the nostalgia zone, and I don't really see much call for it. That said, selecting Sellers with eBay Stores permits you to only search within Store listings.

## Sort By

The Sort By subsection (Figure 5-9 on page 93) is the exact same pull-down option you'll find at the top right of your search results page. One of the goals of having an entire page dedicated to tweaking eBay search is to allow you to make all your search adjustments in one place, which is why they've replicated these search refinements here. I explained the Sort By functionality on page 38 in Chapter 3; here are the six pull-down options again:

1. Best Match
2. Time: Ending Soonest
3. Time: Newly Listed
4. Price + Shipping: Lowest First
5. Price + Shipping: Highest First
6. Distance: Nearest First

### View Results

The View Results subsection (Figure 5-9 on page 93) offers three choices in a pull-down menu that are pretty self-explanatory:

1. *All Items.* This is the default view you usually see when the site returns search results.
2. *Picture Gallery.* This showcases larger pictures in a tiled array for a more visual shopping experience.
3. *Show Item Numbers.* This just adds the item number to the standard default search listing.

If you gravitate toward the Picture Gallery feature, I can't blame you—most people (myself included) love to view the listing photos as large as possible, and the Picture Gallery view allows us to do that. Scrolling quickly through many listings is easier with photos, and if something catches the eye, the details are just a click away.

### Results Per Page

The Results Per Page subsection (Figure 5-9 on page 93) offers four choices in a pull-down menu that allows you to set the number of items that are displayed per page. The options are 25, 50 (the default), 100, or 200 items per page. The more items on a single page, the longer you'll have to scroll to see the bottom (and the longer it will take to load). Use 25 or 50 if you have a slow internet connection, such as browsing while on a plane or a cruise to the Mexican Riviera. For the high-speed internet available to those of us living a less exotic lifestyle, try 200 items per page. When the search results in more items than the value you've selected, navigation links will appear that allow you to move to the next x number of items.

### On eBay Motors

The truth is that you can search eBay Motors using the Find Items tools I've covered previously. The On eBay Motors options (see Figure 5-11 on page 96) are simply another clever and tidy Advanced Search *user interface* that access the same data.

The subsections within the On eBay Motors interface include these tools, which also exist in Find Items:

- Enter Keyword or Item Number
- Title and Description
- Completed Listings
- Items Near Me (in Find Items this is called Located)

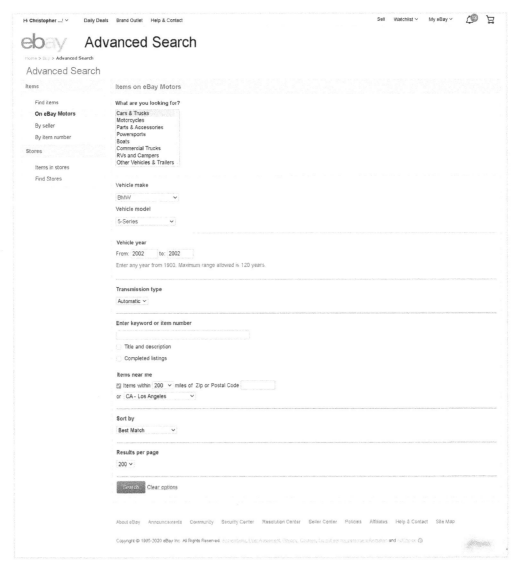

**FIGURE 5–11.** This is the On eBay Motors section within eBay's Advanced Search page. I've filled in a search for 2002 BMW 530i cars located within 200 miles of Los Angeles, California.

- Sort By
- Results Per Page

Now here's what's unique to the On eBay Motors section:

1. *What Are You Looking For?* From here, you'll select from the list of motor types:
   - Cars & Trucks: When selected, options appear to choose Vehicle Make, Vehicle Model, Vehicle Year, and Transmission Type.

- Motorcycles: When selected, options appear to choose Motorcycle Make, Motorcycle Model, and Motorcycle Year.
- Parts & Accessories: When selected, options appear to choose Part Type, Vehicle Make, and Vehicle Model.
- Powersports: When selected, an option appears to select Powersport Type.
- Boats: When selected, an option appears to select Boat Type.
- Commercial Trucks: When selected, options to choose Type and Class appear.
- RVs and Campers: When selected, options appear to choose the Type and Length of the RV or camper.
- Other Vehicles & Trailers: When selected, an option appears to choose Other Vehicle Type (including aircraft, golf carts, buses, etc.).

2. *Select a Popular City.* The On eBay Motors Advanced Search has a tool that determines eBay Motors' most thriving cities and allows you to narrow your search down to one of those areas.

Keep in mind that if you decide to bid $25,000 or more, you'll need to provide eBay with a valid credit card. It won't be charged, but it helps weed out less serious buyers.

---

## eBAY MOTORS TIPS: WHAT YOU SHOULD KNOW

- Dealers will do their best to match the vehicle you requested to the vehicles that are available for purchase. If your exact vehicle isn't in stock, they will help you find a similar car at a similar price.

- Prices don't include government fees and taxes, finance charges, dealer documentation fees, title and license fees, emission testing charges, or dealer-installed accessories.

- You won't pay for the vehicle on eBay. All financing and payment details will be worked out with the dealer.

- If you change your mind about options and features, talk to your dealer to negotiate a new price for your vehicle.

- Contact your dealer with any questions about the vehicle you selected.

- Sellers can offer escrow services using https://www.escrow.com for an additional fee to protect both parties and ensure a smooth transaction.

---

Here are my recommendations when making vehicle purchases:

- Apply common sense to everything you do, every time you buy anything.
- Shop around—it's easier than ever to compare prices.
- Prepare a list of questions and ask away—there's no better time to become familiar with the vehicle than before you commit to buy it.
- Personally inspect and if possible test-drive the vehicle.
- Check the seller's feedback carefully.
- Calculate additional costs such as registration and taxes.
- Think carefully before having a car shipped to you from a distant city without an inspection—this practice is for savvy, experienced buyers.
- Consider paying for a professional inspection whether you're buying locally or traveling to pick up the vehicle.

For motor vehicles and real estate, your bid is considered nonbinding, unlike almost every other part of eBay, where a commitment to buy is a binding, legal contract. When you bid on items in these categories, you're expressing a strong interest, but no contract is formed. Properties and vehicles are high-cost items that involve complex details and are often subject to a variety of laws. You have the right to back out if the vehicle isn't what you expected or is different than represented. Remember that you can simply change your mind.

This concludes our nickel tour of Advanced Search—but that's not the end of our journey. There's a few more things to cover in this already hefty chapter.

## LEVERAGING GOOGLE IMAGES

I'm fond of Google products. I use Google search, Gmail, Google Drive, Google Calendar, and Google Meet as useful and profitable tools for my eBay business. But Google also has a terrific, very powerful, and free reverse image search tool in Google Images. Head over to https://www.google.com and select the Images menu at the top right of the homepage. You can reverse search images using Google Images in two ways:

1. Drag and drop an image from your computer directly into the web page, and it will search the internet for matches automatically.
2. Click the camera icon to the right of the search box and:
   - Paste the URL of an image on the internet; or
   - Click the Upload an Image tab and select an image from your computer (using the method in Step 1 is faster).

Reverse searching images like this can be very useful for both buyers and sellers. It allows you to quickly and easily:

- Identify a particular style of fabric, pottery, pattern (think tartan, etc.), or just about any object you'd like to research and understand
- Identify famous people from their pictures so you can search their name and find related eBay items, autographed memorabilia, and other collectibles
- Pinpoint the month and year of a magazine cover and identify many types of publications from a scan or picture captured on your phone (see Figure 5–12 on page 100)
- Determine the make and model of a vehicle

You'll find many other creative ways to use Google Images to turbocharge your eBay buying and selling.

## POWER BUYER TIPS

You'll discover that virtually everyone thinks they are an eBay expert. But the eBay you log onto today looks very different from the eBay I first used in 1999—and it's equally different from the eBay of just a few years ago. Customer tastes and habits change over time, and so does the eBay user interface. But here are some time-tested tips that you can rest assured work well today and will continue to be helpful well into the future:

- *Haggle!* Even if a seller hasn't enabled Best Offer on their listing, ask if they'll consider accepting a lower price. If they say no, click Add to Watchlist and keep an eye on the listing (on My eBay > Watchlist). Check back in a bit, and if the item still hasn't sold, ask the seller again. There's no harm in trying, and many sellers are more willing to make a deal when their item has gone unsold for a long time. Be courteous and diplomatic when communicating with everyone.
- *Maintain your cool.* It's rare you'll discover anything that's really rare on eBay, so being outbid on an item is OK—you'll see another one listed again soon. Your goal with auctions is to score a great price, so you need to know when to stop raising your bid.
- *Bid weirdly.* Never place even-dollar bids on auctions. You only have to outbid someone else by a penny to win. Bid $10.01 vs. $10.00. Bid in odd numbers.
- *Don't bid early.* Wait until the last moment to place your bid. Experienced auction buyers use tools like AuctionStealer to place their high bids seconds before the auction ends. Bidding early offers no upside, and if you plan to snipe without the benefit of an automated sniping tool like AuctionStealer, be sure you have a fast and reliable internet connection.

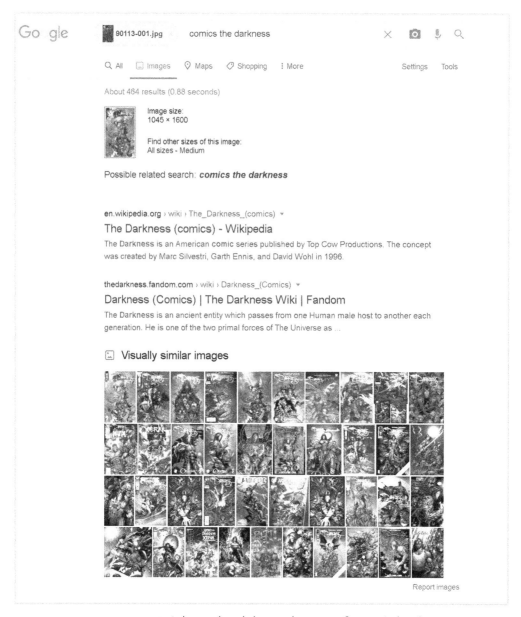

**FIGURE 5–12.** I dragged and dropped a scan of a comic book
cover into Google Images and voilà! It correctly identified the comic.

- *Ask the seller about a Second Chance Offer.* If you were outbid on an auction, the seller may send you a *Second Chance Offer*. With a Second Chance Offer, a nonwinning bidder gets the opportunity to buy the item at their last bid price. The seller can initiate a Second Chance Offer up to 60 days after the auction ends. Second Chance Offers generally occur in three situations:

1. The winning bidder didn't pay, and the seller was unable to resolve the issue.
2. The listing had a reserve price that wasn't met.
3. The seller has more of the same item available.

In a few eBay Motors and Business & Industrial categories, the seller can specify the offer price, as long as it's less than or equal to the item's reserve price. Many sellers aren't familiar with Second Chance Offers, so you can make the first move: message them immediately after the auction closes and let them know that you'd welcome a Second Chance Offer.

- *Ask for combined shipping discounts.* Scope out other items that may interest you from the same seller and ask if they'll combine items for a shipping discount. It also pays to be familiar with shipping rates so you can detect if a seller is padding the cost. Sellers receive healthy discounts off the published shipping rates from eBay, and they can pass those discounts along to you. The key is to ask!

- *Never reveal everything you know.* It's never a good idea to show your hand when you know more than the seller. One aspect of eBay you'll find enormously satisfying is the hunt that leads you to undervalued items, commonly referred to as "sleepers." These are difficult to find, but they do happen. As a seller, I've made my share of mistakes. In one year alone, I failed to put the keywords *sterling silver 925* in the title of a brooch listing that I ran as a penny auction. The bidders must all have been skeptical, because the auction ended with a high bid of just a few dollars. The brooch would have easily fetched $25 to $50 with the proper keywords. In my haste to list a fancy art glass vase, I put it up with a starting bid of only $49.95, and it sold with just one bid. I later discovered that it was a rare Loetz piece worth north of a thousand dollars. I listed a very nice hardcover of Stephen King's wildly popular book *It* that also sold with a single bid for $49.95; it turned out to be a first edition worth $200. The buyer arbitraged it right back on eBay, on the very same account he used to buy it from me. Had any of these very smart and fortunate bidders reached out with questions, I would have almost certainly realized my mistake. Sometimes you just have to keep quiet, bid, and hope that the sleeper is really what you think it is—you may strike out, but the few times you strike gold will make up for it. Be sure to use separate accounts for buying and selling so that you don't accidentally reveal to the seller that you made a bunch of money off their inexperience or error.

- *Bid locally—especially on the big stuff.* Bid on items that are close to you and ask if you can pick them up. Even if the answer is no, you'll still save on shipping due to the shorter distance. Always buy light but bulky items from sellers close to you. Carriers will charge *DIM weight* for big parcels, which is the amount of space a package occupies in relation to its actual weight. DIM weight is also cheaper for shorter distances, which is why you should buy featherlight items like bubble wrap from an eBay seller in your trading area instead of across the country.

- *Retracting bids.* Look, it happens to all of us. Whether it's the result of clumsy fingers or too much eggnog, we've all typed in the wrong amount when bidding. You are only permitted to retract bids if you entered the wrong amount (such as $200 instead of $20), if the seller made substantial changes to the listing, or if you can't reach the seller. Then you may retract your bid if there are at least 12 hours left before the listing ends (then you can retract all your bids); if the listing is ending in less than 12 hours, you can only retract your most recent bid if you placed it less than an hour ago. Click on Help & Contact at the top of the homepage or most eBay pages and type "retract" into the search box, then select Retracting a Bid and follow the instructions on that page.

# Chapter 6

# Partnering with eBay
# (Make Money Selling Nothing!)

No lie. You can actually make a living selling stuff on eBay without selling stuff on eBay. Have I caught your attention? The eBay Partner Network is a wonderful affiliate marketing program that allows you to promote products to the more than 187 million active eBay buyers in 190 markets around the world—and make a healthy commission for doing so.

You can start earning money immediately by simply sharing links that you can generate with a few mouse clicks. I'm not overstating the simplicity of eBay's affiliate program—it's quick to get started and easy to earn money. But how much you earn depends on the amount of time you're willing to invest and the skill you apply toward product selection and price—if you link buyers to higher-priced goods, you'll earn more on each sale generated from the links.

The eBay Partner Network is unlike many other retailer affiliate programs because eBay manages the program in-house, allowing them to pay more generous commissions because there's no intermediary taking a cut. Approval to join is very easy, and you can get up and running quickly. To get started, scroll to the bottom of the homepage and click the Affiliates link in the Sell section. If you already have an eBay account, you can sign up using your existing login. Once approved, you can start earning money immediately.

In the U.S., partners can promote virtually any eBay page and monetize it using a trackable affiliate link generated by the tools available at the eBay Partner Network portal or using a web browser plug-in or script (more on this later).

## HOW eBAY PARTNERS PROFIT

Here are a few ways eBay partners can earn commissions:

- *Written reviews.* A simple and effective affiliate sales tool is to write a review for a consumer product you love and then a means to buy it. A review should include both a link to the product being reviewed and another link to your eBay Store. If you don't have a Store subscription, then use a link to your listings. When your own inventory lacks breadth of variety, then link to an eBay search results page for products that may be of interest to readers.
- *Video reviews.* Some people prefer to watch videos rather than reading text reviews.
- *How-tos.* Post written or video tutorials for DIY projects such as quilting, crochet, crafting, home improvement, and other projects, with links to purchase the equipment, supplies, and other materials needed to complete the project.
- *Fan sites.* Build a blog or social network with turnkey solutions such as WordPress or Ning and create posts about your favorite celebrities, promoting official fan merchandise and autographed items with affiliate links. You'll see an example of a fan site that uses the eBay Partner Network to make money later in this chapter.

Partners are encouraged to promote eBay's daily deals, sales and other events, and trending items to earn maximum commissions—these are opportunities that eBay has determined garner strong interest from potential buyers. Blogging, posting on social media, and opt-in email marketing are all proven ways to generate affiliate money. For example, when *Stranger Things* first launched in 2016, I noticed a ton of eBay links on social media and blogs that led to memorabilia related to the show, and countless *Star Wars* fans link to eBay within their YouTube videos, in their email signatures, and on their personal and business websites.

Success ultimately boils down to creating exceptional content and driving quality traffic from people who are ready to buy. These prospective buyers don't need to be existing eBay members—they can sign up on the spot or make guest purchases without registering for an account. My point is that you can make money marketing to existing family, friends, colleagues, or strangers without needing to know if they've made eBay purchases in the past. I find it surprisingly easy to make respectable money through the eBay Partner Network.

## HOW MUCH DOES eBAY PAY?

I'm leading into this with a discussion about money because most get-rich-quick systems lure you in with a lot of exciting sales talk before asking you to pay a fee to participate in their system or pony up membership dues. These guru founders claim you can enjoy a cocktail on your yacht without ever having to lift a finger. I don't believe in get-rich-quick schemes because they don't work. All affiliate marketing programs require that you work hard to promote their links to people who are likely to buy the items in those links. You can't just set it on autopilot.

If you join the eBay Partner Network, you can rest assured you will be paid, and paid *on time*. They don't charge you anything to participate, and they pay you for persuading someone to buy on eBay. With so many items for sale, there's something for everyone. You need only hone your matchmaking skills.

The Partner Network doesn't disclose how much their top affiliates make, but I've seen many influencers talk about their incomes, and for those whose claims appear credible, it's possible to earn six and even seven figures. Of course, those influencers who are earning more than a million dollars on the network also have millions of social media followers, and they shamelessly push, prod, and promote in every post they make.

You don't need millions of followers in order to make good money as an eBay affiliate, but you are more likely to attract a consistent and captive audience if you develop a strong bond with them because of your passion, knowledge, and active engagement in a distinct niche. Some affiliates focus on high-quality content that attracts many views, while others work on high-volume content (i.e., the shotgun approach). There's virtually an unlimited number of places you can promote affiliate links, but selling via social media remains top of mind. Facebook, for example, had 1.66 billion active daily users in 2019. YouTube had more than one billion active monthly users the same year.

Instagram, Tumblr, and TikTok all have equally impressive numbers. It's important to never put all your eggs in one basket, or you may wake up one day to find that your affiliate revenue stream has suddenly dried up. Remember Vine? When was the last time you logged into MySpace? New social media sites will pop up in the future, and some of the most popular ones today will eventually wither and become irrelevant or die altogether.

While social media is by far the greatest and growing opportunity I envision for eBay affiliate profits, there are folks operating successful email newsletters, personal and business websites, and even people who use eBay's APIs to create their very own dynamic shopping and recommendation sites.

So what's the bottom line? As I write these words, you can earn up to 4 percent, or as much as $550 per referral (see Figure 6–1 on page 107 for a more detailed breakdown). I found the eBay Partner Network application painless and eBay affiliate links quick to set up. It's easier than you might think to drive sales because a lot of people use eBay every day. If you're transparent about it, friends, family, and colleagues will gladly click affiliate links that you've generated and shared with them, knowing it helps you out financially and costs them not a single penny more.

The Partner Network pays you a commission on all sales attributed to the links you promote within the *cookie window*. Everyone who clicks your affiliate link will have a temporary cookie placed in their browser, and that tracking cookie will pay commissions to you for all sales within the next 24 hours.

Not every sale is eligible for commissions. Charity items, eBay gift cards, and a small number of daily deals in the U.S. and Canada are ineligible.

As Figure 6–1 on page 107 makes clear, your commissions vary depending on the category. Let's say that your co-worker Mariam fell in love with the 256GB red iPhone 12 and

## A WORD OF CAUTION

Don't just sign up and start spamming everyone everywhere. The Partner Network has rules against that. You'll need their written approval before you begin promoting links using email, SMS, instant messaging, or internet relay chat. You'll also have to ask permission before using paid traffic sources (such as Google Ads) or building software applications that promote eBay Partner Network links. You should read the Network Agreement located at the bottom of the eBay Partner Network portal page (the link for the portal is at the bottom of eBay's homepage or go to https://partnernetwork.ebay.com).

The Federal Trade Commission (FTC) also requires that affiliate links be accompanied by simple and clear language to inform consumers that your post contains an ad—using terms like "advertisement," "ad," and "sponsored." See http://ftc.gov/influencers to learn more about federal disclosure laws.

| Category | Subcategory | % of Sale | Cap (USD) |
|---|---|---|---|
| Business & Industrial | Business & Industrial | 2.5% | $225 |
| Collectibles | Art & Antiques; Coins & Paper Money; Crafts; Dolls & Bears; Entertainment Memorabilia; Miscellaneous Collectibles; Pottery & Glass; Sports & Leisure; Stamps; Toys, Hobbies, & Games | 3.0% | $550 |
| Electronics | Cameras & Photo; Cell Phones & Accessories; TV; Video & Audio; Video Games & Consoles | 2.0% | $550 |
| | Computers; Tablets & Networking | 1.5% | $550 |
| Fashion | Clothing, Shoes, & Accessories; Health & Beauty; Jewelry & Watches | 4.0% | $550 |
| Home & Garden | Alcohol & Food; Appliances; Baby; Miscellaneous Home & Garden; Pet Supplies | 3.0% | $550 |
| Lifestyle | Gift Cards & Coupons; Miscellaneous Lifestyle; Musical Instruments; Sports; Tickets & Events | 3.0% | $550 |
| Media | Books; Comics & Magazines; DVDs & Movies; Music | 3.0% | $550 |
| Parts & Accessories | eBay Motors | 4.0% | $100 |
| | Vehicle Parts & Accessories | 3.0% | $550 |
| Real Estate | Real Estate | 1.0% | $100 |
| All Other | All Other | 4.0% | $550 |

**FIGURE 6–1.** Here's the eBay Partner Network rate card* showing the very generous commissions for referring *converting* traffic to a listing, a search page, or other eBay pages. *At the time we went to press.

told you she was about to buy one. "Wait, let me send you a link that gets me paid when you buy it and costs you nothing extra," you say. She uses your affiliate link, generated with the Bookmarklet Tool (more on this on page 109), and voilà! You've been paid.

How much did you make? Well, let's do the math. Mariam's new iPhone cost $979, and eBay pays a 2 percent bounty on electronics. That's $979 × 0.02 = $19.58. Not too shabby for a few moments of your time. If Mariam shares the link with her friends, each purchase everyone makes within 24 hours of initially clicking on the link will generate an additional $19.58 in bounty for the same $979 item. Making easy money can be addictive, and you may find yourself really getting into this affiliate thing!

## THE GADGETS AND GIZMOS THAT GENERATE AFFILIATE MONEY

Here are a few of the features and tools available for you if you join the eBay Partner Network:

### Sales and Events Widget

Promote what's trending and hot using ready-made Sales and Events Widgets. Whether it's helping animals, fighting cancer, or the latest trend in consumer electronics, eBay offers an ever-changing array of themed and focused promotional tools. You'll find the Sales and Events Widgets on the eBay Partner Network homepage immediately upon signing in (see Figure 6–2 below). With a click of your mouse, you'll be able to share landing pages relevant to the products eBay has identified as flying out the door.

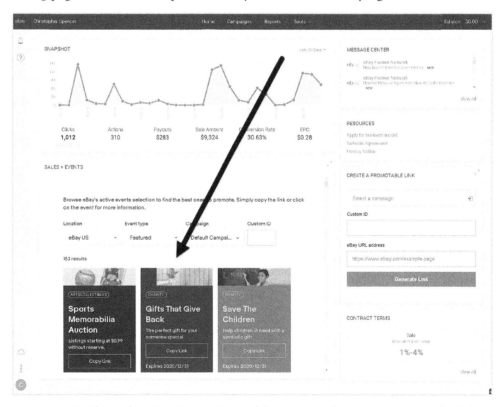

**FIGURE 6–2.** This is the eBay Partner Network homepage; the arrow points to the Sales and Events Widgets section. These special links point to landing pages featuring eBay's trending, bestselling products as well as items being sold to benefit good causes.

## Campaigns

While this feature is optional, creating campaigns allows you to track and manage distinct categories of affiliate traffic. The eBay Partner Network recommends using campaigns to better analyze your performance data to see what is working—and what isn't. Some partners have unique campaigns for different eBay product categories, while others use them to track performance on different parts of their site. Campaigns are also used to track retail events like "Black Friday 2020" or "Email Campaigns." Just click the Campaigns menu from the eBay Partner Network homepage to get started. Figure 6-3 below shows how to add a new campaign.

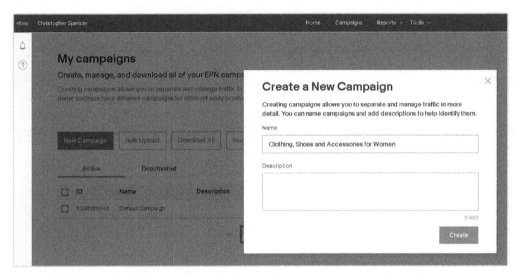

**FIGURE 6-3.** Here's the Create a New Campaign screen, which allows you to record affiliate tracking and revenue to suit your business strategies and processes.

## Bookmarklet Tool

Yes, it's a funny name, but the Bookmarklet allows you to rapidly create trackable hyperlinks to any page on eBay in seconds. This tool is compatible with Google Chrome and Safari. To learn more, click the Tools menu on the eBay Partner Network homepage and then click Bookmarklet Tool. There, you'll find easy-to-follow installation instructions (see Figure 6-4 on page 110). Once installed, simply click the Bookmarklet while you're on any eBay listing page to generate an affiliate link to share with someone you think would be interested in buying that item. You can also use the Bookmarklet to generate an affiliate link from any eBay page that you feel would interest a prospective buyer, such as search results pages.

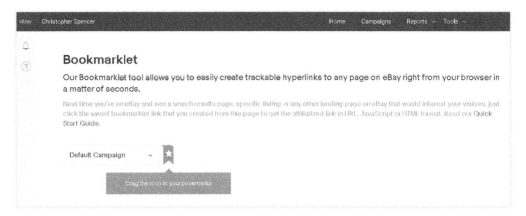

**FIGURE 6–4.** The Bookmarklet Tool is easily installed into the bookmarks bar of your Google Chrome or Safari browser using drag-and-drop. Once installed, clicking it from any eBay page generates an affiliate link for that page.

### Link Generator

If you don't want to use campaigns, the Bookmarklet Tool will do a great job of generating links and keeping your life simple. But if you want more flexibility in tracking your affiliate activity, including campaigns, eBay's Link Generator may be the best solution. With this tool, you create trackable hyperlinks to send traffic to eBay item pages, search results pages, Stores, and more. The Link Generator produces promotable links in the form of a URL, HTML, or JavaScript and a QR code; the last can be scanned by a phone or other mobile device with a QR code reader. Most phones natively support QR code scanning—give it a try if you're not already using them. Grab your next can of Coke and scan the tiny QR code that's printed on it, and see what happens. Figure 6–5 on page 111 shows the Link Generator in action converting an eBay item listing URL into an affiliate link, and Figure 6–6 on page 111 shows the QR code feature for the same URL. If you're also an eBay seller, you can generate a QR code to promote your own listings or eBay Store and put it on your business card, letterhead, fliers, community bulletin board, and wherever else your heart desires. If you operate a brick-and-mortar location, post the QR code and a call to action (e.g., "Shop our jewelry on eBay—scan this code with your phone to visit our Store") to not only generate profits on the merchandise you sell, but also earn affiliate commissions. To learn more, click the Tools menu on the eBay Partner Network homepage and then click Link Generator.

### Smart Links

Automatically optimize your affiliate moneymaking on HTML-based web pages with Smart Links. A tiny line of code will convert all your past and future links to eBay into

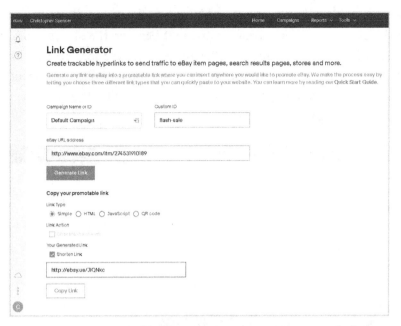

**FIGURE 6–5.** Here's a link produced by the Link Generator using my Default Campaign and the custom ID *flash-sale* used for segmentation and tracking. Notice I've checked the Shorten Link option to produce a tidy little link rather than an endlessly long URL.

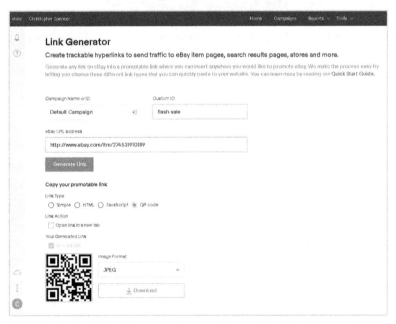

**FIGURE 6–6.** Here's the QR code generation option enabled for the same URL shown in Figure 6-5 above. The downloadable QR code is useful when sharing printed materials. Scanning the code instantly opens the eBay page with the affiliate tracking enabled.

monetized links that track your affiliate relationship and pay you. The Smart Links tool generates the code for you—just copy and paste it between the <head></head> tags of the web page where you want links to eBay to be converted into affiliate links. You'll find the code generator and a quick start guide when you click the Tools menu from the eBay Partner Network homepage and then click Smart Links. Figure 6-7 below shows the page for generating the code snippet.

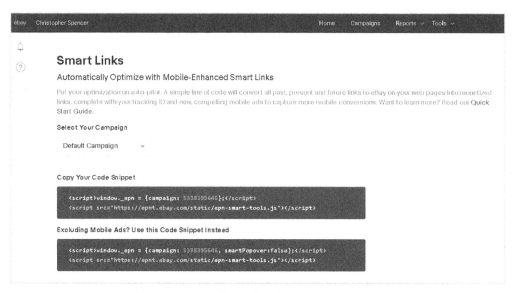

**FIGURE 6–7.** Here's the Smart Links code snippet generator. The snippet is then placed between the <head></head> tags on the desired web page.

## Smart Placements

Generate, store, and edit dynamic banners of various sizes (even custom sizes you choose) to place on your websites. What's clever about Smart Placements is that you can promote "Mandalorian plush" one week and with a few keyword changes promote "Christmas ornaments" the next—without having to replace the code on your page. Creating banners is easy; Figure 6-8 on page 113 gives an example of how to generate a banner, and Figure 6-9 on page 113 shows what the banner looks like once the code is installed on a website. You'll find the code generator and a quick start guide by clicking the Tools menu on the eBay Partner Network homepage and then clicking Smart Placements.

## Smart Share

This is a browser extension (also referred to as a plug-in) that is only available for Google Chrome that works on both Mac and PC computers. Once installed and configured,

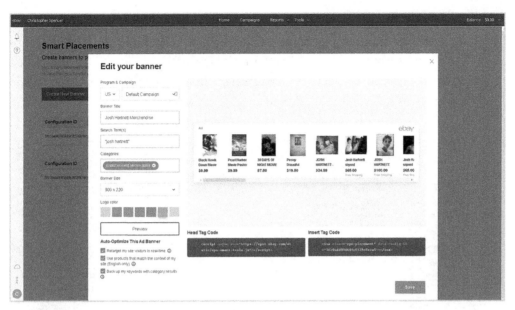

**FIGURE 6–8.** Here's a Smart Placement banner (900 x 220 pixels) that was generated for the Absolute Josh Hartnett unofficial fan website.

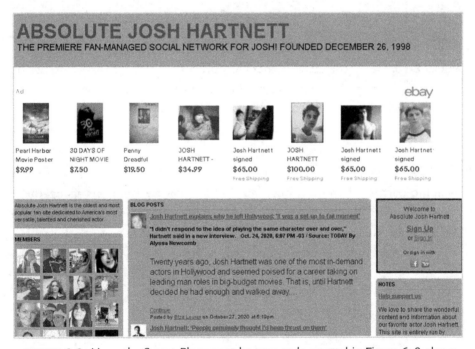

**FIGURE 6–9.** Here, the Smart Placement banner code created in Figure 6–8 above is installed on the Absolute Josh Hartnett fan site. The banner automatically generates dynamic ads that, when clicked, link to relevant eBay listings that are available for purchase—with revenue paid to the site for the referral.

you just look for products and pages you love on eBay, click the Smart Share extension icon, and share the link that's generated (Figure 6–10 below). Smart Share links are automatically associated with your eBay Partner Network account so that your hard work is tracked, and you are paid! To install Smart Share, click the Tools menu on the eBay Partner Network homepage and then click Smart Share.

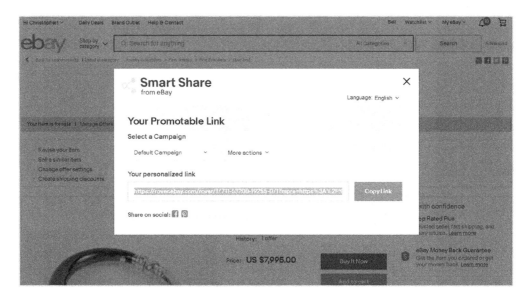

**FIGURE 6–10.** Here's the eBay Partner Network Smart Share browser extension in action. It's similar to the Bookmarklet Tool with a few added features and is available for the Google Chrome browser.

### eBay Developers Program APIs

High-volume partners have developed *distributed commerce* solutions using the eBay Developers Program APIs. Distributed commerce is when potential buyers are able to find, select, and purchase products within an existing ecommerce platform (i.e., an app or a site). In case you're new to the term API, it refers to *application programming interface*, or a computer interface that allows a third-party tool (app or site) to connect to eBay and perform specific tasks. For example, an influencer with a site that reviews men's fragrances can also offer a custom shopping experience, where visitors can buy fragrances, men's suits, accessories, shoes, and so on, all of them for sale on eBay, without ever leaving the site. An API-based distributed commerce solution keeps customers on the original site while still earning affiliate revenue for the influencer. There are Buy APIs, Sell APIs, Commerce APIs, and Developer APIs available on eBay—all free and each tailor-made for a purpose. Some highly skilled partners can earn millions of dollars using eBay's APIs. To learn more or to sign up for eBay's APIs, click the Tools menu on the eBay Partner Network homepage and then click eBay APIs.

### Creative Gallery

This is where you can download attractive logos and colorful banners focused on specific eBay categories (see Figure 6–11 below). The eBay logo is iconic and instantly recognizable. Pairing approved logos and banners along with relevant content yields conversions and sales. Make certain you use one of the eBay link-generating tools to ensure all logos and banners track your affiliate relationship. Access these logos and banners by clicking the Tools menu on the eBay Partner Network homepage and then click Creative Gallery.

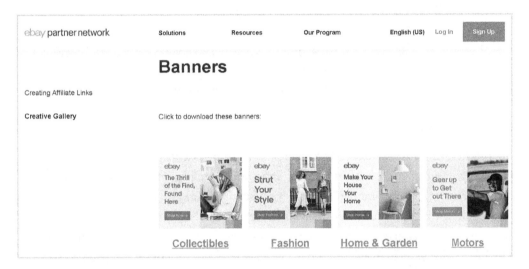

**FIGURE 6–11.** Various standard-size banners are ready-made for you to use. This is the eBay Partner Network Creative Gallery, where affiliates source category-specific banners to use with their promotions.

## GETTING PAID

You can sign up and start earning commissions right away with the eBay Partner Network, but to move those tidy profits into your hands, you'll need to provide payment instructions. Earnings will accrue at eBay until you indicate how you'd like to be paid. Click the current balance on your partner account at the top right of the eBay Partner Network homepage, then click Bank Account and fill in the required fields. If you prefer to receive your funds through PayPal, remember that you'll pay a 2 percent processing fee, capped at $20. I recommend selecting the Autopay option. See Figure 6–12 on page 116 to see the Bank Account form filled out and configured for Autopay.

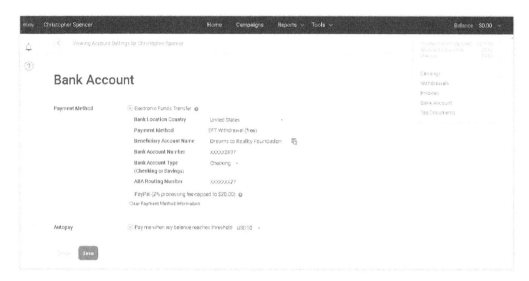

**FIGURE 6–12.** Here's the Bank Account form where you'll enter your account details so you'll receive timely payment—note the Autopay feature. I donate all my earnings from the eBay Partner Network to my favorite nonprofit organization.

## SNAPSHOTS

My mother, Carol Anne Rizvi, M.D., is an accomplished doctor and a fiscal conservative who taught me the value of education and money management, among many other things. When it comes to money, she told me, "Be sure to always measure what you make!"

You'll measure what you make as an eBay affiliate partner through dynamic snapshots and reports. I'll talk about snapshots first. A snapshot of your affiliate earnings is always available at the top of the eBay Partner Network homepage. Snapshots are adjustable, and you can select from a variety of time frames or enter a date range manually (see Figure 6–13 on page 117). The snapshot contains the following analytics for the time frame you select:

- *Clicks.* How many times your affiliate links were clicked.
- *Actions.* The number of times purchases were made within 24 hours of clicking your affiliate links.
- *Payouts.* The commissions you earned on the sales.
- *Sale Amount.* The gross merchandise volume for the sales made using your affiliate links.
- *Conversion Rate.* The actions divided by the clicks—in other words, the probability that someone who clicks your link is likely to make a purchase. The higher the percentage, the better the quality of your promotional efforts, because the person who clicked was actually interested enough to buy the item.

**FIGURE 6–13.** Here you can see a snapshot on the eBay Partner Network homepage. The arrow points to the pull-down menu that allows you to filter by preset date ranges or a specified custom date range.

▪ *EPC.* Short for *earnings per click* and is calculated by dividing the total cost of your clicks by the total number of clicks.

Every user you send to eBay receives a cookie on their system; the eBay Partner Network will pay you a commission on all attributed sales within the following 24 hours. A cookie (also called a web cookie, internet cookie, or browser cookie) is a minute amount of data stored on your web browser after visiting a website that allows remote servers to remember *stateful* information, such as items added to the eBay shopping cart, or to record your browsing activity, including which pages were visited in the past.

The eBay Partner Network uses last-click payout methodology, which means the last affiliate link a user clicks before making a purchase is the one that gets the commission. Even if a buyer is within your 24-hour cookie window, after they click another affiliate partner's link, that partner will get credit for those purchases, not you.

## USING REPORTS TO TRACK YOUR PROFITS

Solopreneurs and small organizations that pick up a little extra side money by joining the eBay Partner Network may lack the time to routinely run and examine reports. But for full-time affiliate marketers, reports provide an important feedback loop that signals if their hard work is generating the commissions they're after. While a snapshot will tell you how much you've earned and a few key metrics within a specific time frame, reports will reveal the details (see Figure 6-14 below). Reports connect the dots and provide important clarity so you can know if your efforts are earning respectable revenue. Reports are accessible via the web or can be accessed through APIs.

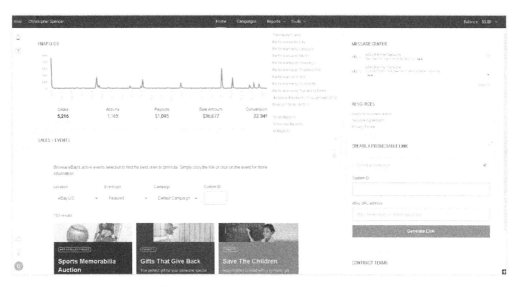

**FIGURE 6-14.** By clicking the Reports menu on the eBay Partner Network homepage, a list of ready-made reports appears in a pull-down menu.

Here's a list of the key reports available:

- *Transaction Detail.* View, filter by date, sort sale data with individual item detail (see Figure 6-15 on page 119).
- *Performance by:*
  - *Day.* Here you'll see metrics grouped by day, including clicks, sales, the number of items ordered, earnings, and a few other data points. These columns appear in all Performance reports, so I won't repeat them in the key points below.
  - *Category.* This report identifies sales by vertical category, which would be analogous to a department in a department store (e.g., fashion); by meta category, which would be comparable to a section of that department (e.g., jewelry and watches); and by leaf category, which would compare to a specific type of product within that section (e.g., pocket watches).
  - *Month.* This report groups sales by month with no transaction details.
  - *Campaign.* Some partners use campaigns to differentiate affiliate traffic for different product categories, while others use them to track affiliate link placements (e.g., on different sites or parts of a site)—this report reveals how each of those campaigns is performing.

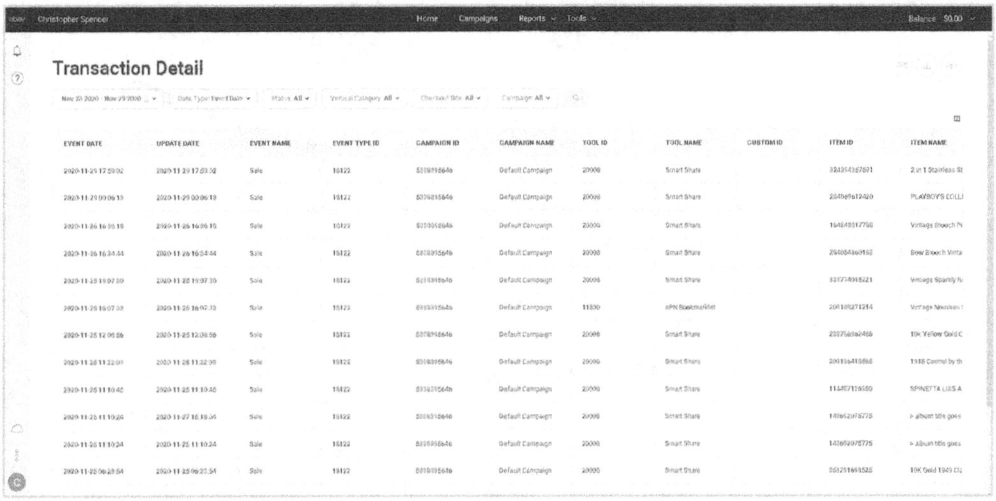

**FIGURE 6–15.** Here's a Transaction Detail report, which offers robust detail of individual affiliate-driven sales transaction data.

- *Checkout Site.* The checkout site for an action that results in a sale is revealed in this report—eBay manages sites in different countries, and when a member in one country buys using an affiliate link, it's trackable by checkout site—so you'll know which country is generating the best results for you.
- *Tool.* This report shows you sales and metrics information for each tool—Bookmarklet, Smart Placements, Smart Share, and Sales and Events Widget.
- *Custom ID.* Highly granular reporting is possible using the Custom ID feature, and when you are deploying Custom IDs (e.g., something like *christmas2020* or *mondaysale*), this report tracks the results of links with Custom ID added using the Link Generator.
- *Top-Selling Items.* Just as the name implies, this report shows which individual products are selling the best as a result of your link promotion.

The Performance reports all have some things in common. They all offer graphical representations of the data and the ability to filter dates, traffic sources, checkout site, and campaign.

You should put report generation on autopilot by using the email icon you'll see at the top right of every report (Figure 6–15 above). Reports can be emailed immediately after you look at them, or they can be (and should be) scheduled to go out regularly. Emailed reports share the same format options as downloaded reports—they can be sent as a PDF, Excel file, or CSV. The Schedule Report configuration options are flexible and robust (see Figure 6–16 on page 120).

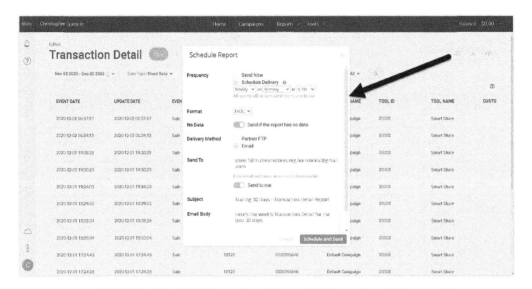

**FIGURE 6–16.** This is the Schedule Report function, which is optional when emailing reports. All reports have an envelope icon at the top right—clicking it launches the email dialogue box and reports can be sent immediately or scheduled in advance.

## TO SHORTEN, OR NOT TO SHORTEN: THAT IS THE QUESTION

There's never a more sincere and dedicated cheerleader for your business than *you*, and in the spirit of self-promotion, below are some affiliate link examples that point to The Dream Store® (eBay user ID: borntodeal), which is my oldest eBay Store, opened on June 4, 1999. I have been fortunate enough to make a great deal of money on eBay, and I now give 100 percent of the proceeds from The Dream Store away to help people in need through eBay for Charity. While this chapter focuses on making money on eBay by promoting other sellers' products, every eBay seller should always maximize their income opportunity by affiliatizing (as we say in the industry) their own product pages before sharing links for them. There is nothing sweeter than double-dipping and making some extra money on your own sales!

Here's what eBay Partner Network links look like using various tools (the good, the bad, and the ugly):

- *Bookmarklet.* https://rover.ebay.com/rover/1/711-53200-19255-0/1?ff3=4&tool id=11800&pub=5575439159&campid=5338395646&mpre=https%3A%2F%2F www.ebay.com%2Fstr%2Fdreamstorealityfoundation
- *Smart Share.* https://rover.ebay.com/rover/1/711-53200-19255-0/1?mpre=https %3A%2F%2Fwww.ebay.com%2Fstr%2Fdreamstorealityfoundation&campid=533 8395646&toolid=20008

■ *Create a Promotable Link* tool (from the eBay Partner Network homepage). https:// rover.ebay.com/rover/1/711-53200-19255-0/1?mpre=https%3A%2F%2Fwww. ebay.com%2Fstr%2Fdreamstorealityfoundation&campid=5338764133&toolid=1 0001&customid=

■ *Create a Promotable Link* tool (with the Shorten Link check box ticked). http://ebay.us/CyDXY8

The last example is by far the most user-friendly URL if you want to share a link on printed materials. The shorten link option rolled out in 2020, but for now it is only available within the eBay Partner Network portal, which takes longer to prepare than the other options. No doubt eBay's engineers will soon rework their affiliate marketing tools to produce cleaner, shorter links across the board. My faster method is to use Smart Share to create a link and then use a URL shortening tool on it. Here are the tools that are currently approved by eBay:

■ Bitly (https://bitly.com/)
■ Ow.ly (https://www.hootsuite.com/pages/owly)
■ Buff.ly (https://buffer.com/)
■ Google Firebase Dynamic Links (FDL) (mobile only)

Here's the svelte URL for The Dream Store I created using Bitly: https://ebay.to/33P3kps (try it out and see where it goes!).

The other option, as we discussed earlier in the chapter, is to create a scannable QR code to link to your product page. Scan the QR code in Figure 6–17 below with your phone and watch the magic!

There's a use case for long links, short links, and QR codes. Use long links when the person clicking won't see them—for example, within an HTML web page where the link is coded into a text hyperlink. Use the short links in emails and social media posts, where the link needs to be visually appealing. Because URL shortening involves redirection technology, there is a very slight possibility the site could go down or users could suffer

**FIGURE 6–17.** I generated this QR code by signing into the eBay Partner Network homepage and using the Create a Promotable Link tool. All purchases made by scanning this QR code result in a sale from one of my eBay Stores and an affiliate commission.

some latency. Official eBay affiliate URLs without redirection shortening are always preferable. Lastly, always use a QR code when sharing your affiliate links on printed pages such as letters, postcards, brochures, etc.

## NEXT STEPS—MAKING BIG MONEY

I am dead serious that you can make big money through the eBay Partner Network. The places you can promote affiliate links are only limited by your imagination. I'll wrap up this chapter by giving you one possible roadmap to a prosperous journey.

Here are my recommended steps for getting started:

- Sign up for the eBay Partner Network.
- Check out all the tools and learn how to use them to generate links.
- Choose a niche—products that you know well enough to promote and talk about with authority—for example, if you're a vinyl record enthusiast, then start by promoting links to eBay's music category.
- Build an audience on social media by blogging, developing a high-traffic website, or building an opt-in email list (do not spam people!).
- Select products you love, sellers you admire, and eBay's themed landing pages to promote.
- Create quality content that fosters an engaged community and promotes your affiliate links.
- Study and become an expert on the topics of keywords and hashtags.
- Engage with others to encourage collaborations—cross-pollination builds audiences.
- Be consistent.
- Test, adjust, and grow your affiliate marketing business.
- Track and evaluate your results (hint: use reports).
- Expand what works.
- Abandon what doesn't work.
- Take calculated risks, but don't bet the farm—apply care and experience to avoid failure.
- Save a little, spend a little, and reinvest a little back into your business.
- Get paid for your hard work.

If at this point you're feeling somewhat paralyzed with fear, remember that unlike selling actual goods on eBay, making money with the eBay Partner Network involves no additional financial investment beyond the money you paid for your computer and the cost of your internet connection. You're simply promoting someone else's stuff. The time and energy you put in will result in profits.

Social media experts recognize that people are multifaceted beings with a wide array of interests, but the most successful influencers identify a narrow niche and promote their content pillars with intensity and laser precision. There's some trial and error in finding your frequency, but it will come. If you've never pursued your own business, it's natural to put off anything that produces anxiety. When we're scared, our impulse is to stay put. According to *Psychology Today*, fear-evoked freezing is a universal response. Don't become intimidated by the fact that your favorite influencers have thousands or even millions of followers compared to your few dozen. Every influencer had to start somewhere, and micro-influencers can often be extremely successful in a very narrow niche.

Your long-term happiness and success in business depends on avoiding the work you hate, banishing unnecessary activity, and doing what you love. If you're burning the candle at both ends, then it should be while running your own business, not working a job and secretly wishing you were doing something else. You don't need to be an affiliate marketing genius to succeed. You'll become more optimistic, more motivated, and ultimately true to yourself if you launch your influencer and affiliate marketing career by pursuing your passion. It just doesn't feel like work if you do.

I've identified the following product and topic areas that I believe would offer attractive earning opportunities for you using the eBay Partner Network:

- *Fashion.* Both men's and women's fashion eternally produces incredible interest from buyers.
- *Food.* Everyone has to eat, and from gadgets to gourmet seasonings, people are insatiably interested in what's new, what's tasty, and how to stay healthy.
- *Fitness.* Everyone's thought about getting into shape at one point, and both men and women are eager for fitness tips and products to support and show off their success.
- *Phones and mobile devices.* According to the GSM Association, which represents mobile network operators around the world, there are 324 million unique mobile device subscribers in North America alone. Although I'm a daily iPhone user, I wanted to give Android a try. I checked out product reviews for Android phones and ended up buying one using the affiliate link provided by the reviewer.
- *Electronics and gadgets.* From home audio to 4K drones and everything in between, consumer electronics always draw strong interest—and smart home, smart speakers, home robots, wireless earbuds, and smart watches are each multibillion-dollar businesses.
- *Jewelry and timepieces.* Nearly everyone on the planet wears something to ornament their body that makes them feel and look good—even timepieces are a functional fashion statement—and the industry generated $78 billion in sales in 2019.
- *Collectibles and art.* Whether it's a first edition book or a fabulous Andy Warhol lithograph, people all over the world love to admire and acquire rare objects.

- *Sports.* From sporting events to sporting goods, there's an endless number of topics, teams (and the fans who love them), and products to talk about.
- *Entertainment.* Movie reviews, TV series recommendations, popular music, and memorabilia are topics that everybody takes an interest in.
- *Health and beauty.* Staying well, looking good, and anti-aging are among the most popular areas for influencers.
- *Weddings and special occasions.* Nuptials and family gatherings are always wildly popular topics among people of all ages.
- *Vehicles.* For some, nothing is too good for their baby (whether it be a car, a motorcycle, or even a plane), and owners are always looking for the next best thing to take care of tire dressings, tune-ups, and other care and maintenance.
- *Home improvement.* With more than $400 billion in U.S. sales in 2020, home improvement will open a lot of doors for affiliate revenue—people are looking for tools, supplies, and tips on how to use them.
- *Home and office security.* High-tech smart security devices are everywhere, and buyers need expert recommendations for high-quality and affordable products.

Those are just some of the topic areas that successful influencers are talking about. Your passion is your path to success with the eBay Partner Network. Transparency will yield the best results—most A-listers are shameless self-promoters who don't hesitate to ask their followers for support.

To begin, just take the leap and pick a topic you'd love to talk about! You can syndicate content across multiple social media channels (just copy and paste), or you can stick to a single platform and build your audience. Be careful about putting all your eggs into one basket (remember Vine and MySpace?). Experiment with video, still images, short form content, longer posts, and hashtags—and keep experimenting until you discover your mojo.

In closing, consider that it's just as easy, or equally hard, to promote higher-value products as it is inexpensive ones. Your eBay Partner Network commissions are calculated on the total value of the sale, so bigger is definitely better. It is far more lucrative to write product reviews or make posts about a luxury robot vacuum cleaner than talk up a standard economy one. So keep that in mind when deciding what to write about.

# Chapter 7

# Become an Incredible eBay Seller

While this guide stands well on its own, I'd encourage you to also read my book *Start Your Own eBay Business, 3rd Ed.* (Entrepreneur Press, 2020), which is written for entrepreneurs who are just starting out. It is more anecdotal and is designed to get the reader to act. I wrote this guide to be more of a brass tacks roadmap for your success as a businessperson on eBay.

## THE KEY POINTS OF eBAY SELLING

Here are my steps for achieving your greatest possible success on eBay:

- Identify your niche—products that you can acquire at a fair price and sell for a reasonable profit.

- Purchase inventory at excellent wholesale prices.
- Take professional-looking photos of your products or use approved images provided by the manufacturer.
- Write eBay ads, called listings.
- Organize and safely store your merchandise.
- Answer buyer questions professionally and quickly.
- Make lots of sales that include a healthy profit margin.
- Pick, pack, and ship your sales.
- Leave feedback for your customers.
- Handle your back-office stuff, such as licenses, accounting, and taxes.
- Save a little, spend a little, and invest a little back into the business.

In order for this to work, you'll need to be inspired to take action, find your passion, source your products, and work your tuchus off. As you continue through the remainder of this book, I'll work hard to help you find that passion and stick with it. Loving your work is important, but so is money. You can't pay for a roof over your head and fill the fridge with hopes and dreams.

I've been selling on eBay since 1999, and I am even more motivated and passionate about my eBay business now than I was when I started. Ecommerce was a novelty back in 1999, and it's ubiquitous today. Everyone I know and everyone I've met has bought something online. According to the U.S. Census Bureau, ecommerce sales represented as much as 16 percent of total U.S. retail sales in 2020.

Not only is there growth opportunity in that 84 percent of U.S. retail sales, but also in the rest of the world. When I ran a report that showed my international sales for 2019, I learned that a stunning 31 percent of my eBay sales shipped internationally. I am an exporter! You can be, too! This high percentage of international sales is due in part to the goods I mostly sell: jewelry, collectibles, and entertainment memorabilia. Buyers are more likely to order products from a foreign seller when they fail to find what they want in their own country. eBay has substantially simplified the export process; I'll explain how a bit later on.

## MAKE SURE IT'S LEGAL AND ALLOWED

Selling on eBay is a global business. You'll want to ship to anyone who is willing to buy what you're selling, and eBay international standard delivery makes it simple. Just print your eBay international standard delivery label, and eBay will handle international shipping for you. Shipping globally is a surefire way to increase sales and a unique benefit of selling on eBay, but make sure what you're selling isn't prohibited. That's where shipping across borders can be tricky. For example, certain art that contains nudity cannot be shipped internationally. Ivory or Nazi items cannot be sold on eBay—while these items aren't illegal everywhere, eBay doesn't allow them on the site. Due to health and hygiene issues, you cannot sell used underwear or socks, even when laundered. You can sell an empty beer bottle but not an uncorked Dom Perignon Rose Gold Methuselah (even if it is worth $49,000!). Alcohol, tobacco, firearms, and a litany of other products are highly regulated and age-restricted by governments across the world, and most are prohibited or extremely restricted on eBay as well. Some FDA-regulated devices may be sold, while others cannot. For example, dental curing lights (which are used to cure, or harden, composite fillings) are permitted as long as the listing includes a statement that clarifies the regulatory status of the item and as long as the purchaser is authorized to buy it (e.g., a dental office or licensed dental professional). Generally, most merchandise that's available over the counter is OK to sell online, but eBay has a few quirks and complexities to deal with.

Even if an item is legal to sell in your city or state, it could be prohibited elsewhere, so eBay has established a *prohibited and restricted items policy*. This is a bit of a moving target because eBay's policies change in lockstep with government regulations in the countries in which eBay operates and change to accommodate the expectations of eBay users. Make sure you stay up-to-date with the policy and check it frequently for any changes. eBay's current list of prohibited and restricted items can be found by following these steps:

1. Click Help & Contact at the top of the homepage on most eBay pages.
2. Type "prohibited and restricted" into the search box.
3. Select the link entitled *Prohibited and restricted items*.

Some prohibited and restricted items include the following:

- Adult items
- Alcohol
- Animals and wildlife products
- Art (some rules about reproductions and sensitive topics, such as nudity and sexual imagery)
- Artifacts, cultural heritage, and grave-related items
- Autographed items (not disallowed, but be sure to read the policy)
- Catalytic converter and test pipes
- Chance listings (e.g., mystery items or a listing that offers you a chance to win something in a contest)
- Coupons
- Credit and debit cards
- Digitally delivered goods (with a few exceptions, like items in online games)
- Drugs and drug paraphernalia

- Electrical and electronic equipment
- Encouraging illegal activity
- Event tickets
- Firearms, accessories, and knives (blade length can be a touchy subject, so study the full policy prior to listing)
- Food (another area that has nuances, so read the eBay policy)
- Gift cards
- Goods from embargoed countries
- Government documents, IDs, and licenses
- Government, transit, and shipping-related items
- Hazardous, restricted, or regulated materials
- Human remains and body parts
- Lock-picking devices
- Mailing lists and personal information
- Medical devices and drugs
- Personal relationships and services (Psst! No mail order brides or grooms!)
- Police-related items
- Real estate
- Slot machines
- Stamps, currency, and coins
- Stocks and other securities
- Stolen property
- Travel
- Used clothing and cosmetics

Don't be scared off by the length of the list. Not everything mentioned is prohibited—many categories are either sensitive or questionable and require a closer reading of eBay's policy. For example, you can sell autographed items with a certificate of authenticity, among a few other restrictions.

I also talked about the VeRO program in Chapter 2—the eBay policies and team protecting the intellectual property rights of others. It's not OK to sell counterfeit merchandise, but you can resell the real deal. The *first-sale doctrine* allows you to lawfully resell legally purchased merchandise even if it's protected by copyright or trademark. (The doctrine is also referred to as the "right of first sale," "first sale rule," or "first sale exhaustion rule.") Whether it's an unwanted watch or a well-played video game cartridge, so long as it's not an illegal copy, you have the legal right to resell it on eBay (subject to other eBay rules). Therefore, a Seiko watch is just fine, but a Feiko is not. If you happen to discover other infringing eBay listings, that doesn't sanction bad conduct on your part (see Figure 7–1 on page 129).

---

## Vintage ███████ Stereo Receiver Owners User Operating Instruction Manual

---

Up for sale is this brand new comb-bound copy of the above listed and pictured manual. All of our manuals are produced with the following features:

Professional monochrome black & white laser printing.

Double-sided duplex printing.

Printed on high quality durable 24 lb weight & 97 brightness white laser paper.

High quality 7 mil thickness clear PVC plastic covers with rounded corners on both the front and back sides.

High quality black plastic combs sized properly for the size of each manual for the binding.

We also can do custom manual or presentation print jobs in black & white using the same process listed above. Please message us through eBay messages with the number of pages of your file, the number of copies needed, and any other specific instructions. We will get back to you asap with a quote (quantity discounts are available), turnaround time, and how to send us your file.

Please note that the item that is in the pictures above is an image of the cover of the scan we use to print in black & white the exact manual that you will receive. Please feel free to ask any questions. This item ships out the same or the next business day after receiving completed payment. Thank you for your interest and for supporting small businesses like ours here in the U.S.!

---

**FIGURE 7–1.** One eBay seller was listing scanned and reprinted vintage electronic owner's manuals for a famous brand that's still in business, which infringed on their copyright. To make eBay a safer place to trade, I reported the listing to VeRO for removal.

## CARVING OUT YOUR NICHE

New to business or new to eBay? You have to start somewhere. I started selling collectible medals on eBay—you can read about it in my first book, *The eBay Entrepreneur* (Kaplan Business, 2006). It's out of print, but you can still find copies of it online. Speaking of business opportunities, out-of-print books represent a lucrative one because eager collectors have difficulty sourcing titles from beloved authors who had small print runs.

When I started my eBay business, I focused on antiques and collectibles and stayed in that space for many years. I rarely bought anything because I worked with my best friend, mentor, and former employer, Mike Richards, who had a seemingly endless inventory of things I could sell on his behalf. Mike sadly passed away in 2015 after a long struggle with cancer.

Mike had a passion for business and was extremely experienced with and interested in antiques, jewelry, fine art, and collectibles. We paired my strong computer skills with his decades of retail and business experience, with great success.

So where do you find your niche? I explored product sourcing ideas in Chapter 4, but you must avoid getting involved in a soul-sucking business idea simply because you think it will be profitable. While it's great to find and follow retail trends, you must also follow your passion.

I have no idea who you are. You might be a teenager like Ben Akrish, who opened his first eBay Store and sold his first item at the age of 18. I helped mentor Ben, and as I write these words, he has 444 items for sale on eBay (see Figure 7–2 on page 131) and supports himself while living on his own and attending college. He started his eBay consignment business, at my recommendation, with zero investment. While the consignor owns the item, Ben sells it, and takes a cut of the profits without having to lay out a single cent. That is a clever and easy way to earn a guaranteed profit.

I take no credit for the idea—I first learned of the consignment model when I started working in Mike Richards' office back in 1985. Mike owned millions of dollars' worth of fine jewelry, antiques, and collectibles and profited just as many millions of dollars by consigning those goods to independent dealers who sold them. Mike and I achieved incredible success with our eBay consignment business, and I am glad that Ben was able to follow our business model with immediate success.

So who are you? You might be (throwing darts here):

- A starving student
- A recent graduate in need of immediate income
- A stay-at-home parent raising children
- Someone who's living solo and wanting to become more financially independent
- Someone who's recently become unemployed
- A senior enjoying the golden years with a bit of time to spare
- A shop owner interested in an additional revenue stream
- The CEO of a big factory with a future focus on direct-to-consumer sales
- A disabled individual who's interested in working from home
- Or a [fill in the blank]

I ventured into my own business at a very young age, but back then I didn't know what I didn't know. Ignorance was bliss. I succeeded only because I was so persistent. I failed many times, but I was young enough that failure didn't sting too badly. I am still willing to take risks, but I am more calculated about it now. As we age, we become more risk averse. We burn our finger, so we stop putting it into the candle flame. However, all business ventures involve some risk, so you'll have to overcome your fear of failure because at some point, you  at something you try in your eBay business. By carefully studying prices, trends, and product availability, your failures should become few and far between as you hone your business acuity.

Back to carving out your niche: start with what you love. Skaters should sell the best and most famous skateboard, skatewear, and streetwear brands. Those obsessed with weddings should avoid the complicated and extremely personalized bridal gown business and focus on wedding accessories and wedding supplies (and, if you're

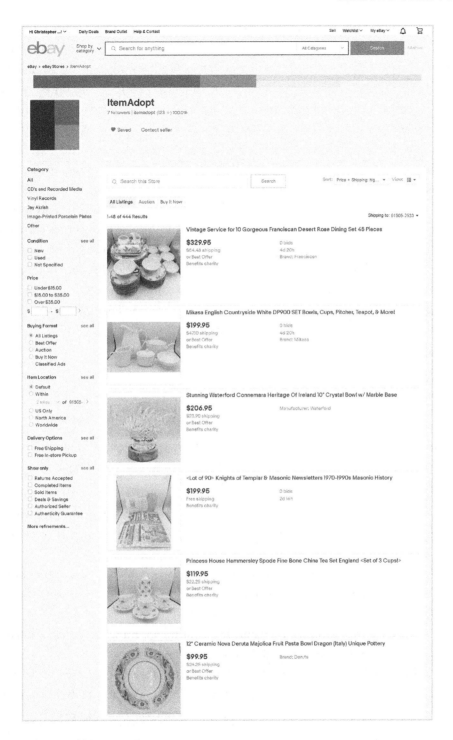

**FIGURE 7–2.** Teenage business owner Ben Akrish's ItemAdopt eBay Store, which is one of two that he operates using the consignment model.

experienced, maybe jewelry, too). Techies should jump into augmented and virtual reality. Gamers should sell . . . well, you get it. Focus on what you love and what products in that niche sell well on eBay. But remember: It is highly unlikely you will discover a unicorn business idea. Popular products made in factories and resold on eBay always face fierce competition. But if you are the factory, then you're sitting pretty because you call all the shots, including deciding who can resell your merchandise.

Trying to predict product trends is like trying to time the stock market. It's very hard. This is one of the reasons I avoid buying inventory and focus on consignment. You open the door to higher profit margins and simply return unsold goods to the consignor. Secondhand merchandise is easier to source for consignment and will yield even higher margins. It is virtually impossible to jump into the deep end with a new mass-market product and compete with the big guys. Consumer electronics sellers, for instance, work on razor-thin margins that are only profitable through huge volume purchasing and well-established relationships with factories.

It will be hard at first to pick the perfect products to sell on eBay. Moreover, if you've never worked in retail, the process might trigger a little panic attack.

Remember that in business:

▦ Competition is always ferocious,

▦ Product markets are saturated, and

▦ Customers want value, selection, convenience, and exceptional service.

I can't let you in on any insider secrets here because in retail there aren't too many secrets to reveal. You'll profit from time-tested ideas, staying focused on your customers, and working hard. Keep these points in mind:

▦ Be flexible and don't get stuck on one idea—success comes in time and from trying out a few ideas, not focusing on just one thing. Be prepared to explore and discover.

▦ Finding stuff to sell involves building relationships, which is slow at first but will start to snowball once you become a trusted and reliable partner with your suppliers.

▦ If you're new to business, focus on local sourcing and avoid being seduced by gurus touting their import and drop-ship schemes.

▦ Popular, high-demand, commodified products make up most of what is sold online, are what everyone wants and needs, and are going to be the toughest goods to source at a steep enough discount to make a generous profit.

I've talked a lot about carving out your niche, but what does that really mean? If you plan to sell new goods, you'll need to discover the white space—the product

## ALWAYS BE READY TO SELL

A lot of people don't like selling, which is why offices are filled with salaried workers, despite the fact that every industry would be dead if their products weren't selling. But the great thing about the internet is that younger people are used to online rejection, which makes them far better at sales than workers of yesteryear. Back in the day, telemarketing and door-to-door sales discouraged all but the most thick-skinned salespeople. Now, fear of rejection is far less of a problem than in the past, because it's practically ubiquitous online. Good salespeople earn a lot of money, and spectacular salespeople live in Beverly Hills mansions.

Successful eBay sellers are always selling. Always be prepared to offer your buyers something extra to satiate their emotional desire to buy.

category on eBay that's lacking inventory. Niche products serve a smaller, more selective audience. This refers to items such as handmade products, unique goods, and products that fill less ubiquitous needs. Small business strategist Bernhard Schroeder is a senior contributor at *Forbes* who follows business trends, and he's identified that successful small business owners focus on long tail products—items that sell in small quantities for a very long time, as opposed to trendy, bestselling products that tend to come and go. Schroeder believes that growth niches address solutions that cannot be resolved by products sold at mass retailers—and they are ideal for the smaller ecommerce retailer. For example, you could focus on organic skin-care products for individuals with unique and problematic skin conditions or plant-based pet treats. Schroeder says to look toward better solutions.

What's popular today can become a zombie product tomorrow. For a good, long stretch, I sold high-quality fossil Baltic amber jewelry on eBay, with an average selling price of $300 to $500 for a necklace. I had equal success with genuine saltwater pearl jewelry. I could not keep either in stock. Then factories in Asia jumped on their popularity and rapidly developed synthetic amber that is almost impossible to distinguish from the real thing. Faux pearls also became so realistic that buying the real deal became much less attractive when women could achieve the same look for pennies on the dollar. I don't always dump my zombie products. I generally keep the prices up. Eventually a discriminating customer comes along and buys the slower-moving, high-quality products. All retailers have to be prepared to pivot and look for what's currently in demand. It's a good idea to sell what you love, what you know, and what's available, but make sure it's not likely to become yesterday's fad.

## RECOMMENDATIONS AND PERSONALIZATION

As big as eBay may seem, it has thrived in part on a unique, personalized experience. eBay makes product recommendations on listing pages, in user emails, and at various points in every transaction. Your ability to establish lasting relationships with your customers and encourage repeat visits to your Store or your listings relies in part on how the customer feels at the end of a transaction.

You can present low-pressure sales recommendations at various points along the customer's sales journey, including:

- Sending a list of relevant product listings that they can buy at a discount and combine with their order before it ships
- Asking customers for their wish list
- Offering repeat customer discounts shortly after the customer has received their latest order
- Setting calendar reminders to follow up with customers using eBay's message system (see Figure 7–3 below)

**FIGURE 7–3.** Here's the Contact link on one of my eBay accounts (borntodeal). Clicking the link leads to the form you can use to message another eBay member. While recommending eBay listings is encouraged, promoting outside sites, merchandise, or offers is a quick path to a warning or account suspension.

Asking for another sale before the buyer receives what they ordered isn't usually unwelcome because the customer is still excited about and anticipating their order. You would be wise to recommend and upsell to everyone who buys from you, but only in the gentlest way, without any pressure.

The eBay Store where I sell jewelry flourishes because I offer special prices and free shipping to existing customers, I always address them by name, and I follow up to offer them links of new-to-eBay items. I anticipate that competition will intensify in the future, so I'm working hard to establish a fiercely loyal customer base with friendly, personalized service. Success in an online retail business depends in large part on your ability to strengthen buying power and improve your margins through economies of scale. It's generally easier to improve profit margins by doing that than to raise prices. The existence of shopping agent technologies such as Google Shopping allow buyers to rapidly compare your prices with those of competing merchants.

This comparison is most viable if you sell a commodified product rather than a unique niche product, such as handmade goods. This circles back to personalization, where offering differentiation is likely to foster customer loyalty, with services included in the price such as engraving, gift-wrapping, bespoke tailoring, etc.

If your ambition isn't to conquer the world but rather to delight customers, have fun, and put food on the table, a business focused on unique buyer experiences will reward you with far more success than following the herd. I love it when I stumble on an eBay seller who has something truly interesting and unique. I recently discovered a seller of jewelry who offers affordable fine jewelry made from pure solid sterling silver that includes personalized birthstones and free engraving included in the price (see Figure 7–4 on page 136). This is a long tail business model that will stand the test of time. It's classic and classy, and it won't become irrelevant like most trendy and fad merchandise.

Recommendations and personalization are core to achieving your goals. Every activity that helps boost your income must command the bulk of your time. And while you're at it, remember to convert product and Store links into eBay Partner Network affiliate links so that you double dip and earn an additional profit from the affiliate commission, as we mentioned in Chapter 6.

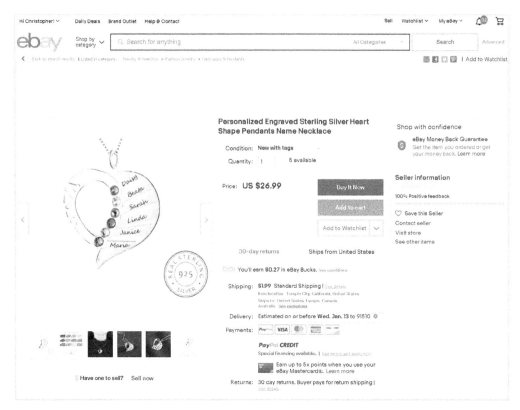

**FIGURE 7–4.** This eBay seller caught my eye. They operate a Store
that offers personalized jewelry. While the items themselves are not remarkable, the
free engraving and choice of stones add a heartwarming, unique touch.

Now that we've looked at the basics of becoming an eBay seller, let's cover some
selling essentials in the next chapter.

# Chapter 8

# Get Down to
# Selling Brass Tacks

By this point, we've discussed listing formats, ideas for product selection, browsing and search, and what it takes to become a seller with a long-term vision for success. And let's face it—reading is no substitute for simply doing the work—you just need to hit the ground running.

But let's get you as prepared as possible first, by walking you through the essentials of putting up listings and managing sales on eBay.

## RESEARCHING PRODUCTS AND PRICING

The amount of research required before you list an item depends on whether the product is a commodity, a rarity, or a handmade item. We'll cover format in a moment, i.e., whether to sell it via auction or at a fixed price. A hasty seller leaves money on the table—sometimes a lot. Experience has helped me avoid making some serious financial mistakes. Take the somewhat ugly little porcelain statue of a nude woman sitting on a pear (not a typo), designed by Nillo Beltrami and made in The Lenci Company factory in Turin, Italy, circa 1930s. A consignor brought this objet d'art to me and asked if I thought it would fetch $100. I had absolutely no idea how to set the price of this piece, but I knew I had to sell it at auction to determine market value. It sold for $17,100 with 34 bids (see Figure 8–1 below). The Lenci sale occurred in 2005.

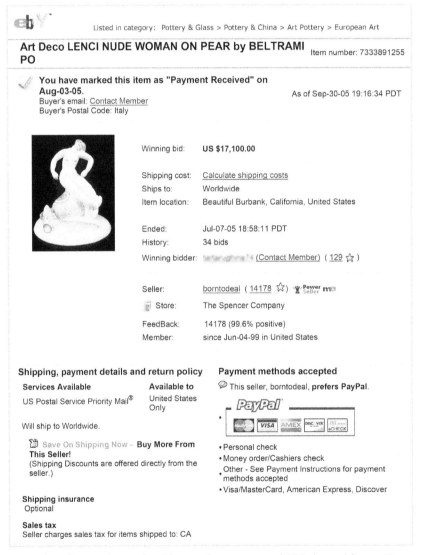

**FIGURE 8–1.** The client estimate for this consignment was $100, but with an eBay auction, I fetched $17,100. Auctions are the best choice for rare collectibles of uncertain value.

I've come a long way since then. I should have done much more research. The internet was slower then. I was hastier in those days. It all worked out, but these days, competition is intense and auction starting prices should be set with care. The consignor was happy, to say the least, and because I earn a percentage of every sale, I made a tidy sum. I have hundreds of similar examples—the week I wrote this section, I sold two rare magazines, one for $4,380 and another for $5,400. The neat thing is that it only takes two determined bidders who are prepared to open their wallets wide to have a highly successful auction.

How do you research an item? A common mistake for greenhorns is to simply type some keywords into the eBay search box and hope for the best. It's a bit like trying to read tea leaves. I explained why mastering Advanced Search is essential in Chapter 5 starting on page 83. Keep these facts in mind:

- Commodified items are easy to find, have plenty of comparable sales numbers, and are easy to price, but margins are usually low, and profits are only made at scale. This is very hard to do for a startup.
- Rare items must be properly identified and valued—haste leaves money on the table, but you can learn to avoid this as you gain experience.
- Handcrafted merchandise is usually harder to sell but typically enjoys healthy margins—while the product category is easily studied, unique items have no comparable sales on eBay.

There are a zillion third-party tools available to check prices, but don't pay for any of them—eBay is so incredibly massive that you'll usually find a *comp* (short for "comparable"). Use eBay's Advanced Search with the Sold Listings check box selected and sorted by Price + Shipping: Highest First (review Chapter 5 if you need to brush up on this).

Try different approaches when searching:

- By ISBN or UPC if available (for movies, games, books, and other products sold at mass retailers)
- By keywords that describe your item
- Browse categories

While there's no one-size-fits-all approach to researching and pricing, here are a few tips:

- Antiques are hard to value and may be just as hard to find—research carefully and gain insights by interacting with experts and collectors, both on eBay and on social media groups focused on antiques.
- Collectibles often have model numbers. For example, all Hummel figurines have a number you can research; a sold listing search for "hummel #347" will provide

comps for the figurine *Adventure Bound* (see Figure 8-2 on page 141). Seek out experts on eBay and in social media groups who can advise on rarity and value. Collectibles exist in multiple verticals on eBay, including entertainment memorabilia, vintage clothes, film cameras and lenses, rare and old sporting goods, collectible dolls and toys, and so on. Each collectible poses unique research challenges that require a time investment.

- Handmade art, ceramics and pottery, crafts, handwork, and cottage trade items like handmade candles and soaps are a challenge to research and price—the most successful sellers of these goods gradually build a loyal audience and promote their creations via social media (remember to also use the eBay Partner Network to double-dip and make extra money); use fixed prices and build in generous margins for slower-moving items like these.

- Clothing, shoes, and accessories are challenging to research and sell because merchandising is a bit more complicated, customer tastes change rapidly, and brands rise and fall out of favor overnight—focus on enduring brands with stable pricing rather than trendy fashions that come and go.

- Collectible (i.e., antique and vintage) vehicles, parts, and accessories require the same careful attention as other antique and collectible items. While late-model vehicles, accessories, and replacement parts are straightforward to research, rare finds require due diligence and loads of research beyond just eBay. Some of the rarest vehicles may only have one interested buyer.

- Dolls, toys, and hobby merchandise is another tough nut to crack due to the many variants, rapidly changing demand, and wild price fluctuations. Commodified items are well understood, but much older, rarer examples warrant loads of research. Some dolls and other toys can be worth huge money (see Figure 8-3 on page 142).

- Jewelry and watches don't just layer in the research challenges you'll face with antiques

**TIP**

It's not a collaboration with eBay yet, but the Google Lens app allows you to snap a picture of your item and pull up relevant information on Google. The technology is also integrated into the Google Photos app; both are available on the Play Store and the App Store. This is particularly helpful for identifying items such as books, games, and movies. This technology is improving rapidly, and it may someday be able to tell you what any object is just from a picture. As it is, it will help you name a celebrity from their photo or tell the difference between Russian niello and Navajo squash blossoms, among many other uses.

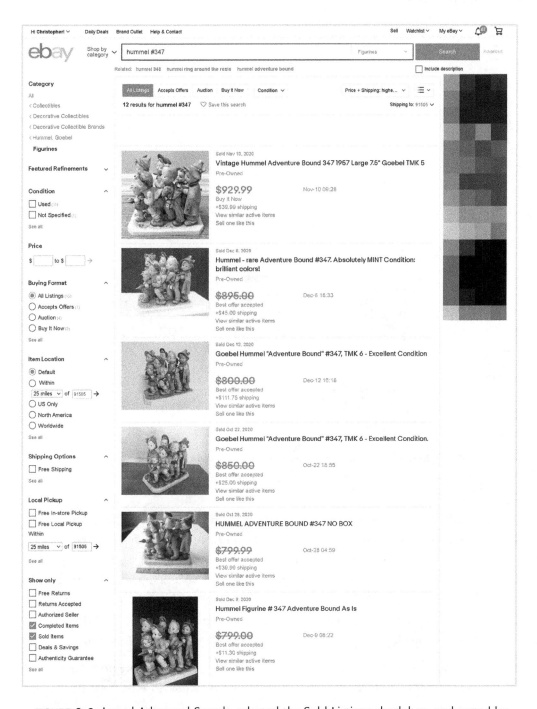

**FIGURE 8–2.** I used Advanced Search, selected the Sold Listings check box, and sorted by Price + Shipping: Highest First. For an item this valuable, I'd run an auction with a starting price no less than $929.99 for a mint condition example. Collectibles tend to go up in value over time, and with only 12 comps on eBay, I consider this item rare.

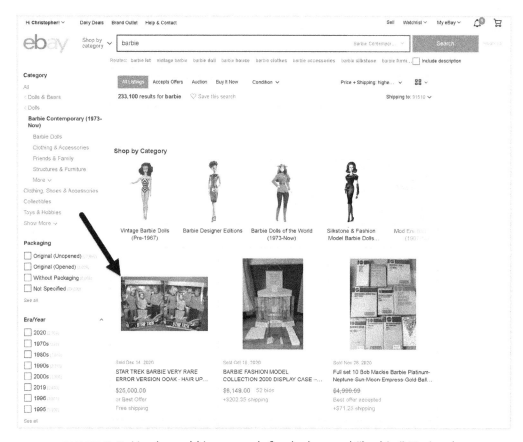

**FIGURE 8–3.** Here's a sold item search for the keyword "barbie." Notice the
*Star Trek* Barbie lot scored a $25,000 sale price.

and collectibles; you also have to consider the emotional reaction buyers have when
they lay eyes on the perfect pendant or the timepiece of their dreams. I refer to this
as *merit*. Items that have merit stand out from the sea of vanilla jewelry and ordinary
watches. When it comes to Tiffany, Jacob & Co, or other branded and commodified
luxuries, price and availability (i.e., rarity) are easy to research. Items of merit may be
harder to study and require more experience when evaluating and pricing. Beauti-
fully handmade jewelry or esoteric timepieces will command a premium.

The above categories are not all-inclusive, but they cover the more popular areas of
merchandise on eBay. But when it comes right down to it, how do you set the price? Here
are my general recommendations for each category, regardless of format (i.e., whether
you sell at auction or at a fixed price):

■ Antiques and collectibles should be researched ad nauseum—these are tough
categories for setting prices. But start high and work your way down. You cannot

recover lost opportunity, but you lose nothing by reaching for the stars. You can always drop your prices later on.

- Price your handmade items sufficiently high to reward you for your time and materials. Only you can set the value of your time. Skill and beautiful workmanship should not be undervalued. Handmade jewelry is especially popular on eBay. According to a highly popular career website, the average annual salary of jewelers in the U.S. in 2020 was $39,177, which would pay $18.84 per hour based on a 40-hour workweek. To earn that much, the necklace you create with $5 in components and 30 minutes of labor should sell for at least $14.42. Talented jewelers make substantially more.

- Unbranded clothing, shoes, and accessories usually sell very cheaply, so stick to popular brands that people crave and price them based on comps from sold item research.

- Commodified goods should be priced close to the highest price commanded for the item on eBay.

- Vehicles, parts, and accessories should be priced based on age and availability. Antique and collector cars warrant the same exhaustive research as antiques and collectibles in any other product category. Be careful not to price rare items too low. Many have only one potential buyer, and rarities command top dollar. Late-model cars should be sold based on comps and using web research such as that offered by Kelley Blue Book (https://www.kbb.com).

- Rare dolls, toys, and hobby merchandise should be treated with extreme care—studying the eBay completed sales is only part of the process. Ask around, seek advice from other doll and toy experts, and test high prices before considering a discount. While some newer dolls and toys can be very expensive, the vast majority of them are commodity items and should be priced using my commodified goods pricing guidance.

- Jewelry and watches are some of the most challenging items on eBay to price. I've enjoyed consistent success selling fine men's timepieces, but women rarely buy my watches, no matter how fancy or sparkling they may be. Antique jewelry with merit flies out the door, but midcentury jewelry, even that made of high-noble metals and precious gems, can sit for years. Rookies can overlook the sometimes wild fluctuations in the precious metals market and fail to adjust their prices accordingly. On a few occasions, my inattention resulted in selling gold and silver jewelry below the intrinsic value of the precious metal. People generally buy jewelry for emotional or sentimental reasons. When it comes to jewelry, it is better to build a loyal following than pander to bargain hunters. The buyer who asks "How many grams does it weigh?" is usually a scrapper hoping you've made an error in determining its value.

The preceding is in no way a comprehensive list—I've just covered the more popular categories. You may come across a mint condition 1979 Sony Walkman tucked away in the attic (*Guardians of the Galaxy* gave vintage Walkmans a price boost) or a late Victorian-era Cantu lace tablecloth in a box in your garage. While most eBay businesses sell mass-produced products, I've always focused on scarce and interesting curiosities that are hard to find yet easy to sell. Speaking of antique linens, check out Figure 8–4 below.

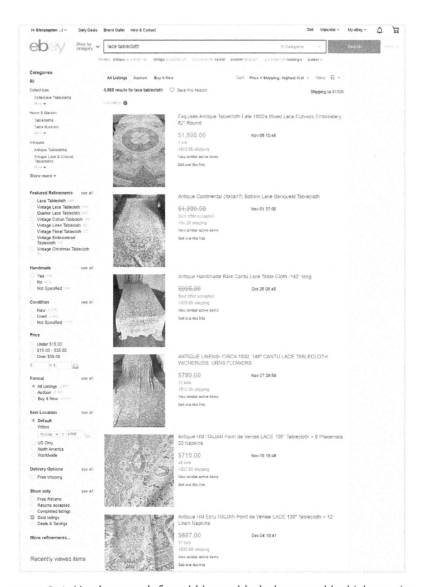

**FIGURE 8–4.** Here's a search for sold lace tablecloths, sorted by highest price. Only sold listings are considered comps. Wow, these are stunning prices. When the value of an item is uncertain, you must use an auction!

Before you list anything on eBay, you must have clarity of rarity and some perspective on value. Never leap before looking. An overwhelming number of my mentees and students have listed rare collectible items on eBay at fixed prices that sold well below their market value. I have never met anyone who felt good about throwing away money. If you're sure, then you're good to go. If you have doubts, hit the books and keep doing your research.

## PREPARING YOUR PRODUCTS BEFORE LISTING

Merchandise preparation (and, later, presentation) makes a big difference to your bottom line. By far the most important factors in determining how much you'll score for rarities and collectibles, for instance, are condition and completeness. Did it stand the test of time? Are the original box and all the accessories present? Is the user guide included? Each "yes" will up the product's price. For most solid or silver-plated items, it's OK (and wise) to polish them to a shine. Some die-hard collectors won't like a shiny Navajo sterling and turquoise ring because the patina (the toning caused by tarnish) brings charm and character to the jewelry. While it's fine to polish a teapot, it's a travesty to clean a silver coin, or any coins for that matter. The rarer an item is, the more caution you should bring to its preparation.

Do everything you can to make what you're selling look great. Your approach to cleaning used items will have a lot to do with their eventual sale price. Today's high-definition cameras take beautiful pictures, but they also reveal an item's flaws. It's plausible that no aspect of presentation affects the salability of an item more than the way in which you clean (or don't clean) it before imaging and listing it on eBay.

To clean, or not to clean: that is the question! And how to clean? Should an item be restored or left alone? Can you do it yourself or will it require a professional? There are at least two obvious benefits of doing it yourself—you pocket more profits, and you sell things faster. It's difficult for

**TIP**

Just as you can't put an egg back into its shell, you can't undo damage you've caused to a valuable antique. Some very desirable antiques, collectibles, and vintage items will lose a lot of value if you attempt to restore or clean them incorrectly. I'm particularly handy and comfortable around tools and chemicals, but I'm also good at researching, and I usually get things right on the first try because I talk to experts. Many experts will respond if you reach out to them—try contacting some of the very smart people on YouTube who give cleaning, restoration, and repair tips.

potential buyers to tell if an item is simply dirty or if it's damaged by looking at a photo. By cleaning, polishing, and restoring, you'll remove doubt and reduce hesitation.

Here are a few possible cleaning methods:

- Dusting
- Mechanical cleaning without chemicals, such as using a slightly damp cloth
- Chemical cleaning
- A combination of methods

Here are some of the tools and techniques I use for preparing merchandise, in no particular order. Be sure you wear eye protection and gloves and cover your skin when handling chemicals:

- *Water.* Water is nature's most elegant and gentlest solvent, so a little spray of water on a microfiber or other lint-free cloth will do wonders for cleaning many things. For products that can withstand a bit of moisture, try a damp cloth first before using chemical cleaners. Be careful not to rub off printing or paint from surfaces by being too aggressive.

>
>
> **TIP**
>
> **Warning!**
>
> This section discusses cleaning and restoration methods that involve readily available household chemicals. That said, some of these products can pose serious danger to your eyes, skin, and lungs. Many are incredibly harmful to domestic animals and wildlife, and some should never be poured down a drain. Please read the labels of these products and use them with care. Always protect yourself when using chemical products and work in a well-ventilated space with plenty of fresh air.

- *Sponges with a scouring pad side.* These are great for rapidly cleaning large surfaces and useful for applying cleaning and polishing solutions. The scouring pad is also useful for eliminating stubborn stains. Scouring pads are abrasive, so test an inconspicuous area on your item if scratching is a possibility.
- *Microfiber cloths.* These are surprisingly versatile and gentle for cleaning soft surfaces and metals that scratch easily.
- *Rags.* These are useful for cleaning less delicate items. These and microfiber cloths can be used many times by running them through the wash, but throw away any that you used for chemicals.
- *Hair dryer.* An ordinary hair dryer is a dirt-cheap and valuable business tool. I bought my last one for $10.97 plus tax with free shipping. It's important to quickly dry merchandise after cleaning it to avoid spots, rust, or corrosion. Use an old cotton pillowcase and a thick rubber band to form a drying tent. Place the items to be dried in the pillowcase, secure the open end over the mouth of the

hair dryer with the rubber band, and turn it on low heat. You can use the air-only setting for products that are sensitive to heat, but it will increase the drying time.

- *Horsehair brush.* This is an indispensable cleaning tool that's great for nooks and crannies yet incredibly gentle on surfaces.

- *Shop vacuum or an ordinary home vacuum with attachments.* These are useful for removing dust when you'd like to avoid breathing it in. Shop vacuums also have a blower feature, which you'll find useful for the initial drying of items after washing them. A shop vacuum with a wet and dry rating can suck up liquids which can come in handy in a variety of situations. Decent-quality shop and ordinary home vacuums can be had for less than $50. Stay away from luxury brands. Buy a brand-name but cheap one and replace it when the suction weakens.

- *Dishwasher.* More items than you might think can be cleaned in the dishwasher. A simple stream of water cut the Grand Canyon, and a dishwasher can remove stubborn dirt from many things. Don't use it for greasy car parts, painted items, or things that are made from iron (they'll rust). Your dishwasher will tidy up a plethora of eBay resale items, including golf balls, plastic sports equipment, hub caps (as long as they aren't greasy), plastic toys, gardening implements, nonferrous metal fixtures, cabinet and drawer hardware, glass globes and shades from light fixtures, desk accessories, flower pots, and anything that will stand up to both a little heat and a lot of water.

- *Cotton swabs.* I love these little cleaning gems. They are great when precision is required and are perfect for cleaning and polishing small and hard-to-reach areas. Cotton swabs can also serve as a small paintbrush when applying touch-up paint or stain.

- *Toothpicks.* A wooden toothpick is an excellent tool for cleaning tight spaces, such as around the edges of a watch crystal. They're also handy for repairing stripped screw holes in wooden antiques and other objects. Fix hinges, drawer pulls, and other hardware by filling the holes with toothpicks and white glue and trimming off the excess with a razor blade. Once dry, redrill the hole for the new screw. They are also great for applying glue, adhesives, and paint on or in small areas.

- *Toothbrushes.* Disposable toothbrushes can be purchased in bulk and are useful for removing dust, mechanical cleaning, and polishing (with or without polishing compounds, cleaners, or other chemicals).

- *Lye.* Used by the food industry, by soap makers, and as a highly effective drain cleaner, lye (aka sodium hydroxide) breaks down organic substances. While it has many uses, I frequently soak pottery and porcelain items in a lye solution to remove old price tags and organic stains. You can also use a weak solution of it in cool water to convert old, caked-on grease into soap, which is then easier to remove. Lye damages aluminum but is safe for most other metals, plastics, and ceramics. You must protect your eyes and skin because it can cause serious burns, so use extreme care.

- *Wright's Silver Cream.* This cream is gentle on sterling and silver-plated items. If minimal tarnish is present, it's fast and effective at removing it. Serious collectors of rarer items do not recommend removing the patina from antique silver items. Pay close attention to how museums handle their antique silver, as well as what your competition is doing, in deciding when to polish and when not to polish. While a natural patina develops over time, some silver artisans apply it intentionally with chemicals (see Figure 8–5 on page 149).

- *Acidified thiourea solution.* This is often referred to as *silver dip* and sold under that name. Museums use this stinky chemical to brighten historical silver items. I don't recommend using it for plated objects, and it's important to read the label carefully. It's great for rapid tarnish removal, but an extended bath can make silver objects look too bright and add a haze to the surface. Practice with something that's not valuable to get the hang of this useful chemical, and work in a well-ventilated area. After tarnish removal, the object should be thoroughly washed (museums use Triton X-100, but dish soap is fine). The surface will have a micro-roughness after cleaning, which can be easily removed by light buffing with a clean cotton diaper (don't laugh; this is how the experts do it) or microfiber cloth. Dry and then immediately bag polished silver items in an airtight container or reusable, resealable plastic zippered storage bags.

- *Brasso.* This is a versatile and highly effective metal polish designed to remove tarnish from brass, copper, chrome, and stainless steel. It is available either as a liquid or as an impregnated wadding pad. My best and highest use for this incredible product is polishing watches. I remove leather bands and ensure the watch is water-resistant, then apply a dab of Brasso and gently scrub with a toothbrush. Rinse well and immediately dry the item. It's also useful for bringing clarity to dull acrylic watch crystals. Brasso has abrasive qualities and will wear down metal over time. Never use Brasso on antiques or collectibles unless you're an expert conservationist and know what you're doing.

- *Ammonia.* Cheap and readily available, ammonia will brighten up dull jewelry. Gold jewelry is alloyed, which means it is mixed with other metals and can discolor over time. A mixture of one part ammonia to six parts of water and a drop of dish soap will bring back its shine after about ten minutes of soaking. Then give

**FIGURE 8–5.** This Navajo sterling silver and turquoise cuff bracelet has an intentionally applied patina. Note how dark specific areas of the cuff are. Polishing silver like this requires patience and care not to remove the artist's deliberate patina from the crevices.

it a thorough scrubbing with a toothbrush, followed by rinsing and drying. Use gloves (latex, nitrile, vinyl, etc.) and a lint-free cloth to avoid adding fingerprints and particles to the jewelry (you tend to only notice these after you've photographed the item and are staring at the image 20 times larger than life on your computer monitor). Buy the plain stuff, not lemon scented.

- *Denatured alcohol.* "Denatured" just means it's ethanol (the kind you drink) with ingredients added that make it unfit for human consumption. This permits this powerful cleaner to be sold at the local hardware store. It's usually sold as camping fuel, but it's also an effective cleaner that evaporates rapidly and leaves no residue. The denaturing ingredient is usually methanol, which is toxic, so protect your eyes and skin. It won't leave streaks and is an excellent general cleaner. Use denatured alcohol on porcelain, pottery, glass, metal, and even wood. Be careful with printed or painted decorations. It's flammable, so use appropriate precautions.

- *Lighter fluid.* Sold under the brand name Ronsonol at most American hardware and department stores, lighter fluid wipes away rust and removes gum, labels, scuff marks, stains, and crayon marks. It leaves a residue that you can then remove with denatured alcohol. It's just as effective as Goo Gone, but less expensive. Lighter fluid is also flammable, so use care in handling.

- *Colored markers.* Invest in an artist's colored marker set and use them to touch up damage on many objects. They aren't a substitute for professional restoration, but they're very useful when there's a small area that just needs a little dab to bring it back to perfection.

- *Nail polish.* They come in an almost unlimited array of colors, are inexpensive, and dry to a hard and durable finish. Use clear nail polish to restore small, damaged areas on lacquered and shiny surfaces. Buy colored nail polish to repair and restore small, damaged spots on shiny painted objects. Be sure to take the item with you so you can compare and match the color in person.

- *Two-part epoxy.* This clear adhesive is extremely strong and won't shrink. It resists water, salt, gasoline, mineral spirits, oil, and many other solvents. Two-part epoxy consists of a base resin and a curing agent. When these are mixed together, they harden. Epoxy adhesive forms a powerful bond with ferrous (based on iron) and nonferrous metals, ceramics, wood, or glass in any combination. Use it to repair broken items acquired for pennies and resell them for big profits. I prefer the Devcon 2 Ton brand, which has less odor than many others on the market.

- *White glue.* While epoxy is my go-to adhesive for truly long-lasting repairs, some stuff just isn't suitable for it. That's when I use ordinary white glue. The generic works just fine. Many antique items have original felt or fabric bottoms that are peeling off due to age. Use white glue to fix them up. From loose product labels to tightening up wooden jewelry boxes, white glue has a plethora of uses in your eBay business.

- *Lotion.* Leather is skin, so I use a little lotion to bring it back to life. Expensive leather items should be professionally restored, but a bit of lotion and a soft cloth will revive ordinary leather. Leather cleaners are much more expensive than a big pump container of store brand lotion. Buy the unscented kind.

- *Acetone.* Be careful with this chemical because it can rapidly ruin certain things. That said, it can be tremendously helpful restoring antiques and collectibles. Acetone will dissolve PVC (polyvinyl chloride) and polystyrene, but not polypropylene, nylon, and PTFE (polytetrafluoroethylene, aka Teflon). I realize I'm getting technical here, but acetone is great for removing residues; polyester and epoxy resins; contact cement; ink; and other unwanted substances from surfaces. It's cheap and readily available at the hardware store under the brand name Klean-Strip.

- *Bleach.* For eBay sellers, bleach can turn dull discards into desirable merchandise. Add one tablespoon of liquid bleach to one gallon of warm or hot water and soak stained ceramics (i.e., earthenware, porcelain, and pottery). Add more for stubborn stains. This works wonders. The decoration must be under the glaze and not painted on the object or it will ruin the paint. Bleach is very effective in removing a plethora of stains. Stained, antique teacups will bounce back to life using this technique. I've restored many Wedgwood jasperware items using a bleach-water solution. Buy the best quality you can afford because cheap bleach is weak. I use Clorox.

- *Dry ice.* This is pure carbon dioxide that's $-109.2\,°F$ or colder. Because it will cool and shrink virtually anything it touches, dry ice is useful for restoring and repairing many items. Dry ice blasting is used in commercial settings to clean statues and equipment and even remove gum from walkways and public areas. Wrap dry ice in a cloth and rub it around and over dents in thin metal to remove dents that have not damaged the paint or finish. Use it to free seized nuts, bolts, and fasteners that have become time welded or to harden gum so that you can remove it easily. Dry ice is so cold it will shrink many materials and break the bond of adhesives. It evaporates completely and therefore is ideal for surfaces that cannot become wet. Be very careful handling it—direct contact with your eyes or skin will cause frostbite and permanent injury.

- *Freezer.* Place books with pages that have become stuck together in a resealable plastic zipper storage bag and freeze them. Often this will release the stuck pages.

- *Steam.* This is another method for releasing stuck book pages, and is also useful for softening old glue. Hold the object over a pot of boiling water until you see results. You can also use steam to rehydrate dried-out leather, which is useful for old leather watchbands, vintage leather shoes, and anything else made of leather that has become brittle from age. After steaming, immediately place the object into a plastic bag and allow the moisture to penetrate and disperse. Don't leave it sealed too long or it will form mold. A day or two should be sufficient. Check daily to see if the leather feels pliant and then remove. After rehydrating, finish the leather with lotion or leather conditioner.

- *Ziploc.* While I don't always buy brand-name products, not all resealable zippered storage bags are created equal. Ziploc brand bags have a superior quality seal and are thicker than most other brands. They are also more expensive, but in this case, you get what you pay for. Dust and moisture are enemies of an inventory-based business. Garages, sheds, and storage units can become a comfortable home for insects, and your customers don't want to adopt an arachnid or cuddle a cricket that's taken refuge in their purchase. For larger items, use clear trash bags and twist ties. A clear bag allows for instant identification without opening.

- *Hydrogen peroxide.* I often use bleach to brighten ceramics, but some materials can't withstand bleach's corrosive properties. Old computers, game consoles, and other electronics that have plastic cases will become yellow over time. If the item comes from a household with smokers, the stains can be quite dark. Depending on your comfort and skill level, you can disassemble these products and soak just the plastic case in hydrogen peroxide. You'll find 3 percent concentration hydrogen peroxide at the drugstore. Use a plastic container for soaking and place it outside in direct sunlight or use an artificial ultraviolet light to catalyze the chemical cleaning reaction. While the sun is a wonderful source of UV light, an artificial light is cheap and allows the process to take place after dark. The light is a necessary ingredient in this brightening process. However, ultraviolet light is harmful to your eyes, and long-term exposure can cause medical problems such as cataracts, so protect yourself. The whitening process may take hours, so keep checking on the progress. Another option is to mix two parts of hydrogen peroxide with one part dish soap and apply it to stains if soaking the entire item is impractical. The soap will help prevent the hydrogen peroxide from dripping away. Cover the item with plastic wrap or place it in a resealable plastic storage bag to keep the solution moist and permit the UV light to pass through to the item. For rapid whitening, you can source stronger solutions of hydrogen peroxide suspended in a gel. Beauty supply stores sell a product called 40 Volume Creme Developer for bleaching hair, which happens to be perfect for whitening discolored plastic as well.

- *Armor All.* Armor All was originally designed to clean and protect vinyl, rubber, and plastic parts on cars. My number-one use for this product is to restore camera lenses and equipment. Rubber will bloom, or form a white haze over time, which is unattractive to vintage camera equipment collectors. Rubber bloom is easily fixed with Armor All. I also use it on natural rubber toy tires and vintage plastics.

- *Vinegar.* Distilled white vinegar is an excellent household cleaner if you don't mind the odor. It's wonderful when partnered with a tea kettle. I warm full-strength vinegar in the kettle and then pour it into items with greasy stains or mineral deposits. Heat accelerates chemical reactions. This technique is useful for removing a cloudy haze from ceramics and glassware, as well as removing mineral deposits from reclaimed antique and vintage kitchen and bathroom fixtures—a product category that is quite lucrative. Mix in some dish soap and use a spray bottle to apply the vinegar-soap mixture to objects. Allow it to work for up to 30 minutes, and then scrub with the scouring side of a sponge or with a toothbrush to loosen up and remove any residual grease or mineral deposits. The best technique for removing alkaline battery leakage from an old electronic device is to carefully dab on a few drops of white vinegar and then clean it off. If you have to scrape the leakage off first, be sure to vacuum away the debris.

■ *Bubble wrap.* I realize most people think of bubble wrap as part of the shipping step, but it's important to protect fragile ceramics, delicate models, intricate decorative items, glass ornaments, and other easily broken items in storage. Some sellers box up the product after they take photos and get it ready to ship. But I have found that many customers buy multiple items, and some ask questions that require further examination of the item. Boxing up ahead of time may present as many disadvantages as advantages, but protecting merchandise from damage is essential, and a bit of bubble wrap will do the trick most of the time.

All that may sound like a lot of time and hassle, but there's no need to rush out and get everything at once. I focus on listing groups of similar items, which allows me to buy only the supplies and tools I need for that project.

Earlier in this section, I mentioned condition and completeness as important factors for scoring the best price for your goods. In addition to cleaning and restoring them, consider the following ideas for improving your eBay offering; use them for inspiration and expand on them with your own thoughts:

■ If a teapot or sugar bowl is missing a lid, source one on eBay.

■ Buy a new charger, cable, and headphones for the phone you're selling. Check the original specs to find replacements as close as possible to the original.

■ Add a fresh battery and new band to an old watch after cleaning it and score top dollar for a fully functional and restored timepiece.

■ Sew a missing button on that coat or blazer to make it far more desirable; if you can't find a matching button, cut off all the buttons and sew on a new set.

■ Find an invisible reweaver to fix moth and cigarette holes in expensive garments you bought for a pittance and raise the resale value sky-high.

■ Pay a professional detailer to transform that jalopy into a beautiful ride.

■ Hunt for a box for that vintage Barbie—the value of toys in an original box is usually much greater, making the time and cost involved in sourcing it worthwhile.

■ Power cords are cheap and there are millions of them on eBay, so learn how to spec out the correct plug size, voltage, and amperage—all details you can easily research online (see Figure 8–6 below). You'll find lots of eBay listings for untested laptops, phones, and other electronics for super-low prices, and they usually just need a replacement for their orphaned power supply.

**FIGURE 8–6.** When purchasing a replacement charger, review the product's original specs and match them. This aftermarket phone charger puts out 1000mA (milliamps), which is sometimes printed as 1A (amp). Newer phones and tablets can handle chargers that put out up to 3A, but that much power would damage an older phone's battery. Every device manufacturer posts their charger specifications online.

## USING IMAGES TO MAKE YOUR LISTINGS POP

As the old saying goes, a picture is worth a thousand words. This adage holds true for eBay sellers, and the most successful of them claim that images are the most important part of the listing. Other factors affect your placement in eBay searches, and we'll discuss those later in the book, but there are quite a few products you can sell with a few well-chosen keywords for the listing title and beautiful product images. In this section, we'll cover imaging essentials (and we'll talk about keywords a little later in the chapter). We'll also talk more about using visual merchandising in Chapter 9.

I use the term *imaging* rather than *photos* because you can capture images using your phone or camera, but also with a scanner. You can also retrieve images from eBay's Catalog, which is a database containing product information. The Catalog contains millions of product entries that have stock images and listing titles and descriptions available for you to use.

While I prefer the higher-quality images of my DSLR camera, the images that mobile phones capture are just so darn good. As phone cameras keep improving, I soon won't be able to argue in favor of my bulkier camera rig. Some of that excellence has to do with the improved AI and software installed on phones. Most of the photography and videography work you do on eBay can and should be conducted with your phone camera. Phones are lightweight, always connected to the internet, and transferring images to a computer or other device is quick and easy. But when I need to show fine detail up close (e.g., jewelry), a DSLR equipped with a high-quality macro lens remains my go-to.

Owning a camera didn't make me a photographer, any more than having a toolbox made me an auto mechanic. Developing an eye for photography wasn't so much an art as a process. The more you do it, the better you will get at it, so start snapping away!

Here are some of the key points to remember when capturing images for eBay:

- Work with what you have. If you don't have a lot of money for fancy equipment, make do. The key is to get started selling your merchandise.
- Use a plain background, and generally speaking you shouldn't put anything in the picture unless it is actually part of the sale. (However, there are exceptions to this rule, as you'll see in the next section.)
- If using natural light, be sure the area is well-lit. You can use large pieces of white cardboard to provide soft, diffuse lighting.
- If you don't have steady hands, it's OK to use a tripod, but it will slow things down. They're very cheap, so having one on hand won't hurt. If you're using your phone to take pictures and can't find a tripod that includes a phone holder, you can buy the holder separately for a few extra dollars.
- Choose your resolution wisely: eBay requires photos to have at least 500 pixels on the longest side, but don't shoot that small. I recommend no smaller than 1000 pixels on the shortest side. Super-high resolution is overkill, though—pick a setting in between that will provide nice, large images but won't take forever to upload. If you pay for data, this will matter to your bottom line. Cameras have resolution settings, but some phones don't permit you to adjust the still image resolution, and that's OK. All modern camera phones will take photos large enough to use on eBay.
- Photos must accurately represent the item.

- Placeholder images used to convey messages aren't allowed. For example, you may not post an image that promotes your company or unrelated products.
- Stock photos aren't permitted for used, damaged, or defective items, only when selling new items.
- Photos may not have added borders, text, artwork, or marketing material.
- Watermarks are never permitted—not even for corporate branding or copyright notices.
- Fill the frame; don't leave a ton of dead space around your item (see Figures 8-7 below and 8-8 on page 157).
- Show measurement or scale using a coin, a ruler, or some other object (see Figures 8-9 on page 157, 8-10 on page 158, and 8-11 on page 158). It's a good idea to both provide scale in the images and give the exact measurements in the listing. Some people prefer visuals, and other people like to read things.
- Capture the details and don't hide the warts. Be sure you reveal everything that's great and also everything that's wrong with the item you're selling.
- Keep things in focus.
- Watch out for the camera's flash—it can leave hot spots and reflections. Natural, indirect light with proper camera settings is ideal for newbies. Once you have more experience, if you choose, you can work with umbrellas and lights designed for eBay or professional studio photography.

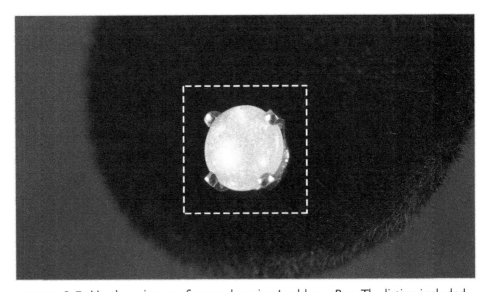

**FIGURE 8-7.** Here's an image of an opal earring I sold on eBay. The listing included multiple photos, including the all-important scale shot (see Figures 8-9 on page 157, 8-10 on page 158, and 8-11 on page 158). The dotted white line shows where the image should be cropped to eliminate dead space.

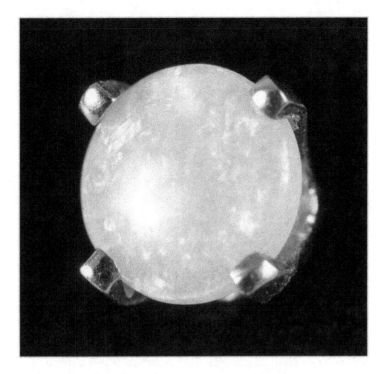

**FIGURE 8–8.** Here's the same image of the earring after being cropped. It's much more impressive-looking and has a much greater impact at this size than in the uncropped image.

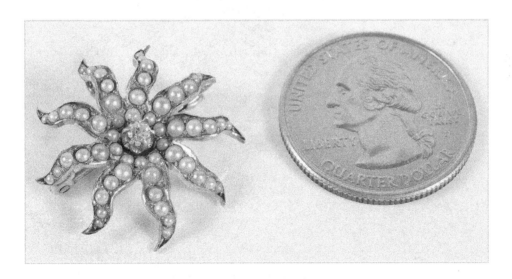

**FIGURE 8–9.** Here's a scale shot using a quarter next to an antique diamond, pearl, and gold brooch. I used a quarter because it seemed appropriate; somehow, I felt a ruler would take the buyer out of the moment. The brooch sold.

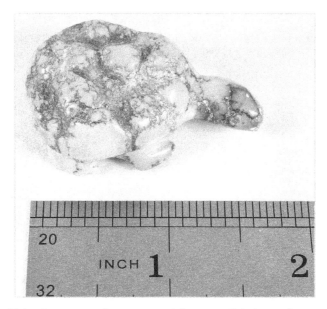

**FIGURE 8–10.** This winsome turtle was carved from a solid piece of gem turquoise by a Zuni artisan from New Mexico. Carvings such as these are called fetishes; they are very popular and enthusiastically collected. Prospective buyers tend to ask for precise measurements, so a ruler was best for a scale shot in this case. This fetish also sold.

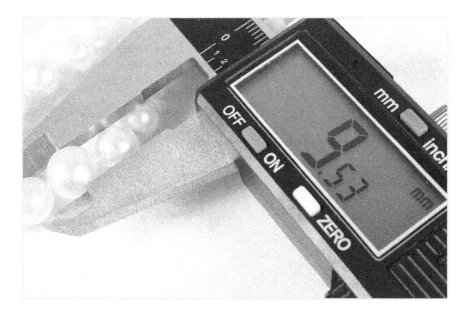

**FIGURE 8–11.** This scale shot clarified the size of the genuine saltwater pearls in this necklace. It was a luxurious necklace with high-quality pearls, so it represented a substantial investment for the new owner. I used an extremely precise digital caliper to measure the pearls and instill confidence in the buyer. The necklace sold.

- You can add up to 12 images on most eBay listings, or up to 24 when listing vehicles. Image hosting is always included at no additional cost with your listing. Make sure you're using one of the accepted file formats (JPEG, PNG, GIF, TIFF, or BMP). Also check that each file is no larger than 7MB. If you're copying from a web address, the photo can be 12MB. While it seems like overkill to me, you can add more images to the listing description by using HTML, but you'll have to host those images with another hosting provider.

- Be sure the item is very clean. Nobody wants to bid on dirty merchandise. Finger-prints show up dramatically in photos because the image is larger than life. Wear lint-free gloves to avoid this. I use latex or nitrile. Vinyl gloves are available at a lower cost but tear more easily than the other two. Show size for rings, length for bracelets, pins, earrings, necklaces, etc. A missing scale shot will hurt your ability to attract a buyer.

- Provide clear photographs of maker's marks, gold, or silver purity marks (925, sterling, 14K, 18K, etc.); or make, model, serial number, and so forth. In Britain, the mark indicating the standard of purity is referred to as the *hallmark*; you'll want to do some research on the anatomy of hallmarks so you don't accidentally sell a solid silver item for cheap thinking it's common base metal. A British assay office hallmark may have a combination of a sponsor's mark, standard mark, fineness mark, assay office mark, and date letter (see Figure 8-12 on page 160).

- It's OK to crop or adjust the brightness, but don't use image editing software to make your pictures look better than the actual product will appear in person. The eBay listing tool has a built-in feature that allows you to crop, rotate, adjust the exposure, sharpen, and *auto adjust* your listing images—that's really all you'll need.

## Indecent PROPosition

Laying a pair of jeans out on a table isn't very appealing. And a necklace dropped in a heap isn't very attractive either. Despite what I said in the previous section about not including extra items in your listing images, some items require props to attract buyers. This is very different from adding a bowl of fruit to jazz up a listing for a coffee table. Buyers will naturally ask "Do the bowl and fruit come with the table?" Apply some common sense to the situation, and be sure to include a description disclaimer if you do decide to add some flair to the staging of something large like a coffee table—which you'd most likely sell with local pickup only: "The bowl and fruit are sold separately."

Some things require support to display them in the correct perspective or to give them stronger appeal. Jewelry props are a must if you sell a lot of jewelry (see

**FIGURE 8–12.** This British gilt (gold washed) sterling silver perfume bottle cap has faint hallmarks around its base, which are essential for converting this seeming piece of trash into a salable item. The hallmarks are (from left to right) "D&LS" (the mark for David & Lionel Spiers, the *makers* or *sponsors*); the lion passant (indicating that this object is 925/1000 fine sterling silver); the date letter (for the year 1884); and the anchor (the Birmingham assay office's mark). This image showing the hallmarks was the sole reason the perfume bottle cap sold immediately to a collector.

Figure 8-13 on page 161). They are very inexpensive, and you can acquire very nice ones cheaply on eBay. For clothing, a mannequin is ideal, and equally inexpensive (see Figure 8-14 on page 161).

Certain items come with their own props—you can use the fancy case that protects designer eyeglass frames as a prop (see Figure 8-15 on page 162). Brand names sell themselves, but items will still move faster when presented in a professional and beautiful way. Don't overdo it, however. You want elegance, not clutter.

## WHICH FORMAT SHOULD YOU CHOOSE?

Back in June 1999, when I registered for my first account on eBay, the auction format was the only option, and it was wonderful. Every item I listed sold for stellar prices. I could start an auction at a penny and always score top dollar. Back then eBay was bigger than any other ecommerce platform. However, customer tastes have changed dramatically since then, and the days of scoring the market price at an auction every single time are over. In

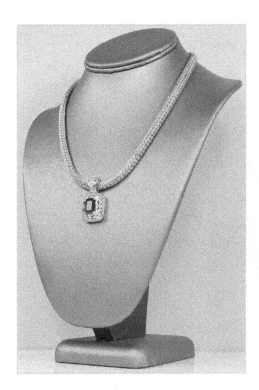

**FIGURE 8–13.** This 18K gold and garnet necklace looks much better presented on a jewelry prop, which is designed to give buyers a sense of what the necklace looks like when worn. The prop cost me $20.99; I sold the necklace for $7,520.

**FIGURE 8–14.** Ralph Lauren's Purple Label suits are their finest Italian-tailored offering. Here is the gallery image for a consignment suit I listed. I used a mannequin to give the jacket shape, with the trousers slung over the shoulder. I sold this *new old stock* (vintage but never used) suit for $1,013.99.

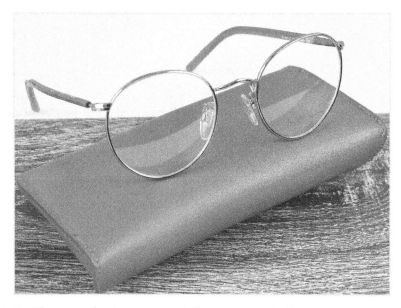

**FIGURE 8–15.** These very fine leather temple frames are ready for some prescription lenses. Here, I've used the case itself as a prop. What looks convincingly like wood is really a ceramic tile I purchased at the hardware store, and the light background is gray photography paper I bought in a roll online. These frames sold for $174.75.

2000, eBay introduced its Buy It Now option, and two years later announced its fixed price format. It even offered the ability to combine the formats in some circumstances.

Making an error selecting your format can have harmful consequences to your bottom line. If you list a one-of-a-kind Roman-Byzantine mosaic at a fixed price, you're potentially leaving thousands of dollars on the table. Putting up new electronics with known values for auction simply delays putting money into your bank account; however, an auction is best when listing a vintage Sony Walkman. So let's look at how to choose your format.

### Auction-Style Listings

Auction-style listings allow you to receive competitive bids from multiple people and sell to the highest bidder (see Figure 8–16 on page 163). The auction format on eBay is generally referred to as auction-style because there's no auctioneer. I use the abbreviated term auction throughout this book because other than eBay's employees and former eBay workers such as myself, everyone else simply calls them auctions. You can list one or multiple items in an auction, and your listing can be featured in up to two eBay categories, which are analogous to departments in a store. Auctions can last one, three, five, seven, or ten days. If you are selling real estate, you can also choose to run your auction for 30 days. There's a feedback rating system in which both the seller and buyer can leave each other feedback, but only the buyer can leave a negative or neutral comment; sellers can only leave positive feedback for buyers. Auctions are ideal for high-demand items, antiques, collectibles, and other hard-to-find objects. For example, a 1925 Auburn Speedster warrants an auction, but a new car probably does not.

A low starting price for an auction will encourage bids, but it's quite possible only one person will bid—remember, there's a lot of inventory and a whole lot of eBay sellers. The starting price of your auction will only rise if at least two people place bids. You can set a secret *reserve* selling price for your item when you make the listing, which is the lowest price you're willing to accept, but many bidders dislike reserves and are frustrated by them because they don't know how much they should bid. You can, and probably should, start with a minimum bid amount that represents the lowest price you would accept without pulling your hair out, just in case only one person bids. If your listing fails to attract any bids, just relist it with a lower starting price or even at the same price—because new people come onto eBay every day, your item may sell the second time around without a price reduction. eBay uses automatic bidding and sets the *bid increment* depending on the current bid price to prevent annoying tiny bids on auctions. See Figure 8–17 on page 164.

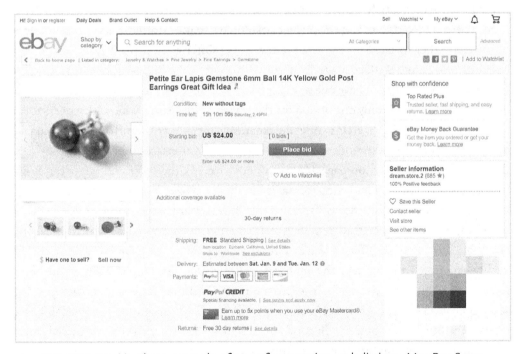

**FIGURE 8–16.** Here's an example of one of my auction-style listings. My eBay Store The Dream Store uses auctions with aggressive starting bids to attract buyers who may also be interested in my other items.

| Current Price | Bid Increment |
|---|---|
| $0.01–$0.99 | $0.05 |
| $1.00–$4.99 | $0.25 |
| $5.00–$24.99 | $0.50 |
| $25.00–$99.99 | $1.00 |
| $100.00–$249.99 | $2.50 |
| $250.00–$499.99 | $5.00 |
| $500.00–$999.99 | $10.00 |
| $1,000.00–$2,499.99 | $25.00 |
| $2,500.00–$4,999.99 | $50.00 |
| $5,000.00 and up | $100.00 |

**FIGURE 8–17.** This table shows eBay's current bid increment amounts.

## Fixed Price Listings

Fixed price listings satisfy a buyer's urge for instant gratification or fill their immediate need. There is no bidding, and the buyer doesn't have to wait until the end of an auction to purchase their prize. You can even add a Make Offer option for buyers who enjoy haggling (see Figure 8–18 on page 165).

Fixed price listings can have one or many of the same product and can be listed in up to two categories. There is only one option for the length of the listing, which eBay refers to as Good 'Til Canceled (GTC). GTC listings automatically renew every month until all available inventory sells or the seller ends the listing. Every time a transaction occurs on eBay (see the Classified Ads section on page 165 for off-eBay trades), the seller and buyer can leave feedback for each other. This listing format is ideally suited for commodities that are readily available and can be replenished or for items that have a clearly understood value.

Using the Best Offer feature allows you to enter both a value at which eBay will automatically accept an offer, as well as a floor price, below which eBay will automatically decline an offer. This sidesteps the annoyance of lowball offers. You can always add Buy It Now to an auction listing for the possibility of an immediate sale; however, once someone places a bid, the Buy It Now option will usually disappear. If the auction has a reserve, the Buy It Now option will continue to be available until the reserve price is met. According to eBay, the Buy It Now option may continue to be available after the first bid for a limited time in some categories—I've never seen that occur in practice and eBay didn't indicate for which categories this applies.

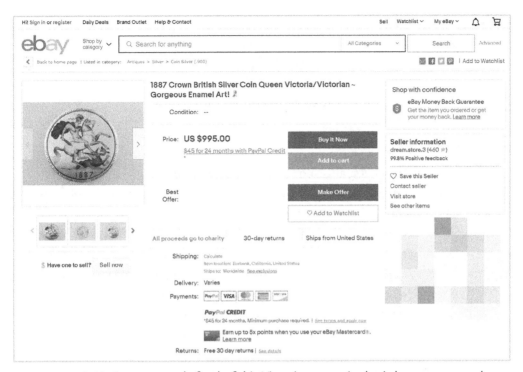

**FIGURE 8–18.** I am extremely fond of this Victorian-era coin that's been repurposed into an art piece. The workmanship and enameling display incredible talent. This is an example of a fixed price listing with the optional Make Offer feature enabled, which signals to buyers that I'm open to a bit of haggling.

## Classified Ads

In the classified ad format, the seller and buyer complete the transaction off eBay. It's a bit more private, but eBay won't mediate disputes if things go south. Ads can run for 30 days or GTC (meaning the ads are renewed automatically). Only a few eBay categories offer the feature:

- Business & Industrial
  - Building Materials & Supplies > Modular & Pre-Fabricated Buildings
  - Office > Trade Show Displays
  - Websites & Businesses for Sale
- Real Estate (note that the fees are different; Real Estate classifieds can also be posted for 30 or 90 days but not GTC)
- Specialty Services
- Travel, excluding the Lodging, Luggage, and Vintage Luggage & Travel Accs (short for accessories) categories

- ▨ Everything Else
  - – eBay User Tools
  - – Funeral & Cemetery
  - – Information Products
  - – Reward Points & Incentive Programs

## Motor Vehicle Listings

While selling a train is actually allowed on eBay, it's more likely you'll want to sell a smaller vehicle. eBay Motors listings let you rehome cars, trucks, motorcycles, powersports vehicles (ATVs, dune buggies, etc.), boats, planes, trailers, and other vehicles. Sellers in the Motors category can use auction-style, Buy It Now, and Best Offer formats with durations of three, five, seven, or ten days. Fixed price listings can also opt for a 30-day or GTC duration. The following QR code (Figure 8–19 below) links to a handy checklist offered by eBay as a guide to selling on eBay Motors.

Selling a collectible or high-demand vehicle on eBay is ideal. Buyers typically pick up their new ride or pay for the shipping costs, so they would need to be strongly motivated to buy a vehicle online that's not located close by. If you're a licensed car dealer, you can contact the eBay Motors dealer team at (877) 322-9227 or motorstraining@ebay.com to discuss special pricing on eBay fees. According to eBay, 7.4 million unique visitors a month look for cars on the site. Is your engine revving yet?

**FIGURE 8–19.** This QR code links to the eBay Motors *Sell your vehicle checklist*, which helps streamline the process of listing your vehicle.

## Auction or Fixed Price?

So now that we've looked at your options, how do you choose? When you're staring at an item you want to list, which will work better, an auction or a fixed price listing?

I won't lie: This remains a perennial conundrum for eBay sellers. I want to get the best price possible in every situation, but there's no hard-and-fast rule for deciding. It takes a bit of knowledge and some courage to come to a decision—don't just throw a dart at the board. You'll get better at it as you gain experience, but you should accept now that you'll make some mistakes along the way. I'm hoping I can help you reduce the likelihood of an error.

## AN EVOLUTION OF AUCTION PRICING, TIMING, AND STRATEGY

Every so often, I'll post an auction for gold earrings or high-demand consumer electronics with a starting price of one cent and see what happens. In the golden days of eBay, I'd score the market price every time I ran a penny auction, but unfortunately that is no longer true. Now, more often than not, I lose money on penny auctions.

Many factors affect auction bidding, including the quality of the listing, the keywords used in the title, the quality of the images, and especially when the auction ends. There are times when buyers are more likely to be on eBay and placing last-minute bids. Shopping is (and should be) a lot of fun, and timing the end of an auction correctly may improve the probability that potential bidders will be in a good mood and ready to buy.

Auction timing is a hotly debated topic on eBay. I've tried short durations and long durations. I've ended auctions at noon and at midnight. In the end, I concluded that there seems to be no pattern to follow. I urge you to do your own experiments and do what works best for you.

Many sellers believe Sunday is the best day to end an auction, because people are more likely to be home and on their computers. While not a hard-and-fast rule, I generally end my auction listings between noon and bedtime EST on Sundays. When you list many items in a similar genre, it's likely your buyers may want to bid on more than one of your listings, so make sure you don't time your auctions to end all at once. Many bidders love to snipe bids at the last minute, so staggering your end times by a few minutes gives them a chance to bid on multiple items ending the same day.

While you're experimenting with the timing of your auctions, keep in mind that offering international shipping, which I do, will change the dynamic of your customer demographics. Many countries thirst for American goods, so consider how your timing will affect customers in those countries. And avoid having your auctions end on a holiday—these are distracting and may result in a smaller number of potential bidders viewing your auction.

Here are some tips that will help you in selecting the best format and in determining how to set your price:

- Never list below a price you can live with, no matter what you paid for the item.
- Start high and work your way down, even when setting the starting price of auctions. There's no benefit to caving to a lowball offer or being in a rush to get rid of something.
- When you have no clue what something's worth, never be ashamed to start with an absurdly high price; you can always lower it later.
- What an item cost should not be a key driver in deciding how to price it—never hold on to a bad buy for years just to be stubborn, and don't be shy about making a huge windfall even if you paid next to nothing. An item's value is whatever someone is willing to pay.
- Only list an item at a fixed price or enable Buy It Now on an auction if you are confident of the item's worth.
- Don't be in a rush to list or get rid of an item unless you have a truly good reason to do so. Conduct price research with care first.

In Figure 8–20 on page 169, I've prepared a flowchart to assist you in selecting the listing format that works best in most situations. Use your own best judgment, as this is merely a guide.

No matter which format you select, keep my second tip in mind, which is to start high and work your way down over time. *New to eBay* goods are more attractive to potential customers. While it may be tempting, resist the urge to do any of the following with new to eBay goods:

- End the auction early to sell the item at a fixed price, even if it's more than the starting price—savvy buyers will know its true value and lowball you.
- Add Best Offer to the listing when it hasn't been up for very long—unless you're in a hurry, give it 30 to 90 days of exposure to eBay's millions of buyers.
- Add a fixed price to auctions (I never do this, but some sellers do)—instead, run a couple of auctions at your desired starting price and see if there's interest.

Before you're tempted to consider an offer to end the auction and sell the item for a fixed price, take a look at how many potential bidders are sitting in the wings watching the listing. You can see this and other useful information about your listing by going to My eBay > Selling > Listings (see Figure 8–21 on page 169). Many bidders come in at the very end of an auction, just before the bidding closes (see Figure 8–22 on page 170).

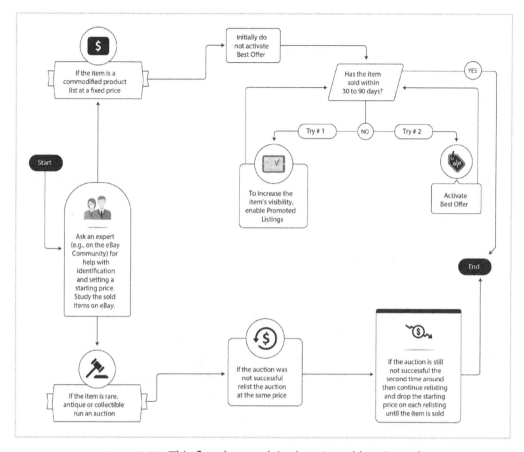

**FIGURE 8–20.** This flowchart explains how I would navigate the listing format selection process and subsequent handling of unsold items. Use common sense and this guide to refine your own work flow.

| Format | Current price | Available quantity | Promoted listings ⓘ | Watchers | Questions | Bids | Views | Time left ⌃ |
|---|---|---|---|---|---|---|---|---|
| ⚖ | $475.00 | 1 | Not eligible to promote | 10 | 0 | 1 | 273 | 2h 11m |

**FIGURE 8–21.** Here's the summary of information found at My eBay > Selling > Listings. This shows just one row, but you can see a spreadsheet-style view of all your listings from the link. This rare magazine auction had a whopping 273 views and 10 watchers 2 hours and 11 minutes before the auction ended. I set the starting price at $475, which was my estimate of value. By choosing the auction format, I allowed for the possibility that demand would push the price higher.

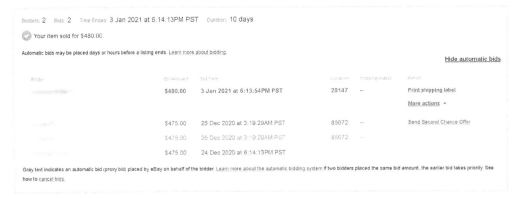

**FIGURE 8–22.** Here's the bid history page for the same auction shown in Figure 8–21 on page 169. Note the final bid price rose only $5 above the starting bid, and the high bidder swooped in to place the winning bid 19 seconds before the auction ended. While the price didn't rise very much, I still made an extra $5, and my estimate of value was spot on.

Most new eBay sellers don't have access to warehouses full of high-demand goods they can buy for a song and resell on eBay. I've been at this for two decades, and I'm still focusing on high-quality secondhand goods, rare antiques, jewelry, timepieces, and other high-potential merchandise. With very few exceptions, I run all these through two or more auction cycles and then move them over to fixed price, initially without Best Offer enabled. After 30 to 90 days, depending on the rarity and size of the item (space costs money!), I add Best Offer to items that are not declining value assets. While this works perfectly with an antique vase, it's not a great idea if you're selling live praying mantises. (Yes, eBay lets you sell these ferocious-looking garden predators—and other bugs, too!)

## LISTING AN ITEM

In this section, I'll walk you step by step through listing an item. If you're computer savvy, reading this may feel like watching paint dry, but even for people with prior experience selling on eBay, each person I've taught this to has stated categorically they were glad I did it. Everyone learns something new. For this exercise, I'll show you how to list a rare 1981 Apple II computer game on floppy disk. I don't use eBay's mobile app; while some sellers find it useful, as a professional eBay seller, I only use a laptop or desktop computer to make listings.

What you'll need to make this listing:

- The item in front of you—this helps you evaluate its condition and completeness
- Images of the item

- A computer with an internet connection
- An eBay account
- A postal scale
- Something to store the item in after listing
- Optionally, a notebook, labels, and a pen, used for manual tracking (you can dispense with these if you prefer to use spreadsheets)
- A credit or debit card (if this is your first listing): eBay will probably ask for your card number to cover any future eBay fees (remember, you can list a certain number of items for free each month)

Now let's walk through making a listing.

### 1. Sign In

You'll need to be signed into your eBay account. (See Figure 8–23 on page 172.)

### 2. Seller Hub

Go to the Seller Hub by clicking the Sell link at the top of the homepage or most eBay pages.

### 3. Open a New Listing

From the Manage Active Listings page, click the Single Listing link.

### 4. Begin the Listing Process

The next page (see Figure 8–24 on page 172) is where you begin the process of creating your listing. You can add a title, description, and item specifics manually or use eBay's Catalog, which will pre-fill most of your listing from a database of millions of products. Retrieve Catalog data by keying in a UPC, ISBN, ePID, part number, or product name. Because creating a listing with the help of the eBay Catalog is very easy, we'll be listing an item freestyle to demonstrate a more challenging process. While it's still easy, you must make more decisions, and it requires additional skill.

A listing starts with the title. Put yourself in your buyers' shoes and think what keywords they might use to find your listing. Titles are limited to 80 characters.

I've come up with my own fun modality for keyword selection that I break down into three layers:

1. The bones
2. The meat
3. The feathers

**FIGURE 8-23.** This is the Listings page within eBay's Seller Hub. If you're new to eBay, you may be asked to opt into the Seller Hub, which is recommended. On this page, you'll find the option to create listings.

**FIGURE 8-24.** Enter a title into the text box. In lieu of the product name, you can also enter a UPC, ISBN, ePID, or part number. The title may not exceed 80 characters in total. eBay will attempt to retrieve information from the Catalog and when that information is available, it will be displayed; otherwise you'll be entering the title and product information manually.

The bones of an eBay title provide the absolute essential keywords relating to that item, such as the brand name, artist, or designer, and a basic description.

Here are three sample bare-bones titles and their character counts:

*Samsung Blu-Ray Player (22 characters)*
*LeRoy Neiman Serigraph (22 characters)*
*Chanel Messenger Bag (20 characters)*

These are perfectly acceptable titles that very well may result in a successful sale. They aren't great, but eBay has so much traffic that it's highly likely an interested buyer may discover these listings. But I prefer to improve my odds by doing better. Let's add some meat to these bones by providing more inform ation, such as size, color, condition, model number, and other important searchable keywords.

Here are the same three examples, with bones and meat:

*New Samsung BD-F7500/ZA Smart 3D Blu-Ray Player with UHD 4K Upscaling (69 characters)*
*LeRoy Neiman Prima Ballerina Open Edition Serigraph (51 characters)*
*New in Box Autumn 2014 Chanel Le Boy Black Caviar Messenger Bag (63 characters)*

These additional high-quality keywords substantially increase the possibility that a potential buyer will find these items, but we still have some room left over. Let's work to make it to our 80-character limit without adding clutter. When basic facts and details have both been exhausted, you can add some feathers. Just as real feathers help birds soar to great heights, feather words in your listing title add flair and excitement. But remember: the meat and bones must always take priority in the title-building ritual.

Let's layer on some feathers to our examples:

*Awesome New Samsung BD-F7500/ZA Smart 3D Blu-Ray Player with UHD 4K Upscaling (77 characters)*
*Gorgeous & Vivid LeRoy Neiman Prima Ballerina Open Edition Serigraph (68 characters)*
*Scarce & Sexy New in Box Autumn 2014 Chanel Le Boy Black Caviar Messenger Bag (77 characters)*

I'm using the Apple II game as my listing example and I've decided on the following title:

*c1981 Beneath the Pyramids Crystalware Crystal Computer Apple II Game Floppy*

In my opinion, the bones would consist of the name of the game *Beneath the Pyramids* and the computer platform *Apple II*. The name of the software series *Crystalware* and the publisher *Crystal Computer* could fall into the bones zone or perhaps I would argue they are meat on the bones. With vintage computer software that's rare and in-demand, I would speculate that buyers don't require the publication year *c1981* or the words *Game* and *Floppy* to find the item on eBay, so those are feather words in my view.

A few additional key points:

- Ditch silly and nonsense words such as L@@K—use the valuable title real estate for meaningful and searchable keywords.
- DO NOT USE ALL CAPS—people find it annoying.
- Be sure your title describes the product even if that repeats the category name.
- Plurals and synonyms are not needed—eBay's search engine figures that out automatically, so you can save the space.
- Punctuation consumes valuable space, so don't worry about commas and periods in titles.
- Make sure you've spelled everything correctly or you may lose discoverability for that keyword—all browsers have built-in spellcheck, so put it to good use.
- Avoid acronyms, abbreviations, and contractions, with a few exceptions (e.g., many folks use "Vtg" vs. "Vintage" to save on space, and there are a few quirky and popular acronyms that sellers and buyers are familiar with. Back in the day, eBay titles were limited to 55 characters, which increased to 80 on September 6, 2011, and sellers used keywords such as MIMB for mint in mint box, NRFB for never removed from box, and a long list of acronyms that are less popular now that titles are longer. As a matter of policy, I avoid all abbreviations in my own listings because eBay is global and many buyers use translation tools to read my listing text and make purchase decisions. I want the translation to be clear so that buyers are not disappointed.
- Your keywords must describe the actual product and not refer to competitive brands or keywords that are included only to increase hits. Keyword spamming, also referred to as keyword manipulation, is not allowed.
- The title may not contain emails or phone numbers. You may only mention a URL if you're selling a domain name or website.
- Profanity isn't allowed in titles or anywhere else on a listing unless it is part of the official title of a CD, DVD, or other media, or if the item is a novelty such as a shirt, hat, etc. and the profanity is obscured in your images or the majority of the word has been replaced with asterisks.

## 5. Listing Form

After you add the title and click Get Started, eBay's listing form appears (see Figure 8-25 on page 175). Your listing is automatically assigned a proposed category and, in

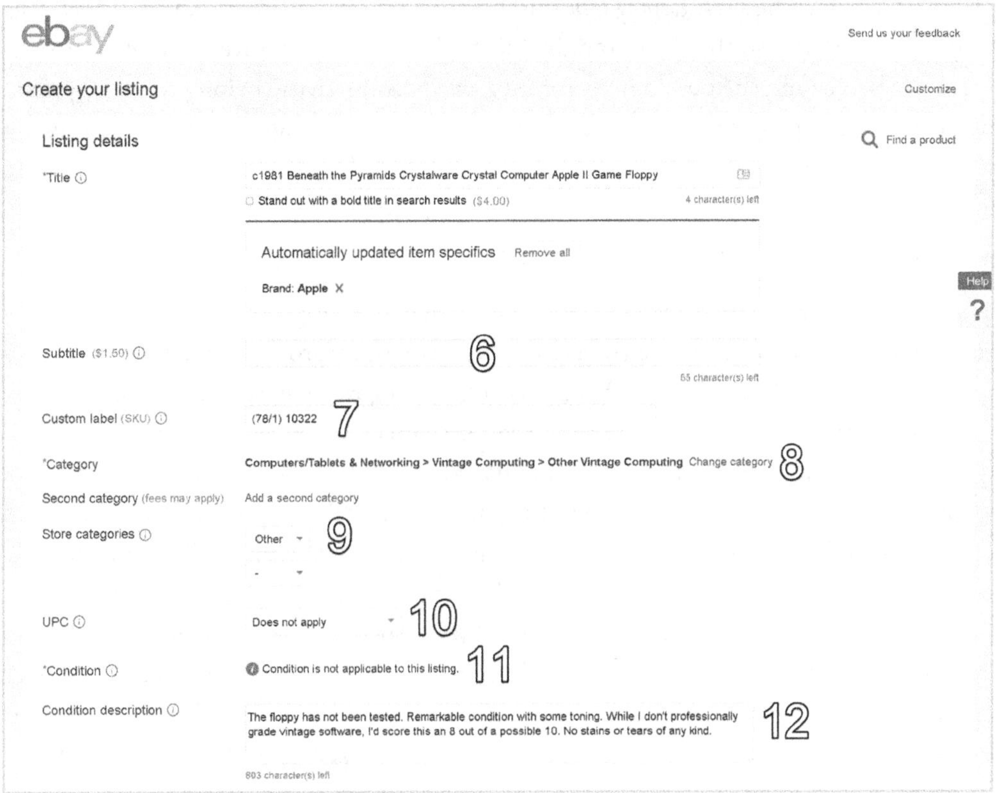

**FIGURE 8–25.** Here's the first group of fields and options within the Listing Details section on the listing form.

many cases, some or all of the item specifics for the listing. My listing for the *Beneath the Pyramids* game goes into the eBay category: *Computers/Tablets & Networking > Vintage Computing > Other Vintage Computing*. From this point on, until we actually list the item, the listing form is a single, scrolling page, but I'll be breaking it down into sections.

## 6. Subtitle

This is something I don't personally use, but many sellers love the *subtitle* as a way to expand on their title when they just don't have enough room. Subtitles cost extra and can be up to 55 characters long.

## 7. Custom Label

This field is an organizer's best friend. In my example, I've included the Apple II game's physical location in my warehouse, which is "78/1" (shelf 78, bin number 1), and

"10322," which is the *stock keeping unit* number, or *SKU* for this item. I've combined this into "(78/1) 10322" so that I can rapidly locate the game in my inventory when it sells. Most problems (and the possibilities for improved productivity) belong to your system, not you or your people's abilities. Use this field as a secret ingredient for maximizing your productivity.

## 8. Category and Second Category

These are initially selected for you but are completely changeable. However, eBay has rules, and the category must be correct for the item, or improperly categorized listings will be ended by eBay. If I'm not happy with the category eBay suggested for a listing, I search for similar items to determine the best choice of category. I was happy with the category eBay suggested for my game listing. If you're catering to buyers who like to browse, add a *second category* (which I rarely do) for added exposure. Additional fees apply if you add a second category. I'll offer an example: When you're listing your 1972 Munich Olympics cuff links, eBay would allow them to be listed in either *Sports Mem, Cards & Fan Shop > Fan Apparel & Souvenirs > Olympics* or *Jewelry & Watches > Men's Jewelry > Cufflinks* or both. eBay will charge an additional insertion fee for the second category and you can decide if it's worth the additional cost. Free insertion fee allocations cannot be used for the second category and you'll always be charged an additional insertion fee for using it.

## 9. Store Categories

This option appears to Store subscribers. These are the virtual shopping aisles or shelves in your eBay Store. While they aren't required, some sellers swear by them. These Store categories, if seller-enabled, appear within your Store page. In lieu of Store categories, sellers may simply display eBay categories, which I find simpler and less taxing from an administrative perspective. I don't use Store categories because they require a little more effort per listing, and over time, that adds up to a lot of lost productivity. But if you love the feature, use it!

## 10. Product Identifier

The choice of category determines whether this field appears. According to eBay, a product entry in the eBay Catalog acts as a fact sheet on the product; it describes a product as it is produced by the manufacturer. The product identifier can be a UPC, an ISBN, or a manufacturer's part number. It's for commodities and newer items. For antiques categories and many others, it won't be applicable. For this field, a UPC is the expected input. However, due to the age of this Apple II video game, there is no product identifier to be found, so I've entered "Does not apply."

### 11. Condition

Also category-dependent, this field offers a variety of pull-down choices, when available. However, condition choices do not apply to this category, because virtually all items being listed here are used.

### 12. Condition Description

Provide a detailed review of flaws, quirks, or issues with secondhand or second-quality goods. Strike a balance between being candid and killing the sale. For the *Beneath the Pyramids* game, I lack an Apple II computer to test it and ensure it works, so the condition description is focused on the physical condition of the game.

### 13. Photos

As you scroll through the next section of the eBay item listing form (see Figure 8–26 on page 178), you can now add your images. They should be clear, candid, and free of manipulation. Remember, borders, text, and additional embellishments are not allowed. You can use a few photo editing tools directly within the listing form: crop, rotate, brighten, contrast, and sharpen are available without using additional software. You can also click the auto adjust magic wand and see what happens. My third image is the back of the printed card that accompanies the software. Although it is blank, I provided it anyway because potential buyers may ask about it. Better to have it and not need it than to not have it when a buyer wants to see it.

### 14. Gallery Plus

This option allows you to display a jumbo gallery image in search results for an additional fee. I'd skip this. The gallery images are big enough already. I have no evidence to prove it is a good investment.

### 15. Item Specifics

In addition to the automatically updated item specifics that eBay gathers from the title you enter, you may be required to add category-dependent data to help buyers find and filter through listings. According to eBay's help documentation, the Best Match algorithm rewards sellers who populate all optional item specific fields with improved placements. Note that I added custom item specifics for Year and Platform.

**FIGURE 8–26.** Here's the Listing Details section of the form showing the image uploader, built-in image editor, and the section for adding item specific information. Your listing must have at least one image. You may add custom item specifics if you think they will enhance the listing.

## 16. Item Description

As we continue through the Listing Details section of the form (see Figure 8–27 on page 179), we now input a description for the *Beneath the Pyramids* game. Select the HTML tab if you're an advanced user pasting a custom design using code. Clicking the Advanced Editing link at the top right of the Item Description box expands the toolbar to its fullest potential. The toolbar offers a variety of font faces, sizes, and colors. There are

**FIGURE 8–27.** Here's the Item Description within the Listing Details section of the form. Note the Mobile-Friendly Checker link at the top right, which shows you what the description will look like on a mobile phone.

also features to bold, italicize, underline, and align text, as well as generate ordered and unordered lists with variable indenting.

The description is a stage where you're delivering your best performance. It's romance or substance and typically a little of both. Writing can be art or technical, but it should not be long and clunky. You're telling a very short story with the emphasis on being short. Tailor your descriptions to what you sell. There's no one-size-fits-all way to prepare a description, and some eBay sellers launch listings with no descriptions at all.

I've summarized products into five essential types to help you decide how to be the best description architect for what you're listing. Most goods fall into these headings:

- Aspirational
- Luxury
- Collectible
- Commodity
- Necessity

An **aspirational** product speaks to an audience that wishes to own it, but the supply is scarce and the potential number of individuals who can afford it is small. These are products that appear inside the pages of fashion magazines and are represented by gorgeous models. An aspirational product may include jewelry, fragrance, apparel, accessories, eyewear, or footwear. I'd consider a Ferrari an aspirational product and you certainly can find Ferraris on eBay.

A **luxury** product may be aspirational, but the marketing strategy speaks more to ego than emotion. The approach may feel similar, but think products like expensive watches, designer baby strollers, crystal-studded phone cases, and products that are by their nature functional, but designed for a wealthier audience. Sellers position aspirational and luxury goods with a lexicon that evokes a strong response and with messaging that engages. Luxury goods may be expensive, but they're generally not rare.

**Collectible** buyers are interesting. They are exceptionally knowledgeable. They can be very price sensitive. Many are bargain hunters. Some philately collectors will pay whatever it takes to acquire a mint condition 1930 Graf Zeppelin U.S. postage stamp. They are not swayed by flowery language and you will find that crafting a listing for collectible item buyers is a stark contrast to aspirational and luxury products. Focus on the item's specifics and condition.

**Commodity** items have a relatively clear and predictable price and are offered by many sellers. Competition also means lower margins. You'll have to somehow differentiate yourself to be seen among the volume of sellers. While a commodity does not have to be a necessity, the buyer is price shopping and comparing carefully. She's looking for a killer deal on the latest generation Xbox for a teenager's birthday present. She knows what she wants and how much she'll pay. A wordy description is a turnoff. Seconds count and she's in a hurry . . . barely reading the description. Seller feedback, item condition, and returns policy matter more than a romantic explanation of the features and benefits. You're selling brands and explaining what's in the box. Measurements are far less important than a sealed package.

**Necessity** buyers are practically twins with commodity customers. The difference is that they're filling a need. While all the other types of customers are probably good with waiting until they win an auction, necessity buyers prefer Buy It Now listings that can be had today. They have no time or patience for extra words. Tell them how large or small, the color and condition. Keep it direct and simple. The make and model number. They know all the brands, and while they are open to buying what they need in a compatible product, brand names rule and generally are the keywords being searched. They need that printer ink today, the truck tire now, and that shower head yesterday.

As I mentioned earlier, there's no one-size-fits-all style guide for authoring compelling copy. Every year that I am in business, I'm continuing to develop the art of the description.

Here are a few more key points to consider when preparing descriptions for eBay:

- Place the most important details first and discuss them right away.
- Leave out irrelevant information.
- Talk about condition and mention any flaws; be truthful but never negative.
- Provide dimensions in inches—feel free to also include metric.
- Provide sizes for rings, clothing, shoes, and anything else where size is important.
- Include the brand name.
- Provide the make and model when appropriate.

- Identify key materials; is it genuine leather or faux leather? Are the rubies natural or synthetic?
- Explain the color even if it's clear from your photos.
- Cover provenance and age.
- Point out the features.
- State the country of manufacture when known.
- Talk about what will be included and what won't . . . a missing power cord may not hurt you that badly because they are usually cheap to buy on eBay, so mention it.
- Mention international shipping, emphasizing that you offer it.
- Discuss returns options if you allow them.
- Don't include links or email addresses—unless the link merely points to a product manual or a noncommercial web page with specifications about the item, and the link complies with eBay's links policy.
- Give yourself limits—while eBay may not limit the length of your description, you certainly should, so keep things brief, relevant, and to the point.

> **TIP**
>
> According to Harry Temkin, eBay vice president and head of seller experience, 64 percent of eBay's global sales are completed on a mobile device. Using the Mobile-Friendly Checker feature ensures that your listing looks just right on mobile.

Provide a backstory for collectible items where possible, but don't fictionalize. Mention certificates of authenticity. That might just seal the deal.

The eBay listing interface will store and recall seller-created reusable templates to reduce unneeded work by prepopulating text. Click the Mobile-Friendly Checker link to preview the item description in a mock mobile phone viewport. Viewport is just a fancy name for the visible area of a web page as seen on a particular browser.

## 17. Format

The Format field opens the Selling Details section of the form (see Figure 8–28 on page 182). Here you can select how you want to sell the item you're listing. Most categories offer two choices—an auction or fixed price listing. A limited number of categories, such as the one we're using to sell this vintage game, offer the classified ad format. I chose the auction format for the *Beneath the Pyramids* game because it's very rare and collectible. I use auctions for products that are aspirational, luxury, and collectible. I use fixed price when selling commodity and necessity items because customers of those products are shopping for convenience and immediate need.

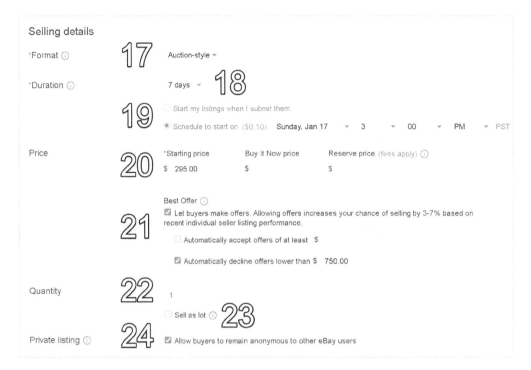

**FIGURE 8–28.** Here's the first part of the Selling Details section on the listing form. For collectibles, starting and ending an auction late Sunday afternoon works best. Not only is eBay traffic very high at that time, but I've also noticed that prices tend to go higher. Perhaps people are inclined to bid more while relaxing at home. While my starting price is very high, this Apple II game is very rare. I can always relist it if no one bids.

## 18. Duration

An auction can run for one, three, five, seven, or ten days in most categories. I chose a seven-day listing for *Beneath the Pyramids*, which gives ample exposure to potential buyers and allows buyers to check with anyone else they need to check with (e.g., a spouse or business partner who may need to approve the spend). A fixed price listing is always automatically set for the GTC duration and will relist every month until you choose to end it. The durations for classified ad listings, if that format is offered in your chosen category, are 30, 60, or 90 days.

## 19. Schedule to Start On

It costs a little extra to do this, but scheduling an auction listing may offer strategic advantages. I decided to pay the extra ten cents for the *Beneath the Pyramids* auction because, in my experience, there's more buyer activity and traffic on Sundays. Many sellers insist ending an auction on Sunday yields the best results. While you can do it, I think it's nonsense to schedule a fixed price listing because they're all GTC anyway. You can schedule a listing up to three weeks in advance.

## 20. Price

For auctions, you enter the starting price and, optionally, a Buy It Now price. You can add a secret reserve price for a fee, but be aware that buyers dislike reserves. I see no point in adding Buy It Now to an auction because it disappears after a bid is placed. When you add Buy It Now to an auction, buyers can either purchase the product immediately or place a bid. In most categories, the Buy It Now value needs to be at least 30 percent above the auction starting price. When someone bids, the Buy It Now option normally disappears. When you've added a reserve, the Buy It Now remains an option until the reserve is met. In select categories, the Buy It Now option may remain available for a limited time subsequent to the first bid being placed. Be certain you can live with the starting price if only one person bids. For fixed price listings, this price is what the buyer will pay when they use Buy It Now. I'm starting this auction at $295, because that's the average selling price for these vintage Apple II games.

## 21. Best Offer

Originally only an option for fixed price listings, it's now available for auctions, too. If you believe an auction item could go higher than the starting price, skip this feature—otherwise, what's the point of having an auction? In these fields, you can enter prices for eBay to automatically accept or decline on your behalf. For auctions, both of these figures should be higher than your starting price, and for fixed price listings, they should be lower than your stated price. If you were to twist my arm really hard, I'd consider adding the Best Offer feature to an auction. I've configured this listing to automatically decline offers below $750, which is more than double the $295 starting price for the auction. I prefer not to have an auction automatically accept offers just in case I acquire some previously unknown intel about the value of the merchandise. The $750 figure is so high that I would be over the moon to receive it, but in my years of experience, it's possible to have auctions finish with a price that's many times the starting figure. Proceed with this feature cautiously. Use it sparingly.

## 22. Quantity

For auctions, like this one, this number will always be one (1). However, for fixed price listings, you may enter your entire inventory, as long as every item you include is identical. Some categories, such as clothing, permit some variations such as color, size, etc. For fragrances, it can be different scents, and so forth. In those categories, you'll enter variation inventory distinctly. Variations save on listing fees and improve the buyer experience by placing inventory with variations in a single listing.

### 23. Sell as Lot

Some sellers tick this check box and enter lot quantities—for example, you may have 996 AAA batteries in stock, but the batteries are shrink-wrapped into packets of 12. In this case, you'd indicate that you sell in lot quantities of 12. I love that eBay offers this option, but I've never personally used this feature in my business.

### 24. Private Listing

You can keep a listing private to protect your buyer. I love this feature and use it often, as I have here in my listing example. As a seller, you might choose to set up private listings when you're selling high-priced items or pharmaceutical products. Buyers may not want purchases of high-value items revealed for fear of being targeted for theft or letting the cat out of the bag in case the purchase is a gift for someone within the household. Health-related information is always confidential and smart sellers enable this feature for health and wellness products. Sellers of certain category items also use this to keep their sales discreet. For example, eBay allows the sale of nude art and risqué photographic images; and often buyers and sellers of these collectibles prefer to keep their deals undercover.

### 25. Make a Donation

The Selling Details section continues with the Make a Donation option (see Figure 8–29 on page 185). Give a little, a lot, or everything to your favorite cause or causes. Sellers can earmark 10 to 100 percent of their items' selling prices to benefit a registered eBay for Charity nonprofit. Love a nonprofit that's not on the list? Just direct them to https://www.ebayforcharity.org to have them register. Your donation is automatically withheld and forwarded to the nonprofit within 45 days. I opted to donate 100 percent of the proceeds of the *Beneath the Pyramids* game to a nonprofit that's close to my heart, Dreams to Reality Foundation®.

### 26. Payment Options

Available payment options depend on a few factors. eBay manages payments for most sellers and funds are deposited to the seller's bank account by daily electronic funds transfer. Immediate payment can be required; however if the Best Offer feature

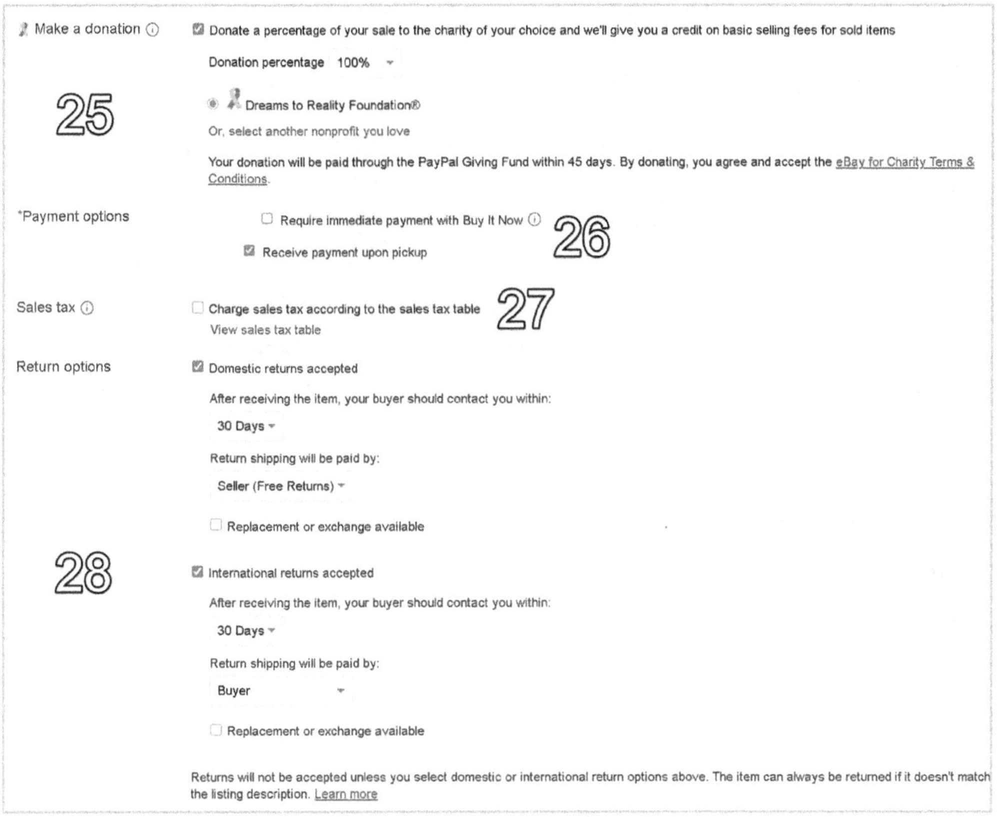

**FIGURE 8–29.** Here are the next four parts of the Selling Details section on the listing form.

is enabled, the buyer can pay within four days, per eBay regulations. You can also indicate here that local pickup is permitted and add additional checkout instructions that will show on the eBay listing page. When the immediate payment option is selected, the local pickup option is not visible, and when eBay manages payments, a tracking number is expected by the system. Payments outside of eBay, for example when a local pickup occurs, are not covered by eBay's Money Back Guarantee for buyers or the seller protections that are extended when deals occur entirely on eBay, including payment processing.

## 27. Sales Tax

eBay now automatically collects and remits sales tax to most states, including California where I live. It's hassle-free, so there's no need to check this box unless you operate your business in one of the few states not already set up for collection. Reach out to eBay support if you're not certain.

---

### eBAY TRANSITIONS TO MANAGED PAYMENTS

From 2002 to 2015, PayPal was pretty much the only way to pay and be paid on eBay for items that sellers shipped out. However, PayPal became a separate company in 2015, and in late 2018, eBay started offering end-to-end payments to sellers. While the transition has been gradual, eBay expects to manage all payments for sellers by 2022. While PayPal will remain one of the payment methods available to customers, eBay now offers many more ways to pay. It's a great move because sellers will no longer be required to have both eBay and PayPal accounts, allowing them to focus on their core business.

---

## 28. Return Options

The vast majority of buyers expect to physically examine what they buy online and have the right to return it if they're not satisfied. While eBay doesn't require you to allow returns, you will be forced to accept an item back if it's not as described in your listing. I'd recommend that you accept returns, and eBay's options for a returns policy are no returns, 30-day returns, or 60-day returns. You can decide who pays return shipping, you or the buyer, but if you do offer free returns, eBay protects you from any monkey business—you can issue a partial refund if an item comes back damaged or missing parts, and eBay will protect you from any buyer claims and remove any negative or neutral feedback. You may offer the same or a different returns policy for international buyers. Here's what I do: if the item is high-margin and lightweight, I offer free 30-day returns for U.S. buyers and 30-day returns for international customers, but the latter must pay return shipping. I allow returns of low-margin and heavy items and normally require the buyer to pay return postage; and I refund the original purchase price, less outbound postage costs when the product comes back in good condition. As of the moment I write this sentence, my return rate for the trailing 30 days was 0.69 percent. I firmly believe I would lose many sales by not permitting returns, so I customarily allow them. Some categories (e.g., clothing) have much higher return rates than others. I'm offering free domestic returns on the *Beneath the Pyramids* game because it's light and video game collectors rarely send anything back.

## 29. Domestic Shipping

This is the beginning of the Shipping Details section of the listing form (see Figure 8–30 on page 187). Here you can offer flat rate local, calculated shipping (based on carrier's rate tables), freight rates (for heavy stuff), or shipping pickup only.

## 30. Services

Sellers may offer one or more different shipping services, and while I might ordinarily offer cheap Media Mail through the U.S. Postal Service for software, I'm using faster, more secure FedEx 2Day for this rare and potentially expensive collectible software program.

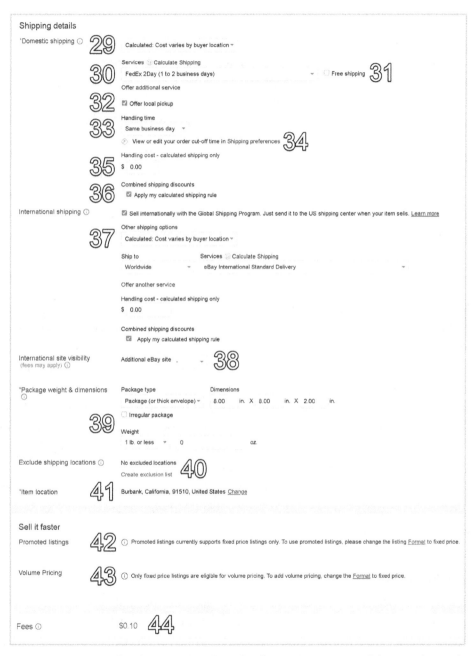

**FIGURE 8–30.** Here are the Shipping Details and Sell It Faster sections of the eBay listing form.

Even if asked, I would not ship this game using a cheaper method. You can add up to four shipping services, although I usually only offer one to keep things simple. When enabled, the system will automatically calculate the shipping cost for the most popular services offered by USPS, FedEx, and UPS.

### 31. Free Shipping

Checking this box enables free shipping. Offering free shipping may boost sales, but it isn't a marketing tool for rare items in the same way it is for commodified goods. Because the *Beneath the Pyramids* game is a rare collectible, I decided not to offer free shipping. When this check box is enabled, it applies only to the first shipping service you've listed on the form; so be careful which one you list first so you don't unintentionally offer free FedEx overnight.

### 32. Offer Local Pickup

When you choose your shipping options, you can indicate that local pickup is the only option for your listing, but here, you can check the box to show you'll allow buyers to pick up their winnings even if you also offer shipping services.

### 33. Handling Time

Seller performance is evaluated based on a number of data points, including *handling time*: the number of business days between when you receive payment for an item and when your package is scanned by your shipping carrier. This setting will be used to inform potential customers how quickly to expect the arrival of their merchandise. It's the promise you make to get your products to buyers in a timely manner. You have to meet this commitment 95 percent of the time to avoid penalties such as a lower seller rating. The most diligent sellers are rewarded with better placements in eBay searches and discounts on eBay fees. You can set this to the same business day or any number of days up to 30. Choose a realistic time frame that encourages purchases but doesn't drive you out of your mind—you may not want to go to the post office or have the carrier pick up every day until your sales volume has grown to a healthy level.

### 34. Shipping Preferences

This is a link that you only have to set once to indicate your time zone, working days, and cutoff time for same-day handling. I have a high order volume, so I ship five days a week, and any order that I receive by 3 P.M. Pacific Time will ship the same business day.

## 35. Handling Cost

If you're packing pricey art in crates or the item you're selling requires a plethora of bubble wrap, you can add a *handling cost* to cover the expense. While it's not unreasonable to do so, buyers are particularly sensitive to the total cost of shipping. Many big-box retailers now offer substantially subsidized shipping, and that has spoiled us. More often than not, I simply consider packing supplies a cost of doing business and pay for them out of the item's profit margin.

## 36. Combined Shipping Discounts

This unassuming check box seems self-explanatory, but there's a catch—you can't simply check it to extend combined shipping discounts to your customers. You first have to configure these settings, and for some reason eBay doesn't prompt you to do this. It's a bit of an insider secret, but when you tell eBay to reward customers who buy multiple items, you'll be earning loyalty and catalyzing more sales. Be sure to enable this feature. To configure combined shipping discounts, make sure you're signed in and then hover over your name at the top left of most eBay pages and click Account Settings. On the next page, under Selling, click Shipping Preferences, then scroll to and allow Combined Payments and Shopping, click Edit next to one or more of the appropriate sections, and do the needful. Then you can come back to this page and check that box.

## 37. International Shipping

These are a repeat of most of the shipping options I referenced (in #29 through #36) for domestic shipments. Unless you have a really good reason not to offer cross-border shipping, every item should have these services enabled. The number of options here can be mind-numbing, so here's how I manage international shipment settings. I ship worldwide and offer eBay international standard delivery on shipments valued at $100 or less (the maximum insurance offered for this program). I enable the Global Shipping Program for shipments with a value above $100. Both of these programs are eBay-managed services where you send the item to eBay's U.S. shipping center and they manage the logistics. However, I only ship jewelry and high-value collectibles registered mail with the USPS. Just as with domestic shipping, consider whether you want to add a handling charge and be sure you've configured and enabled combined shipping discounts. If you already activated combined shipping rules (eBay refers to this as *calculated shipping rules*), then you're all set—you won't need to configure international combined shipping separately.

## 38. International Site Visibility

For an additional fee, your listing will appear on the eBay U.K. site. I decline this option because eBay buyers across the world can buy from the U.S. site, and they do!

I recommend you test eBay's additional concessions and determine if they are worth the added cost to you. If you become a super-high-volume seller, these fees will add up quickly.

### 39. Package Weight & Dimensions

Here's where you indicate the package type, dimensions, and weight, which for mailing *Beneath the Pyramids* are 1 lb. or less and 8 inches by 8 inches by 2 inches. The number-one rookie mistake when it comes to shipping is failing to consider the physical size of the package, as opposed to its weight. The larger a package is, the more room it takes up on a truck, plane, or ship—and the more shipping will cost as a result. Dimensional weight, or DIM weight as it's called, is used to determine freight charges for large parcels that consume more room on a vehicle. Automated carrier equipment will calculate the DIM weight if you forget to enter the package dimensions when you prepare the shipping label. It's important to measure the parcel or estimate its dimensions so that you are collecting enough money (or raising the price of the item sufficiently) to cover the shipping cost. There's a check box in this section for irregular packages, but this is used so rarely it's hardly worth mentioning. Stick to using standard packaging such as boxes, padded mailers, envelopes, etc., and avoid irregularly shaped shipments.

### 40. Exclude Shipping Locations

Clicking Create Exclusion List in this section allows you to block orders from countries you don't want to ship to (e.g., those with unreliable postal systems that may lose your parcel). If you only ship domestically, you can block buyers who are off the mainland. This may be appropriate if there are shipping concerns, such as sending certain items to deployed military personnel who use APO/FPO addresses. You can also block entire continents with one click or select individual countries where you'd prefer not to ship. You can safely ship to any country eBay will ship to using eBay international standard delivery (210 countries as of 2021) or the eBay Global Shipping Program (more than 100 countries as of 2021.) Both of these shipping methods offer reliable overseas shipping. You can (but should not) block buyers who only have a P.O. box. Rather than block a country or a region and lose out on potential business, speak with your preferred carrier about ways to guarantee delivery such as Registered Mail (I have never lost a Registered Mail shipment) and using preferred air shipping services from private carriers.

### 41. Item Location

This may seem silly at first, but many large sellers have separate office and warehouse addresses. The item location is used to calculate shipping costs and the estimated time for delivery to the buyer, so make sure you enter the location from which the item will actually ship. If you drop-ship, this should be the location of the drop-shipper's facility.

## 42. Promoted Listings

This feature, which allows you to pay a fee to boost your item's visibility, is only enabled for fixed price listings (see Figure 8–31 below). Paid promotion is the new normal for ubiquitous, commodified items. If your profit margin can handle it, you should enable this feature and pay for premium placements. I have tested this feature extensively, and it works very well. While you can set rates per item, you can also select an existing Promoted Listings campaign with a preset rate. (We'll talk more about Promoted Listings in Chapter 11.) You'll find a link to the Promoted Listings dashboard in your Seller Hub.

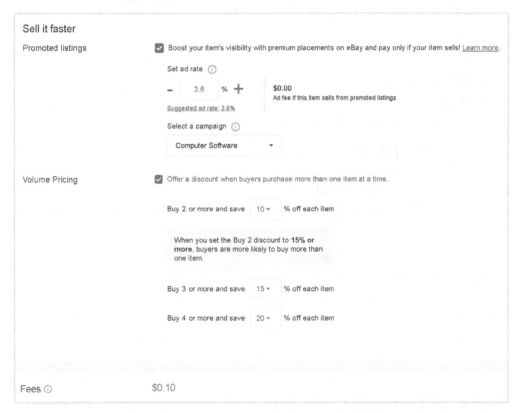

**FIGURE 8–31.** Here's the Sell It Faster section with the Promoted Listings and Volume Pricing features activated. These options are only enabled for fixed price listings, not my video game auction, so I'm just including this screenshot to show you how they work.

### 43. Volume Pricing

Offering discounts for buying more than one of the same item is also only available for fixed price listings. It's a good idea to offer a healthy volume discount for products you can readily and rapidly restock. Smart wholesalers will extend you better pricing once your volume increases, so moving more product out the door can result in better deals from your wholesalers.

### 44. Fees

This listing adventure is nearing the end. The fees are displayed so you know exactly how much you'll be paying for the listing. This total will represent the insertion fee plus the cost of optional listing upgrades. Optional listing upgrades include:

- Setting a one- or three-day duration
- Adding a bold title
- Gallery Plus (increasing the size of the Gallery image), in select categories
- Adding a second category
- Listing Designer
- Scheduling the listing
- Adding a subtitle
- Setting a reserve auction price
- Adding international site visibility

Figure 8–30 on page 187 indicates a charge of ten cents, which covers my fee for the *Beneath the Pyramids* game listing, because I've already exceeded the number of zero insertion fee listings this month. The final value fee is what you pay eBay for a successful sale.

Once you've finished filling out the listing form, you're faced with four choices (see Figure 8–32 on page 193):

1. *List Item.* Click this, and away you go!
2. *Preview.* Why not? Let's see what the listing will look like before it goes up on eBay (see Figure 8–33 on page 193).
3. *Save as Draft.* This option is a lifesaver if you've run out of time, need to check on pricing, have to capture more images, or are having an assistant draft listings and need to review them yourself before they go live.
4. *Cancel.* Be warned! Clicking this means all your hard work will be gone forever. Only cancel if you've decided not to sell the item, or if the cat got to your Ming vase before you could finish listing it!

In case you're curious, I sold *Beneath the Pyramids* for $635.00. The same buyer bought 27 items from my Apple II software auctions and spent a total of $9,863.44. I had

**FIGURE 8–32.** Once you've completed the listing form, you have these four options at the end of the page. It's a great idea to click the Preview button and ensure that everything looks just right before clicking List Item. Use caution with the Cancel button—that makes all your hard work disappear forever, and then you'll need to start over.

**FIGURE 8–33.** Here's what the listing for my Apple II game looks like when clicking Preview. While you can revise or end listings after publishing them on the site, both those decisions happen in public. Why not simply perfect everything to ensure the listing looks beautiful before launching it?

rescued the software for these auctions from the trash while visiting a client of mine who had asked me to pick up some other items to sell for her on eBay. They were in a paper bag outside her building, sitting in a pile destined for the dumpster. After she received her windfall from the sales, less my consignment commission, she never threw anything away again without asking me first.

## SELLER HUB: YOUR eBAY NERVE CENTER

An eBay seller's nerve center is called the Seller Hub as first introduced on page 171. From the Seller Hub, you can access eBay's many seller tools, manage your listings, and grow your sales. The Seller Hub provides the launching pad to discover:

- Your listings and orders
- Orders reports
- Promoted Listings
- Promotions Manager
- Global Shipping Program
- Features to manage your eBay Stores
- Competitive listing guidance

Sign into your eBay account and take a look at the Seller Hub. If this is your first time there, you may be asked to opt in to the tool. Use a desktop or laptop instead of a mobile device—you'll want the larger screen. If you're not registered yet, this would be the time to get it done. From the homepage, hover over (but don't click) My eBay at the top right. In the drop-down menu, click Selling. The Seller Hub will open. See Figure 8–34 on page 195 for a view of the Orders tab on the Seller Hub—this is where your sales appear when they're ready for shipping.

From the Seller Hub dashboard, you can quickly springboard to the many other seller resources eBay offers. Figure 8–35 on page 196 provides a quick breakdown of Seller Hub tabs and what they contain.

The Seller Hub is modular and customizable. In fact, many eBay pages that relate to the management of eBay seller activity have a discreet Customize link that allows you to tailor the view to your liking. When you click Customize, you can move the information panes around on the page or remove them entirely. You can add back removed panes at any time. If you don't care about something, just hide it.

While there are an endless number of possibilities with eBay's Seller Hub, most of us will use it to check which buyers still owe us money and to email them reminders, check in to see which orders are waiting to ship, look up order histories, and handle

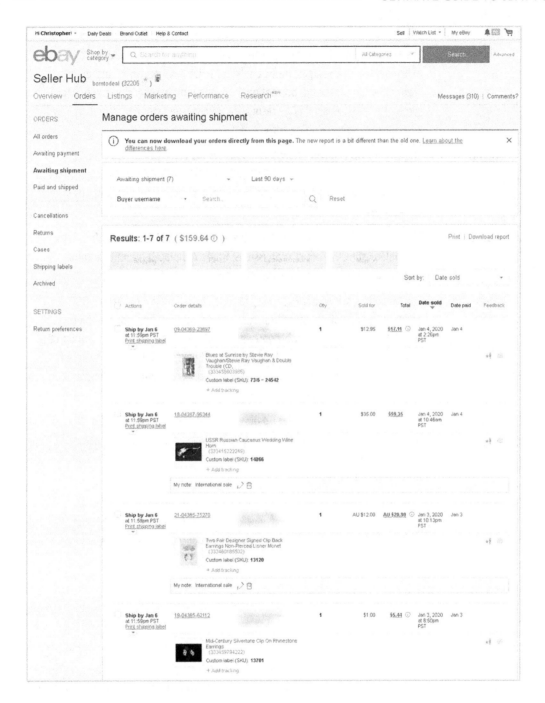

**FIGURE 8–34.** Here's a view of the Orders tab on the
eBay Seller Hub—items that have sold and are ready to ship appear here.

| Overview | The Overview tab displays tasks, sales statistics, order information, links to listings across all stages, traffic analytics, seller resource shortcuts, eBay account health scorecard, promotional offers, monthly seller limits, feedback summary, links to useful eBay resources, selling announcements, and an account summary including current fees. |
|---|---|
| Orders | The Orders tab displays filters to view orders awaiting payment, awaiting shipment, paid, and shipped, as well as cancellations, returns, cases, a list of purchased eBay shipping labels, archived orders, and a link to adjust return preferences. |
| Listings | The Listings tab displays filters for active listings, unsold listings, draft listings, scheduled listings, product submissions, listing templates, optional automation preferences, and optional business policies. |
| Marketing | The Marketing tab is more of a way for eBay to sell their eBay Stores than a resource. It has links to Store branding and promotions and, for non-Store subscribers (which is probably you right now), Promoted Listings. If you don't have a Store and click on anything but the last link, you'll be asked to select an eBay Store subscription level. Wait until you have a consistent supply of items to sell before opening an eBay Store. |
| Performance | The Performance tab provides 90-day sales insights, listing traffic and click-through analytics, a summary of eBay selling fees, and the current status of your seller performance (such as seller level, defects, late shipments, and unresolved buyer cases). |
| Research | The Research tab is another excellent tool for eBay Stores. It has links to Terapeak product research (only available for Store subscribers), recommendations for listing improvements, sourcing guidance, and restocking advice. |

**FIGURE 8–35.** This table lists the various Seller Hub tabs and their uses.

routine selling activity such as approving an occasional buyer request to cancel an order or reprint a shipping label that's been misprinted or spoiled.

But here are a few other features you may find interesting after you've listed and sold some items. Try these out for fun:

- From the Listings tab, click the Customize link and make it your own by adding, removing, and rearranging fields to show only what interests you. Don't like the result? Click Restore Defaults and everything returns back to the way it was.

- From the Marketing tab, click Promotions and generate retail excitement by launching a sales event.

- Also from the Marketing tab, give Promoted Listings a test drive by creating a new campaign. Try signing up to spend just 1 percent of your final sale price and see how many new sales you can score with a tiny ad budget. You can always increase that number once you've become a believer.

- Become better informed about your eBay business by exploring the options within the Performance tab. I love the useful visual aids available here, including detailed charts and tables explaining my selling costs, listing traffic, and sales trends.

While I encourage you to explore, don't lose sight of your North Star—make sure you have a focus and direction that keeps you on track. The goal is to have fun and be profitable with your business. Banish needless activity and focus on what brings the sales across the finish line.

# Chapter 9

# Stunning and Stimulating Buyers with Visual Merchandising

Something most eBay sellers don't employ that nearly every brick-and-mortar retailer uses every day is *visual merchandising*. Visual merchandising is an essential tool for business promotion, and every eBay seller should enhance their listings with free and low-cost visual merchandising techniques. While I received no formal training in this field, I have examined many thousands of listings made by other eBay sellers as well as perused retail stores in cities across the world. Much of this is trial and error, but there are time-tested techniques that work, and I'll share them here with you.

## VISUAL INTEREST IS EASIER DONE THAN IMAGINED

Merchandising will delight your customer to the point of taking action. Their initial response will generally be to browse around and gain a greater sense of who you are and what you have to offer before they make a purchase. Keywords and listing item specifics will attract buyers through discoverability, and the listing images will do much of the work to woo them and catalyze the purchase.

Creating visual interest isn't difficult. Here are a few basic tips to follow for compelling listing photos:

- Have an ample source of light.
- Get close and avoid excess background, so that the item takes up all the space in the photo. eBay lets you crop surplus background, but don't rely on that tool—go ahead and get ready for your close-up.
- Set up a clean and clutter-free background.
- Use a clear, basic image for the gallery and then capture every angle for the additional images.
- Avoid having yourself appear in the photos. If you can see your reflection, try various angles until you are no longer visible.
- Take a generous number of photos so you can choose the best ones when you're making the listing.
- Make sure the product is clear and in focus.
- Use a mannequin to display clothing and props for jewelry and watches.

Try different presentations until you've found what really works for your sensibility and helps lead buyers to checkout. I demonstrated eBay's Advanced Search tools and explained how to display and sort sold listings in Chapter 5. The sold listings provide a big, beautiful window into eBay that permits you to see what works and what doesn't. Have a look at Figure 9–1 on page 201, which is my search results for the keyword "blazer" displaying sold items sorted by highest price first. Notice the stark contrast between sellers who present their blazers in the best possible light and those who simply lay an expensive bespoke masterpiece on a table without even taking a few moments to steam or press it.

The blazer images offer immediate clarity on what you need to do to be competitive. A mannequin, shirt, and tie are all reusable and make a world of difference in merchandising a gentleman's fine blazer. If you're selling expensive clothes you can afford to take some time with your merchandising.

A fine, form-fitting garment deserves a presentation with great panache. According to visual communication scientist Jernej Zupanc, the eye's retina is an extension of the brain containing 150 million light-sensitive rod and cone cells. Half the human

**FIGURE 9–1.** This Advanced Search result shows completed listings for the single keyword "blazer," with the search results sorted by price, highest first. Most of the items have been handsomely merchandised. My favorites are those displayed with a mannequin, shirt, and tie to round out the presentation. The use of an image of a runway model (bottom left) is clever but impractical for most sellers. Remember to secure written permission to use other people's images even if they are from the factory.

When you create listings, you've consented to allow both eBay and other eBayers permission (via the user agreement) to use your images and product details.

brain is related in some way to visual processing, so it is unsurprising that a pleasing presentation and images so often seal the deal.

I like to try different things. If something hasn't sold within 30 to 90 days, I may decide to capture all new images and relist it. Merchandise that attracts a smaller audience, such as niche collectibles, may sit for a while until an interested buyer happens across it. An example would be American Brilliant Period cut glass, where a wonderful piece in excellent condition will attract few buyers but command a high price. Glass and crystal are notoriously hard to photograph and require patience. Wear the wrong clothing, select an inappropriate background, or work in a cluttered room, and prospective buyers will be messaging you asking "Why does that comport dish have a reddish hue?"

I subscribe to top magazines to give me inspiration for visual merchandising. The topics of these magazines include home decorating, fashion, lifestyle, hunting, automotive, and a plethora of others that provide me with amazing retail intel. I also constantly look over other sellers' imagery for ideas. As long as the price you're asking is reasonable and you're not in a hurry to sell, try out a few ideas on your listings and see how they work.

## WORKING WITH DISPLAYS

There are an endless number of bloggers and other purported experts offering to pass on their wisdom about visual merchandising. But few true working experts sell their own master classes. Courses and systems will just slow you down while quickly emptying your wallet. Teach yourself instead.

It's remarkable how quickly and easily a product comes to life when displayed in an interesting way. Here are a few tips I've curated when it comes to using inexpensive displays and free materials to generate visual interest:

- Use jewelry props to bring sparkle to wearable art.
- Fit clothing over inexpensive mannequins to give it shape and provide visual context. Use ordinary jumbo binder clips to gather up loose fabric and secure it—but make sure the clips aren't visible.
- Add a shirt, tie, and even cuff links to help a man visualize himself in a fine blazer or bespoke suit.
- Drape a $3 piece of colored velvet over a cardboard box to connote luxury when capturing images of curious old collectibles and antiques.
- Stuff repurposed gift tissue into handbags, messenger bags, and backpacks to provide shape.
- Display small objects on an attractive wood cutting board to add a winsome look.

- Pick up a variety of inexpensive, large ceramic tiles at the hardware store, with interesting colors and patterns ranging from dark to light, to use as backdrops.
- Pick up a roll of seamless photography background paper. These papers come in various colors and patterns—some even have photographic images printed on them. Stick to relatively simple designs. Once the paper is soiled or torn, cut off that part and unroll a fresh section.
- Add a realistic artificial fruit assortment in a bowl to provide context. Even a set that looks totally edible won't set you back much, lasts for years, and will repay you after just a few sales.
- Pick up a used, artificial Christmas tree—the smallest one you can find—at any thrift store. Use it to merchandise fine, collectible antique and vintage ornaments and other seasonal decorations.
- Small, heavy objects such as a paperweight, a bag of marbles or bolts, a smooth stone, or lead-free fishing weights can all be used to hold items down or prop them up during photography sessions. If you have to shoot large items outdoors, sand-filled bags offer a useful way to secure items from falling over or blowing away if it's windy.
- Attach a tiny dab of reusable adhesive putty to keep a ring floating on an attractive ceramic tile or other choice of background. Be sure the putty isn't visible.
- Display pretty china plates on a dish easel. The presentation looks elegant, and your neck won't get stiff from trying to capture an overhead shot.

While accumulating all the above-mentioned props, displays, and supplies sounds a bit overwhelming, they're all affordable, and you'll earn the money back very quickly. An inexpensive plastic footlocker is a convenient way to store everything and keep these essentials close at hand.

## USING CONTRAST AND COLOR

Appealing, eye-catching photography requires you to use contrast to direct the eyes to focus on the subject. A compelling composition sells better. Colors with opposite characteristics contrast strongly when placed together. Swiss expressionist painter Johannes Itten said of complementary colors, "They incite each other to maximum vividness when adjacent . . ."

Here are a few basics:

- Bold colors offset weaker colors.
- Dark colors contrast against light colors.
- Warmer colors contrast against cooler colors.

Before you invest in a bunch of colored backgrounds, consider what you'll be selling. If you're selling commodified products, they are very likely to be considered for the Google Shopping feed. Having products displayed on Google Shopping costs eBay a tremendous amount of money, and sellers pay nothing for this exposure. If all you'll ever sell is brand-new sneakers, you'll want to follow eBay's guidelines for inclusion in Google Shopping, and that means using a simple white background. While Google Shopping generally requires images to be shot against a white background, I have seen certain products, such as collectibles and clear glass, that are staged on colored and black backgrounds.

If you're not selling merchandise that's likely to appear in Google Shopping, then go ahead and have some fun with colors. To determine if your item is Google Shopping-friendly, just try googling what you're selling. For example, try searching "sneakers," and

## GETTING A PASS THROUGH GOOGLE SHOPPING'S PEARLY GATES

Here's what you should be doing to make sure your listings are approved for Google Shopping:

- Capture high-quality images.

- Verify that the images you are using are at least 800 by 800 pixels (I go larger—I recommend no smaller than 1000 pixels on the shortest side), on a white background that has no text or watermarks.

- Use listings that have single-quantity items (vs. multiples or bundles).

- Prepare well-written product titles with robust and relevant keywords.

- Steer clear of marketing text such as "free shipping," ALL CAPS, or gimmicky and unusual characters.

- Avoid acronyms that might confuse buyers.

- Input as many item specifics as you can. (Google will only display merchandise in the Clothing, Shoes, & Accessories categories when you provide the item specifics for Color, Size, Age Group, and Gender.)

- MPN, GTIN, ISBN, or UPC should be included when known. Include manufacturer details and colors.

you'll notice that with a few exceptions, the results are displayed on white backgrounds. Now type in "hummel." You'll see a dramatic difference in the images—lots of colored backgrounds and less professional-looking images.

For one-of-a-kind items that aren't slated for the Google Shopping feed, I love to use colored backdrops that pop. Try premier velvet (not the cheap or stretchy kind) for a black background. Buy the good stuff. It's worth the extra money and you'll get years of use out of it. Fabric remnants are a good source for deals; if you can't find any on eBay, try the local fabric or craft store. Velvet looks rich in photos. Cotton or microfiber will tend to look lighter in pictures. I am also extremely fond of crimson, indigo, and plum velvet. Photography paper is great for a smooth look; ceramic tiles are cheap and come in an array of colors. Natural wood, burlap, and other everyday household materials offer color, contrast, and texture.

Don't be afraid to try different ideas. Look at other eBay sellers and popular magazines for inspiration.

Capturing that perfect shot can be especially challenging for certain types of products, and for the neophyte, working with these troublemakers can be downright intimidating. Here are a few of the agitators and how to wrangle them:

- *Glass and crystal.* Photographing any reflective object such as glass and crystal introduces new challenges. One neat trick with glasses—if you have two identical glasses, put one upside down and set the glass to be photographed on top of it. The bottom glass will give the appearance that it's a reflection. Lights, whether camera flash or a continuous light source, will look unattractive on the reflective surface. Use a piece of white foam board or white background paper to diffuse and direct your light source. This creates a nice, defined look with excellent contrast.

- *Shiny jewelry (or shiny anything, for that matter).* The returns I generally receive on jewelry are due to the occasional complaint that the color didn't match the images on eBay. This could be because of differences in monitor settings, but I hate disappointing customers. So how do you make sure the gold in your photographs looks the correct shade of yellow (or rose, green, or white, as the case may be), and the gems have the same vivid color and sparkle that the buyer will experience in person? When shooting with a DSLR or mirrorless camera, be sure to set the white balance according to the manufacturer's instructions. Proper lighting and a quality image sensor will ensure beautiful color and contrast. Try using daylight-balanced bulbs for lighting and a light tent as a diffuser. Experiment with different backgrounds. I use ceramic tiles, high-gloss black acrylic, wood, and props to complement the jewelry but not upstage it.

- *Tiny items.* I bought a special close-up macro lens for my camera to bring itty-bitty things into focus. Newer phones have a built-in macro feature, which is essential for capturing sharply focused images.

- *Very light-colored items.* Needless to say, the background must contrast with the item. I scratch my head when I see eBay listings with images of a very light product on a light background. Perhaps the seller doesn't realize how badly that hurts their prospect of selling the merchandise. If what you're selling isn't transparent or reflective, like glass or crystal, then place it on a high-contrast opposite, like dark gray or black. You will see these combinations on Google Shopping when searching product feeds from eBay listings.

> **TIP**
>
> Some sellers, when photographing jewelry, may wonder why all their beautiful diamonds have little specks of color on the facets—it's probably a reflection coming off their clothing. The solution: keep a lab coat handy and throw it on over your street clothes. Voilà! No more color conundrum.

Contrast and color are essential elements for engaging people's moods. While high contrast and vivid colors provide an energetic feeling, low contrast and subdued colors will tend to relax or induce a dreamy feeling. Play around with colors until you settle on what works. The great thing about digital photography is there's no film to waste—you can always reshoot items when they haven't sold and try different approaches to contrast and color.

## EMBEDDING VIDEOS

Videos have had an on-again, off-again relationship with eBay. In the early days, sellers could provide links or embed videos. Due to various abuses, including inappropriate content and unscrupulous attempts to divert business off eBay, the policy has become much stricter. That said, the ability to provide product videos is extremely powerful. If a picture is worth a thousand words, a video is worth a million.

Using videos in your eBay listing involves gingerly navigating the minefield of the eBay *links policy*. Review eBay's complete links policy by following these steps:

1. Click Help & Contact at the top of the homepage or most eBay pages.
2. Type "links" into the search box.
3. Select the link entitled *Links policy*.

Here are some key points relating to videos in listings:

- Videos must be a product review, demonstration, or installation video, but cannot include adult content or divert buyers off eBay

▨ Videos can only be embedded within item descriptions and are only permitted from the following sites (subject to change, etc.):

- YouTube (my preferred video service)
- Vimeo
- Brightcove
- Ustream
- Screencast
- Kizoa
- Dailymotion

Use a video when photos fall short of getting the job done. The juice must be worth the squeeze, however. Ask yourself:

▨ "Is there enough profit potential in this product to warrant the time required to record, edit (if needed), upload, and embed a video?"

▨ "Would a video truly enhance the customer experience, or is this item simple enough that a video isn't necessary?" Most things probably aren't complicated enough to need a video, honestly.

▨ "Is this item complex enough that a video explaining how it works may actually avert customer frustration and a return?"

▨ "Does a video provide a more compelling sales presentation than still images alone?"

I like to use video when the product is highly collectible, is a high-ticket item, has complex moving parts, or, in the case of jewelry, if it would throw off a nicer sparkle in a video than in photos.

As of this writing, eBay does not allow a YouTube video player to run in its listings. The link must open a new window to play the video. In essence, you can include a clickable thumbnail image that opens a new window for the video. If you have a Google account, you have instant access to upload videos and quickly link them in your product listings. You can also use HTML5 code to embed a cloud-hosted video file, which allows the viewer to watch and download it. I'll show you both methods. When adding or revising an eBay listing, you'll need to be on the HTML tab of the Item Description editor (see Chapter 8, page 179).

▨ *YouTube.* Create, edit, and upload your video to YouTube. If you're new to this process, check out a tutorial—on YouTube, of course! You can put a unique SKU or other identifier in the video title or description to help with managing and pruning videos once items are sold. Click the Share link just under the video

> **TIP**
>
> According to eBay, active content, such as JavaScript and and the now obsolete Flash, hinders mobile purchases, creates longer load times, and increases security vulnerabilities. Active content is not permitted on eBay, but you can include a link to your product video or use an embed method with HTML that does not contain active content.

player. In the pop-up window, click the Copy link (see Figure 9–2 below) to copy the video's URL. Then head over to any of the many free eBay YouTube video embed code generators. Generally, I use ISDNtek's converter (https://www.isdntek.com/tagbot/YouTubeConverter.htm), but you can google to find others.

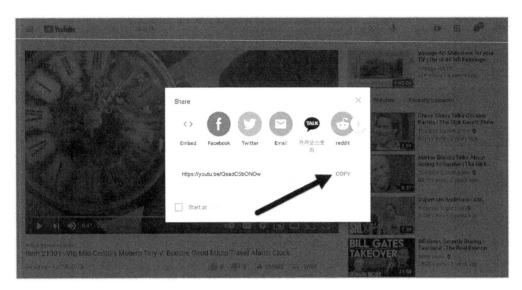

**FIGURE 9–2.** This is the sharing options pop-up window on my YouTube explainer video for a really mini musical travel alarm clock. Do not click on the Embed option because eBay does not allow that type of code. Click Copy to grab the video's URL, which you can then paste into one of the many available free video embed generators. This neat collectible alarm clock sold for $211.38.

■ *HTML.* The ideal scenario is to be able to play a video directly from your listing description, but eBay currently prohibits that. However, here's a neat trick. Host your video at any good ISP, copy the URL of your hosted video, and add this code to your eBay description: *<video width="480" height="320" preload="" controls="" style="font-size: 14pt;"> <source src="VIDEO FILE URL HERE" type="video/mp4"></video>* This code, when added to your listing description using the HTML tab, will embed and allow video playback without opening a new window (see Figure 9–3 on page 209). It preloads the video in the

**TIP**

Preview your video embed before launching a new listing or saving revisions to a running listing. You cannot change the description once an item has received a bid, so be sure you prepared and pasted the code correctly before committing to it.

background and displays it neatly in the listing description, ready for playback (see Figure 9–4 below). If you already operate a website, you can host your videos there—just delete them once the item has sold to save on storage space. I found hosting plans for as little as $1.42 per month simply by searching "web hosting." If you're interested, check out more HTML and CSS code examples at W3Schools (https://www.w3schools.com).

While adding videos to your listings takes extra time and should be reserved for special, high-value, intriguing, or more complex items, it can be a wonderful sales tool that increases buyer engagement.

**FIGURE 9–3.** Here's the Item Description section you'll see when creating an eBay listing. Notice that the HTML tab is selected, allowing you to enter code directly. The arrow points to the start of my video embed code. The long URL, beginning with "https" and ending with "mp4," belongs to the video that I uploaded to my ISP. Check with your service provider to make sure they can handle lots of traffic and if streaming videos is included in their price. You'll notice the text is set off by <div> and </div> tags.

**FIGURE 9–4.** Here's the video and video player generated from the HTML5 code I entered, as seen from the eBay listing description. You can always adjust the width and height values in the code I provided if you want a larger player to display.

## COLLECTION-BASED MERCHANDISING

Just as store windows are a vital aspect of brick-and-mortar visual merchandising, an eBay Store's merchandising is the digital window that entices a potential buyer to browse and hopefully buy from you. Collections are an essential component of apparel merchandise and are used in many other product categories as well, including kitchen gadgets, indoor and outdoor décor, motor sports, and sporting goods.

Social media platforms offer insights into the latest trends. If you're a trendsetter, create your own vibe and flaunt it. Here are a few ways to promote your collections:

- *Custom Store categories.* Every eBay Store comes with optional Store categories that allow you to organize your Store listings into collections by type of item, theme, size, color, genre, format, and so forth. To add and edit custom Store categories, hover over My eBay at the top of the homepage or most eBay pages, and then click Selling. Scroll to and click the Manage Store link. Click the Store Categories link on the left side of the page to get started. You'll need to assign custom categories to your listings when creating them or edit existing listings to add the new category. You could, for example, deploy a custom category called "Daily Deals."

- *Build HTML.* While this is not the easiest way to eBay, if you're comfortable with HTML, adding a bit of fancy code can boost your collections-based sales and increase customer loyalty. Use the product description to build links to other eBay listings that form your collections. More experienced HTML coders have developed beautiful product description templates with clickable images to other products within a collection, so buyers can shop collections quickly and easily. Fashion sellers recommend complementary clothing, shoes, and accessories; comic sellers provide clickable thumbnails that link to other comics from the same series or universe; electronics sellers offer color-coordinated accessories; and so on.

- *Curate your own style.* You don't need an MBA in fashion merchandising to do a wonderful job promoting collections. There is no wrong way to do this. Assemble your favorite items into a collection, and someone with similar taste will buy them. Base your collections on themes, trends, top eBay products (based on your research), customer favorites, top-viewed items, and bestsellers (that's not the same as customer favorites, which is based on reviews). Collections help buyers find what they want or didn't know that they wanted and give them an exciting and enjoyable shopping experience.

## PROMOTION BY OCCASION

The fancy term for marketing to specific audiences is *customer segmentation*. One way I segment is by using different eBay accounts. For example, I operate an eBay account that has a Store subscription and focuses on upscale fine jewelry. That's only one of ten accounts I'm using. Having themed accounts makes it easier for me to promote listings related to occasions.

eBay sellers don't have to think about their seasonal promotions as far ahead as big-box retailers do. Their logistics are a lot more complex. That said, it's nice to organize and launch merchandise that honors occasions such as Valentine's Day or holidays such as Christmas. I offer gift and presentation boxes at no charge with orders that are likely to be gift items. I also accommodate special requests, the most common being to ship *blind*, which means that the package appears to be coming from the person giving the gift. I also never include prices on my packing slips anyway but always leave the document out upon request.

## CELEBRATING THE SEASON

While seasonal retailing is kissing cousins with promotions by occasion, it is handled slightly differently. In the brick-and-mortar world of big retail business, managers plan a few seasons ahead and make their purchase commitments long before products appear on the sales floor. This advance planning ensures availability of the products that are likely to do well, leading to improved sales, higher availability, and delighted customers. As an eBay seller, you too should get into the habit of formally planning out your seasonal merchandising. Stock up on products in advance and plan two to three seasons ahead. Give your eBay Store a makeover for every season and work some promotional magic that celebrates the holidays.

What makes for stunning and stimulating visual merchandising? You must work hard to be creative, but when you hit a creativity roadblock, look at what's selling in your Store and on eBay, ask questions, and study the trends. Pour over magazines, watch ads, and take field trips to retail stores to harvest ideas.

I'll wrap up this chapter with a few closing tips:

- Develop strategies that highlight promotions, clearance sales, seasonal merchandise, and holidays.
- Appeal to new audiences simply by rearranging existing images on your listings.
- Move merchandise around to stay on trend.
- End (or pause) listings for a set time and relist them later to capture a new audience.
- Retire failed ideas rapidly and accept failure as a necessary ingredient for success.

# Chapter 10

# Masterful Customer Service

Whether you run one auction or a thousand fixed price listings, the customer experience needs to be extraordinary. Expert communication with people requires experience (and intuition), and if you're new to running your own business, you'll make mistakes along the way. Don't be too hard on yourself, because we all do. For the most part, the people you'll encounter are decent and honest, but the occasional bad egg does come along to throw a wrench in your day. Never let those few bad experiences place a dark cloud over your business or affect your positive interactions with your other customers.

Your new and loyal customers are on the prowl for quality stuff, fair prices, and fantastic customer service. Many times, a buyer's first purchase is an audition—a test to see how you perform. An exceptional experience means repeat purchases.

Delivering excellent customer service means having fun and keeping things light and relaxed. Great customer service is rare, and fabulous customer service is memorable. Prompt communication begins with you and is one of the best ways to put a smile on your buyer's face.

## COMMUNICATING ON eBAY

Here are the communication basics—you can skip this section if you've already mastered eBay's messaging system. The messaging system works like most email inbox applications, allowing you to receive and respond to messages. You may archive or delete messages once you're done handling them. If you'd like to contact another eBayer, you know their user ID, but have not yet received a message from them, here's a quick way to accomplish that:

1. Type the URL https://www.ebay.com/usr/user ID and insert the user ID of the person you're messaging.
2. Click Contact.
3. Select "This is not about an item."
4. Click Continue.
5. Compose your message.
6. Add up to ten photos (optional).
7. If you'd like to receive a copy, check the box "Send a copy to my email address."
8. Click Send Message.

While eBay does not disclose individual message limits, there's a limit to how many messages you're allowed to send each day so that eBayers are protected from spammers. I speculate it is directly correlated to your sales volume. Any time you sell an item, you'll see a contact link on the listing. Use this link to recommend additional products you're offering and encourage buyers to add additional purchases into the same shipment.

You can customize the way eBay notifies you about selling and buying activity by clicking on My eBay > Account > Communication Preferences and editing the Seller section. As your business grows, your email inbox will quickly become flooded, and you'll soon want to turn off all the friendly eBay alerts so you can manage your orders in a, well . . . more orderly fashion. Here's how to find your orders in the morass—specifically those that are unpaid sales:

1. Hover over My eBay at the top-right-hand corner of most eBay pages.
2. Click Selling.

## FREE RETURNS—THE PATH TO POWERFUL PROFITS

I don't know any sellers who love returns, but I don't hate them. My return rate is very low and always has been. In my experience, that rate doesn't rise when I offer free returns or extend the returns window. A no-returns policy, on the other hand, does reduce sales, and I've proved repeatedly that offering free returns increases sales. Offering free returns on light items is cheap and a catalyst for greater profits. Just don't offer free returns on bulky or heavy items if the freight costs are significant. You'll regret it.

Also keep in mind that eBay's got your back—sellers who offer free returns can keep up to 50 percent of the selling price if the item comes back in a condition different from when it shipped out.

3. Click the Orders tab.
4. Click the Awaiting Payment filter.

If you don't mind killing trees, you can print a hard copy of this page using the Print link. But go ahead and save a tree by downloading a CSV file using the Download Report link.

The orders shown by the Awaiting Payment filter are unpaid. Volume sellers should bookmark this page and come here daily to check on payment status. Now's a good time to send a gentle payment reminder to your buyer (we'll talk more about dealing with unpaid listings a little later in this chapter). eBay requires buyers to pay for the items they win or commit to buy within four days, and in most cases, I send a payment reminder every day for unpaid items. Click the Send Invoice link under the Actions column (see Figure 10-1 on page 216). If the same buyer ordered multiple items but didn't use eBay's cart feature to place the order, you will need to combine the purchases, figure out the new shipping rate based on the combined weight, and edit the shipping costs. If you forget to combine shipping, the buyer will either complain or pay in disgust and leave you a low DSR for shipping and handling charges. When you send the invoice, make any promised adjustments or discounts.

### TIP

Don't want to lose your place? Right-click on the Send Invoice link (you can do this for any hyperlink) and select the option to open the link in a new tab or window. That way, when you're done sending the invoice, you can close the tab or window and you're right back where you started.

**FIGURE 10–1.** Send invoices for unpaid sales from the Orders tab in your Seller Hub by using this link.

This is also a good time to do a little cross selling! Encourage additional purchases with a friendly message and offer discounts and free shipping by including the new item in the same package as their original purchase. I'll cover cross selling in more detail in a moment.

Offering same-day shipping makes it harder to offer customers a chance to buy additional goods before mailing their purchase. A Top Rated Seller can display a Top Rated Plus seal prominently on their listings if they offer same-day or one-business-day shipping and handling time and 30-day or longer free returns. Unless there's a compelling reason, don't offer same-day handling time. One-day handling gives you a little breathing room to communicate and make product recommendations.

Here are some of my tips for communicating well with your customers on eBay:

- *Respond fast.* Stay connected to your eBay email on your mobile device at all times. This isn't a 9-to-5 job, it's your business, so think like a business owner. The faster you reply, the quicker a sale will occur or you will resolve a customer service issue—and that means more money in the bank.

- *Keep your promises 100 percent of the time; 99 percent isn't good enough.* As a corollary to that rule, only make promises you can keep. No matter how good or bad a situation seems, always tell your customers the truth. Trust is priceless. Use a calendar to follow through on anything you've promised—an online service such as Google Calendar is a reliable tool for staying on top of your many tasks and details.

- *Be helpful and outgoing, and don't act aggressive or be sarcastic.* Jokes, even harmless ones, may be misinterpreted. Remember that eBay is a global marketplace. Many buyers are in another country, and their messages are often automatically translated by eBay. Keep your communication unabbreviated, clear, and friendly.

- *Give your business a personality.* You're not a big-box company, so don't act like one. Small businesses have an advantage over large ones when it comes to their customer service. Boring businesses fail and fun firms flourish.

> **TIP**
>
> Occasionally, buyers will ask you to hold their shipment, but failing to meet your handling time, even at the buyer's request, is an order defect that can hurt your Top Rated Seller status or, even worse, cause eBay to restrict your selling privileges. Communicate with your buyer and offer a few solutions. You can cancel and relist the item with a longer handling time, cancel and relist when they are able to pay, or ship immediately and ask them to put a mail hold on the package with the post office (or shipping carrier).

- *Keep tabs on your regulars.* Know who they are and welcome them when they come back. In my Gmail, I can always search for an eBay user ID and check a buyer's purchase history. I remember repeat customers and lead off the conversation with "Welcome back."

- *Business involves risk.* When a situation goes south, you may have to eat the cost. Forgot to buy the shipping insurance and the candy arrived crushed? Issue the refund quickly. Waiting on a small insurance payment for a damaged product? Refund the customer now and get the insurance money later. Why should they wait? They will appreciate knowing you stand behind your business.

- *Be a great listener.* When someone pitches a fit in an email, respond with empathy and always offer solutions. Let them vent.

- *Avoid the words "can't," "don't," etc.* Always talk about what you can do for your customers.

- *Apologize for your mistakes or any time something doesn't go as planned.* It's that simple.

Customers want to do business with companies that treat them well. Good word about a great company spreads like wildfire to friends, family, and colleagues, while rotten service can end you. Customers have set expectations based on the service they have received from other online sellers, eBay or otherwise.

I can't say this enough. With more than a billion of items for sale on eBay, if you wait for a day to respond to someone's questions, they will have already bought from someone else. If you own a cell phone, you can receive email notifications about eBay questions and respond to them anywhere. An instant response means a greater chance at a sale. With each passing minute, odds are they've already moved on. Timeliness is even more crucial when dealing with existing customers because they've already made a commitment to do business with you.

> **TIP**
>
> You can always contact your buyer from the item listing page, but another quick way to reach out is from the Orders tab within the Seller Hub. Click the pull-down menu from the Actions column and click Contact Buyer.

## THE ART OF CROSS SELLING

Cross selling is an art form that has existed for centuries. If you're a fan of *Aladdin*, you'll remember the lively Agrabah Marketplace where Jasmine and Aladdin first meet. Merchants in similar bazaars all over the world have developed cross-selling skills that have been passed down through the generations. Did they teach this when you were in school? They didn't in mine. You will see videos on YouTube explaining how to hustle. That's just a cheeky way of saying cross selling. I ask and offer, but there is never any pressure involved in my cross-selling approach.

Perhaps the only way to achieve sales growth in your eBay adventure is to encourage more purchases from your existing customers. Big companies are cross-selling you every single day. How many times have you heard a cashier at a fast-food restaurant ask you "Do you want to make that a combo?"—a simple yet effective marketing device that really works.

Try my five time-tested tools for cross selling:

1. *Stalk the buyer.* OK, don't actually stalk your buyer. Your initial cross-selling attempt should occur immediately after the sale and before shipping the order. Click the feedback number next to your buyer's user ID and click on the Received as Buyer tab on their profile (see Figure 10–2 on page 219). While you can't see exactly what items they've purchased, you can click the user IDs of the sellers who

left them feedback and view the type of merchandise they offer. This will give you clues for your next step.

2. *Curate.* Based on your intel and what the buyer purchased from you, curate other items they might be interested in. While it may be tempting to serve up a whole buffet, take a more measured approach. If you have a wide variety of merchandise for sale, focus on related items. In addition to the listing link, include the title

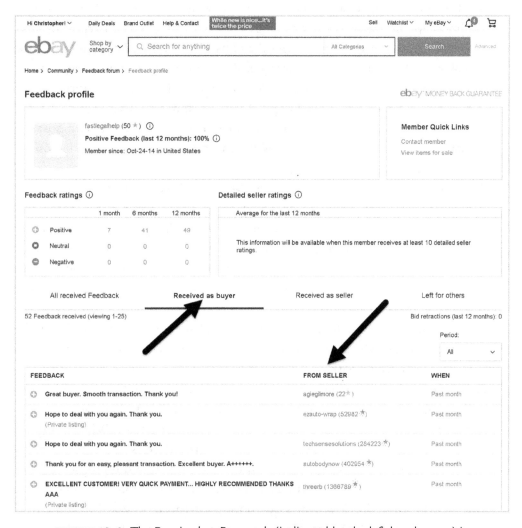

**FIGURE 10–2.** The Received as Buyer tab (indicated by the left-hand arrow) is selected, revealing the most recent sellers who have left feedback for this user. Clicking the user ID for each seller (under the right-hand arrow) and viewing their items for sale provides clues regarding the buyer's interests.

of the item when preparing to send your message (see the next step). If the title sparks interest, they can click on the link to investigate further.

3. *Suggest.* Now it's time to send a message with your product suggestions. Keep your messages brief. According to technology market research firm The Radicati Group, the world exchanged more than 306 billion emails per day in 2020, so weary eyes tend to read short messages and skip over long ones. All communication on eBay must take place on its secure and native messaging system. Prepare a friendly recommendation message sharing what you've curated. Address customers by their first name, and be sure to mention that you handpicked the links for them, indicating how important their business is to you. Add an incentive for making additional purchases before you ship out their current order, such as free shipping on each additional item added to the same shipment. Give them a bit of time to respond—not everyone is glued to their computer 24/7. If you're selling noncommodified products, such as antiques, collectibles, and jewelry, set your handling time to as long as two days to allow for your suggestions to be considered and accepted.

4. *Gift.* Almost everybody loves to receive gifts. Don't you? Cross selling is most effective when customers are happy with their initial purchase. Including a free gift with purchases, while not a guaranteed cross-selling home run, shows that you care about your buyers and helps create customer loyalty. What you give is less important than the sentiment of the gift. A few complimentary reading comics with a large order of collector issues, some locally sourced hard candy, or a little tchotchke such as a key chain are all nice considerations. Gifts should either be relevant to the purchase or simply a treat of some kind. Hannah Yonce, the talented woman who helps with my business, is an eBay seller herself; she sends a pack of bubble gum with each of her orders.

5. *Personalize.* This is in the same vein as including a little gift, but it costs very little. Buy blank note cards in bulk, which are readily available at a very low cost, and include a pleasant thank-you note with each order. While not quite as meaningful as a handwritten note, a printed note is still a nice way to express appreciation. These should only be used if you're shipping a boatload of orders every day. Business cards are very inexpensive nowadays; you can also write your thank-you message on one of those. Resist the temptation to do what every desperate seller has done in the past and ask for feedback. Every buyer receives an automatic reminder from eBay to leave feedback, and a satisfied customer will leave you positive feedback. If you start wheedling for five stars in your thank-you notes, an unhappy customer may leave you not-so-nice feedback instead.

## HANDLING CUSTOMERS WHO HAVEN'T PAID

So you made a sale, but payment hasn't arrived and you're getting nervous or angry? Chill out and think hard. What could be the reason? A broken computer or lost phone? A sudden illness? A family vacation? Did someone forget to pay the internet bill? Don't get testy; instead, be proactive. Within 24 hours of the end of the listing, send a gentle reminder: "Hello, Javiera, thank you for making this purchase, when can I expect to receive your payment?" If payment is still nowhere to be found by the second day, send another polite note: "Javiera, I hope all is going well with you, however, I still have not received your payment for this purchase. Could you please respond to me and let me know your intentions? Thank you." If you're wondering how I knew the buyer's name is Javiera, I can see the full name and address of all my customers by clicking the Order Details link on the item listing page.

Still being ignored? You can enable Preferences for items awaiting payment so that orders that remain unpaid after four days are canceled automatically.

Here's how you configure Preferences for items awaiting payment:

1. Hover over your name in the upper-left-hand corner of most eBay pages.
2. Click Account Settings.
3. Under the Selling section, click Selling Preferences.
4. Click Edit next to Preferences for Items Awaiting Payment.
5. Enable Automatically Cancel Unpaid Items.
6. Select the number of days buyers have to pay for items before eBay automatically cancels them, between four and 30 days.
7. Optionally, enter the user ID of anyone exempt from your unpaid item requirements.
8. Click Save.

Deadbeat bidders can be a drag, but I encourage you to be pragmatic and practical. If the customer wants to cancel the deal, do so without hesitation. The buyer can still return the product under eBay's Money Back Guarantee by trumping up a phony reason for doing so—and you'll end up paying freight both ways. You're much better off canceling the sale and relisting the item.

## HANDLING BUYERS WITH URGENT QUESTIONS

Let's talk about what happens when you have a winning bidder in a fiercely bid-up auction who never asked a question prior to bidding, but now sprays a firehose of questions at you. Even worse, they've already paid, and you must ship within the handling time stated on your listing. They seem dissatisfied with their purchase already, and they haven't even received it yet. Perhaps the underbidder isn't quite as fussy and would love it if you sent them a Second Chance Offer, which allows you to sell the item to the underbidder(s) when the high bid isn't honored or when you have more than one of the same product available. The underbidder pays their original bid price when you send a Second Chance Offer and they accept it.

Here's how to make a Second Chance Offer:

1. Hover over My eBay at the top-right-hand corner of most eBay pages.
2. Click Selling.
3. Click the Listings tab.
4. Click the Ended filter on the left-hand side of the page.
5. Perform a search for the listing or use the pull-down filters to find it.
6. Click the title of the listing to bring up the full listing page.
7. Click Make a Second Chance Offer.
8. Select a duration for the offer between one and seven days.
9. Select the username of each person to whom you wish to send the offer to.
10. Add an optional personal message.
11. Click Send.

You can make as many offers as you have product to sell. Buyers will receive your offer at a Buy It Now price based on how much they bid on the listing. You may send up to 20 Second Chance Offers at one time.

When it comes to dealing with demanding people, try to answer all the buyer's questions honestly and quickly in the friendliest way you can. If you're getting the clear sense you can't satisfy the buyer, then you can ask "Do you want to cancel the order? No hard feelings if you do, I'll be happy to take care of it." If the agreement to cancel is mutual, here is how to cancel an order:

1. Hover over My eBay at the top-right-hand corner of most eBay pages.
2. Click Selling.
3. Click the Orders tab.
4. Click the All Orders filter.
5. Click the pull-down menu under the Actions column.
6. Click Cancel Order.
7. Select Buyer Asked to Cancel the Item(s) in This Order.
8. Click Submit.

Do not select the Out of Stock option or you will suffer an order defect that will adversely affect your eBay account. Remember to send the underbidder a Second Chance Offer as quickly as possible to increase the chances they'll still be interested in buying the item.

## "YOU'RE BANNED FROM THE CLUB!"

You can block difficult customers to avoid having to deal with them again in the future. Here's the process for doing that:

1. Click the Site Map link at the bottom of the homepage (under the section Tools & Apps).

2. Navigate to the section Sell and click Block Bidder/Buyer List under the Sell Activities subsection.

3. Click Manage Blocked Buyer List.

4. Type the buyer's user ID in the text box (you can block up to 5,000 users in total).

5. Click Submit.

If you later decide to unblock a buyer, simply return to the same page and delete the member's user ID from the list. Use CTRL + F to search for their user ID if the list is long.

## HANDLING BUYERS WHO WANT TO RENEGOTIATE

I'm always puzzled when buyers message me "What's the lowest price you'll take for this item?" It's not against eBay policy, but virtually all my fixed price listings have the Best Offer feature enabled. Why not just press it and enter an offer?

That doesn't bother me. What concerns me greatly is the buyer who wins an auction and then decides to haggle before paying—or, even worse, who receives the item and wants to keep it but demands a discount anyway for some vague or off-the-wall reason:

- "The condition wasn't as good as in your pictures." (I don't retouch my eBay photos.)
- "The quality isn't as good as I had expected." (Then why not just return it?)
- "There aren't any batteries, and I had to buy them and they were expensive." (I didn't say batteries were included; I said it worked.)
- "It didn't come with the case." (It's used, and I didn't show a case in my photos.)
- "The color isn't the same as your photos." (Screens vary.)

Sometimes these complaints are just tactics to get a discount. This sort of renegotiation is common among resellers, who intend to turn around and resell the item either in their brick-and-mortar store or online. Major collectors, too, tend to spend more money than they should, so they frequently ask for discounts. When I ask these buyers if they want to return their purchase, the answer is usually "No, I want it, but I think you should give a discount of $X because of the (whatever excuse they are using)."

Sometimes, of course, you should give a discount—for example, if you accidentally overcharged for shipping and they call you out on it, then you owe them a discount to make the buyer whole and bring the shipping charges in line with what you paid.

Any business you run for long enough will have snags along the way. Use your good judgment in deciding how to handle complaints. If you had underbidders, encourage the buyer to return the product. If the value of the item is low (say, $5 to $10), don't risk negative feedback—just refund their purchase price.

Did the buyer threaten you with negative feedback or lousy DSRs? As long as the message was sent to you on eBay, you can probably get feedback removed if you were subject to what eBay calls feedback extortion. The illegal act of feedback extortion involves an attempt to extort merchandise or services that you never promised in the eBay listing, or a demand to return, receive a refund, or another item not promised in the original listing or eBay's Money Back Guarantee. When you become the victim of feedback extortion, end all communication with the buyer and contact eBay.

Here's how to reach eBay support if you're a current eBay seller:

1. Click the Help & Contact at the top of the homepage or most eBay pages.
2. Scroll to the bottom of the page and click Contact Us or Contact Us (depending on your Store level and selling volume, you'll have the option to call or use the chat bot)
3. Follow the instructions, and eBay's support number or chat bot option will appear during eBay's customary support hours (this may vary throughout the year).

While on the subject of feedback, you can't press your customer to give positive feedback, post specific DSRs, or revise feedback in exchange for:

- Receiving the product that they ordered from you (feedback and DSRs are 100 percent optional)
- Providing a refund; whether partial or in full
- Financial compensation
- The shipment of additional merchandise

Buying and selling on eBay is a privilege, not a right. You'll have to stay in the good graces of eBay to continue using the site.

When you're asked to accept an unusual method of payment, be on high alert. Common online scams involve phony cashier's checks and fake money orders. When I started on eBay in 1999, I accepted checks, money orders, and direct credit cards, but eBay allows buyers to pay with a card, a checking account, PayPal, and a plethora of other digital payment methods, which has made mailed in payment options unnecessary. Promptly report suspicious emails to spoof@ebay.com.

## THE FUNDAMENTALS OF FEEDBACK

When you purchase or sell something on eBay, you can leave feedback about the transaction. (If you comment on something unrelated to the transaction, the other person can request that eBay remove it.) Feedback is the heart of the eBay system. It's

---

### EXPLORING SELLING MANAGER PRO

Selling Manager Pro is a subscription eBay service that allows you to manage products, track inventory, store listing templates, generate sales reports, and here's the big one—fully automate feedback for buyers. It's $15.99 per month to add to your account, or free with a Premium or higher eBay Store subscription. Learn more about Selling Manager tools in this way:

1. Click Help & Contact at the top of most eBay pages.

2. Type "selling manager" into the search box.

3. Select a subscription, if desired.

The feedback automation is a time-saving tool that eliminates needless work and improves customer relations. Buyers appreciate positive feedback and many are downright offended if you don't leave one promptly after they pay for their goods. Your Selling Manager Pro subscription will ensure that every buyer receives a positive, customized feedback comment after successful payment is received.

To automate feedback, follow these steps:

1. Hover over My eBay at the top-right-hand corner of most eBay pages.

2. Click Selling.

3. Navigate to the Feedback pane.

4. Click Manage Automated Feedback.

5. From this page, you can edit stored comments and configure automated positive feedback for buyers.

---

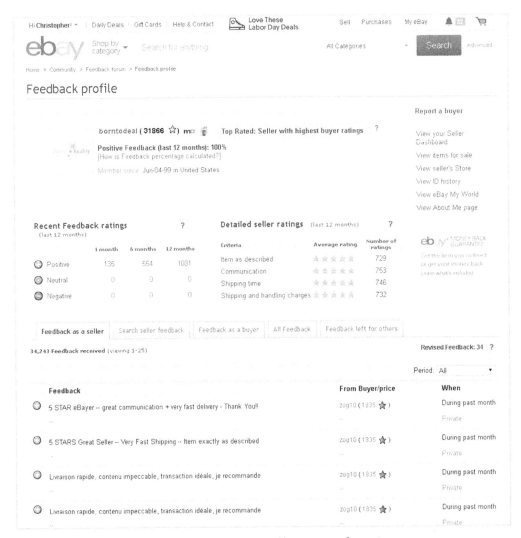

**FIGURE 10–3.** Here's the feedback profile on one of my eBay accounts.
Notice the buyer who commented in French—my sales in 2020
were 81 percent domestic and 19 percent international.

how buyers and sellers get to know one another in a meaningful way. Feedback lets your trading partners know what kind of eBayer you have been in the past and is an indicator of your future behavior. Figure 10–3 above shows the feedback profile on one of my eBay accounts.

Not long ago, sellers could leave negative feedback for buyers, but too many sellers were retaliating against buyers who left them a bad comment. Today, sellers can only leave a positive rating for buyers, but sellers sometimes still use the comment space to go after a buyer.

Although there is some debate among sellers about when you should leave feedback, eBay encourages you to do it as soon as payment is received or has cleared. Some eBay sellers believe you should wait until the buyer has left you feedback, but it's not really a huge deal. I'll talk about it a little more later on in this section.

Sellers can never revise their feedback, but buyers can change negative or neutral feedback to positive at your request. If you were attacked with negative feedback but later entered into a peace accord (e.g., made a refund, fixed the offending issue, etc.), you can ask the buyer to revise their feedback. To do so, you should go to the Site Map at the bottom of most eBay pages, navigate to the Community section, and under the Feedback section, click Request Feedback Revision. Once you request a revision, the buyer has ten days to act on the request before the feedback becomes permanent unless the buyer violates a rule that allows for feedback removal.

In the same Feedback section of the Site Map, there are also links that allow you to make your entire feedback profile private (I have never really understood why this feature is helpful or who would use it), follow up on feedback you left, and reply to feedback received. If a stubborn buyer won't budge, you can get in the last word by posting a reply to their negative feedback comment. Calm and rational responses to bad feedback are viewed as professional and responsible in the eyes of future customers, but unhinged remarks will discourage people from doing business with you.

When I make eBay purchases, I really don't expect seller feedback, but some buyers take great offense if you don't leave a nice comment for them once they've paid. Go ahead and leave positive feedback the minute you receive payment. Some hardheaded sellers insist that the buyer leave them feedback first. I've even received emails from sellers asking me to leave feedback so their automated system will leave one for me. I never do. I think it's kind of rude.

As a personal rule, I never ask an eBay buyer for feedback and I don't think you should, either. That's not to say you should become Silent Bob. It is 100 percent appropriate to message your buyer after tracking shows the parcel was delivered with a friendly message: "Hello Tecoya, I see the package has arrived. I wanted to reach out and make sure the box was undamaged and everything arrived in good condition. Please let me know if you need anything else. I hope you enjoy your new Gorham dinner plates."

There's a well-known saying among eBayers: *If you ask for feedback, you might get feedback you don't want.* What if your customer was just too lazy to return the undersized shirt (oops, did you measure it correctly?) or just didn't want to be mean and mention the hairline crack you missed on the antique teacup (maybe it's time for you to get new glasses)? Pressing for feedback is like poking a stick at a sleeping lion. You might live to regret it.

# Chapter 11

# The Art of Promotion

The eBay site is big. Really massive. There are 1.7 billion listings on the site at any moment. When eBay was a small company, you didn't have to be as knowledgeable about the site in order to make sales. These days, a savvy eBayer will need to navigate more possibilities and learn all the ropes to become a big time seller. eBay has evolved over the years to fit the needs of different kinds of merchants. Useful advertising programs and innovative tools allow skilled sellers an opportunity to sell more. Learn to use them to your advantage and you will thrive on the site. In this chapter, I'm offering you a master class on eBay promotion.

## THE POWER OF PROMOTED LISTINGS

I explained how to add the eBay Promoted Listing feature to an individual listing in Chapter 8 (see Figure 8–31 on page 191). The Promoted Listing feature has become my new normal for securing a prominent spot within the eBay search results (see Figure 11–1 below).

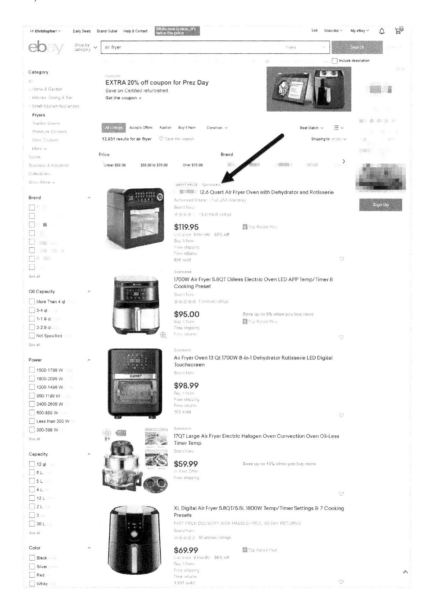

**FIGURE 11–1.** The word "Sponsored" appears above the title of a listing that has employed the Promoted Listing feature. You'll often notice that Promoted Listings have a number indicating how many items have been sold.

Organic listings are those that are not promoted and will appear just below the Promoted Listings in eBay search results. You're only charged for a Promoted Listing when the item sells. While you can always promote individual listings when you create them, you can also skip that step and promote listings in bulk by running campaigns. Here's how:

1. Hover over the My eBay link on the homepage or most eBay pages.
2. Click Selling.
3. Assuming you've already opted into using the Seller Hub (see Chapter 8 on page 194 on how to do that now if you haven't), click Marketing and then click on Dashboard.
4. If you've never been here before, click Create Your First Campaign.
5. You can click Select Listings Individually or click Select Listings in Bulk (I usually do the latter).
6. Now select the eBay categories for the items you want to promote or upload a CSV file with the listings you want to promote. Using CSV files isn't hard, but I usually choose the simpler method of promoting all my listings at one rate or selecting a rate based on the item category.
7. Click Continue.
8. Select the ad rate from the list of possible choices.
9. Click Continue.
10. Provide a name for your campaign, for example "1% Ad Rate."
11. Click Launch.

After creating a Promoted Listings campaign, it will appear immediately, and very rapidly these listings will start to see elevated search action (see Figure 11–2 below).

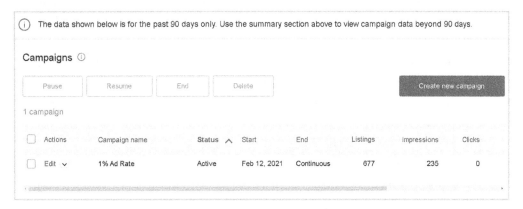

**FIGURE 11–2.** Here's a campaign for Promoted Listings showing a lot of impressions just 30 minutes after I started it.

You'll notice that I've set my ad rate to 1 percent. While eBay has a list of trending ad rates that are usually higher than that, I have discovered that a modest 1 percent will result in healthy additional sales, and I don't even notice the cost. Every seller can afford 1 percent. In one month of my fixed price sales, 44 percent of those sold via Promoted Listings.

Looking at Figure 11-2 on page 231, you'll see that there's an edit option (bottom-left corner). You can always modify your ad rate strategy to:

- Apply the rate that eBay suggests. It's set by eBay (and they don't explain their method) to offer you the optimal balance between ad performance and cost. See Figure 11-3 on page 233.
- Adjust the suggested ad rate by setting it below or above the recommended rate with an optional limit cap preventing you from spending more than your max. Setting a bump above the suggested rate will potentially display your listings more often than your competition.
- Apply a single ad rate. This is useful if you have a fixed ad budget, and for our example, I'm setting the rate at 1 percent, which will do a nice job of promoting your listings at very low cost. Try gradually increasing the rate to see how it improves your sales. I don't know anyone with an unlimited advertising budget, so be practical and spend as much (but not more) than you can afford.

The order details page will indicate when an item was sold via Promoted Listings (see Figure 11-4 on page 233).

eBay's technology determines the listings that are displayed and their placement based on the ad rate  how relevant the listing is to the buyer's search, the listing's quality, and other proprietary factors that eBay keeps a secret.

Here's how the Promoted Listings fees work:

- The seller sets the ad rate between 1 percent and 100 percent of the item's current fixed price. Ad placement probability and display frequency rises when the ad rate is increased.
- eBay's suggested ad rates are calculated  based on factors such as item attributes, seasonality, past performance, and current competition for each of your listings.
- A fee is only charged if the buyer clicks on one of your promoted items and then completes a purchase within 30 days.
- There is never a cost if the item remains unsold.
- The payments tab and seller invoice display the ad fees so that you know how much you've paid.

One last note: if a buyer clicks on your promoted listing, eBay only charges you the ad fee if they buy the item within 30 days of first viewing it.

**FIGURE 11–3.** Modify your Promoted Listings campaign if it doesn't seem to be working for you. Apply eBay's suggested ad rate, adjust the rate, or set a single rate for all the listings in the campaign. Start at 1 percent and see how you do.

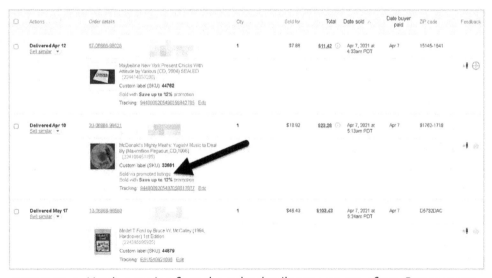

**FIGURE 11–4.** Here's a section from the order details page on one of my eBay accounts. eBay indicates when a sale is attributed to a Promoted Listings campaign.

## MAKING OFFERS TO WATCHERS

It is easy for neophyte entrepreneurs to fall prey to the seemingly invincible fallacy that eBay or other ecommerce businesses are a set it and forget it activity. There aren't any active businesses that offer passive income. If you want to become wealthy, you have to work hard.

There's a discreet Add to Watchlist link in the upper-right-hand corner of every listing for members who are interested in the item but not yet ready to bid. eBay won't tell you who these watchers are, but you can send offers to them. I send offers to members who are watching my fixed price listings on a daily basis, and during busy shopping seasons, I send offers two and sometimes three times a day to ensure all new watchers receive my offers.

Here's how:

1. Hover over the My eBay link at the top of the homepage or most eBay pages.
2. Click the Selling link.
3. Click the Listings tab—Manage Active Listings is the default view.
4. If visible, click the Send Offers—Eligible button under Quick Filters. (If you can't see it, it means you currently have no one watching your listings.)
5. From the filtered results (see Figure 11-5 on page 236), you can send offers on individual listings to watchers or select multiple watched items to send offers in bulk (see Figure 11-6 on page 236).

## OTHER WAYS TO TURN LURKERS INTO BUYERS

Let's say you have a superhot item listed at the maximum retail fixed price. That's OK! It's even better if the listing has multiples of the same item available. People use the watch feature for many different reasons, and often they simply forget about the items on their Watchlist. In some cases, you can prompt a sale to these watchers without sending a formal offer. I'll explain how in a minute. Here are some of the reasons someone would watch a listing:

- They are considering buying it very soon, or they're stalking the auction to snipe it (place their bid at the last moment).
- They are kicking the tires but for some reason aren't ready to commit—perhaps they'd like to see how the auction progresses or if the seller drops the price on a fixed price listing.
- They are evaluating multiple sellers of the same item.
- The item caught their interest, and they're merely admiring it without actually planning to buy.
- They are selling the same or a similar product, and they are monitoring your business to collect intel.

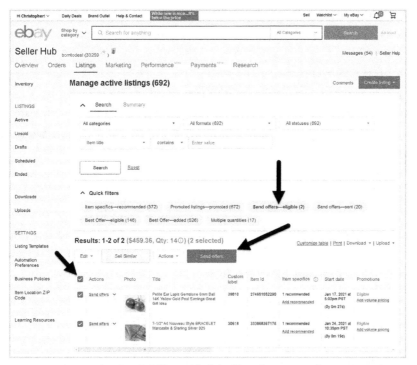

**FIGURE 11–5.** The Send Offers—Eligible filter (top arrow) appears when your fixed price listings have watchers. Select individual listings or all at once (bottom-left arrow) to send out offers (middle arrow).

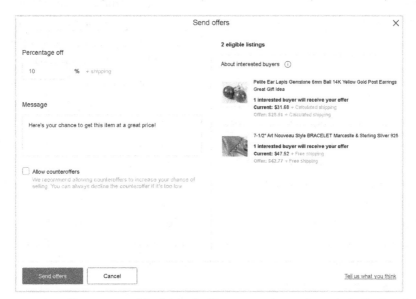

**FIGURE 11–6.** You can send individual offers or, as shown here, in bulk. Sending offers on individual listings (not shown here) lets you enter an offer price or a percentage off. You can include a message and, optionally allow counteroffers.

While it is impossible to know these eBay lurkers' true motives, you can benefit from eBay's marketing systems to trigger their renewed interest and score additional sales. I explained how to send offers to watchers in the previous section, but there are other ways to transform a watcher into a buyer.

All watchers receive persuasive marketing emails from eBay every time a fixed price listing is reduced by at least 5 percent. For popular products with a boatload of watchers, that means eBay becomes your virtual assistant, inviting your secret admirers to consider romancing your merchandise.

As we discussed in Chapter 10, you will spend a fair amount of time answering people's questions about your listings. While most of these questions never result in a sale, each message is an opportunity for you to make an offer. When responding to messages sent from a fixed price listing, the Send an Offer button appears (see Figure 11-7 on page 237). This is available only for fixed price listings, not for auctions.

Here are some tips about making offers:

- You can make an offer to a potential buyer on an item you are selling for the exact asking price on the listing in order to combine that item with an existing order that's already paid for. This is useful because you cannot send a combined invoice for new purchases once the buyer has paid. Let's say, for instance, you've sold several baseball cards to a collector, they paid, but they've discovered another card that interests them. The problem arises if you normally charge shipping on the products you sell and the buyer asks you to combine the additional item with their paid order so they can avoid additional postage. When the buyer messages you from that listing, click Send an Offer for the full price of the additional item, and in the offer message indicate that you will be combining it with the existing order. Once the buyer accepts your offer, send an invoice with the shipping cost set to zero, and instead of printing a new shipping label, simply enter the tracking number from the initial order into the new order.

- It's relatively common for a buyer to ask for gift wrapping or a gift box. This can be a bit awkward because not every seller offers these services and helping out with gift options takes additional time and costs money to keep the supplies on hand. If a buyer messages you before making a purchase with such a request, click Send an Offer for the item price plus the additional cost of the gift wrapping service or gift box. Let's say you're selling a fancy ballpoint pen for $75 and you'd like to ask for an additional $10 to handle the gift wrapping. To cover the additional service, send an offer for $85.

- A seller can retract an offer or counteroffer if the wrong amount was entered, if there are 12 hours or more left before the listing ends, or if the listing is ending in less than 12 hours and you placed your most recent offer less than an hour ago.

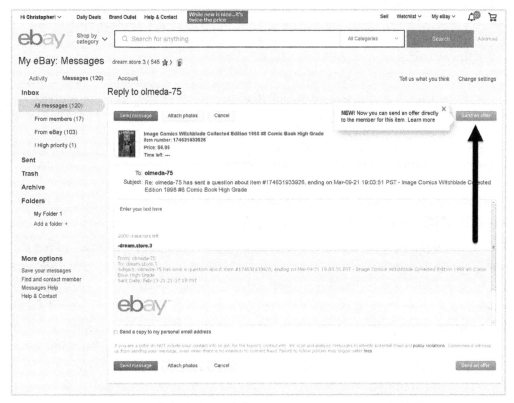

**FIGURE 11–7.** I clicked the reply button on a message I received from a prospective buyer within the eBay messaging system. Note the Send an Offer button at the top right—use this marketing tool to persuade buyers to make a commitment by making an offer they can't refuse.

If you're using the eBay desktop site, here's how to retract an offer or a counteroffer:

1. Go to Bids/Offers in My eBay.
2. Find the offer you'd like to retract.
3. Select Review Offer, then select Retract Offer.

You can also cancel your offer on the item page by selecting Review Offer and then Retract Offer.

To get the most out of the offer process, follow these recommendations:

- Fair offers are the most likely to be accepted.
- Don't take things personally—if you aren't interested in their offer, make a fair and reasonable counteroffer or simply decline with a polite message explaining your position.
- Include a message for the other person.

- Add a message for the seller. You catch more flies with honey than you do with vinegar. Look for the Add Message to Seller option.
- If you're the prospective buyer, then check the listing date. Sellers become more motivated as time marches on.
- For most categories, you can make up to five offers; eBay tallies expired, rejected, and retracted offers against this limit.

Auctions also allow this time of haggling before the auction ends; I'll discuss that in the next section.

## HANDLING OFFERS ON AUCTIONS

If I had a dollar for every message I've received that said "Will you take $XYZ and end the auction early for me?" I'd easily be six figures wealthier. The vultures come out every time they discover I list a juicy find for auction. Informal offer messages are most aggressive when you've listed a rare item at a low starting price, and an expert collector thinks they know something you don't. Every seller I've spoken with who received an informal offer this way and didn't accept it went on to sell the item for a higher price—in some cases much much higher. The Lenci figurine I showed you in Figure 8-1 on page 138 sold for an incredible $17,100 with a starting bid of $100. This isn't necessarily an extreme example, either. I've had many auctions shoot to the stars this way.

I explained how to enable offers on auctions in Chapter 8 and provided Figure 8-28 on page 182 to show where to check the box and enter optional upper and lower limits for automatically accepting or declining offers on auctions.

Now let's talk auction offer tactics. At the time this book went to press, the ability for sellers to enable the Best Offer feature on auctions was very new. I've experimented with the feature and noticed that most buyers think it works the same as for fixed price listings, in that they almost universally make offers below the starting bid. When that occurs, you should decline or counteroffer. Include a polite message informing them that the Best Offer on auctions means they can offer more than the opening bid amount. However, there is nothing stopping you from accepting an offer lower than the opening bid if that's what you want to do. You can also ignore the offer; if not responded to, an offer on an auction will expire automatically after 48 hours. While ignoring an offer might be considered rude, you might consider a lowball offer to be rude. Is tit for tat really that wrong? In lieu of ignoring offers you consider nonsense, consider setting a floor price and have eBay automatically decline offers that fall below it.

Personally, if the item is new to eBay I won't enable offers. I will enable it on the relisting if it doesn't sell the first time around. Any offers received will help guide you toward a starting price on the relisting. Here are some possible ways to approach offers on auctions:

- Accept an offer at or above the starting price.
- Decline the offer and see where the auction price lands.
- Relist the auction with a starting price equal to the highest offer you received when the initial auction was running, and send a message and auction link to everyone who made offers.

Now if you'd rather not waste your valuable time with nonsense offers that fall below your absolute minimum price, you can let eBay decline automatically (see Figure 11-8 below).

Some purists on the eBay Community discussion boards complain that allowing offers on auctions goes against the spirit of the format, but I like the intel it provides—it helps me learn what potential buyers are thinking and how to better set the starting bid when relisting an unsuccessful auction.

## SETTING YOUR PRICES TO SIGNIFY QUALITY

Pricing is a complex topic. Knowing how to set an auction starting price or how much to ask when listing at a fixed price isn't always easy. I've noticed that much older individuals,

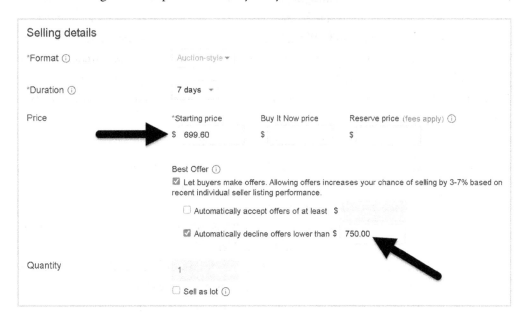

**FIGURE 11-8.** Here, I've listed a very nice Navajo sterling silver and turquoise cuff bracelet and set the opening bid to $699.60 (top arrow). While I'm allowing offers, I've told eBay to automatically decline all offers lower than $750 on my behalf (bottom arrow).

people who received an item as a gift, and those who inherited items are likely to list at a price that's low. The price you paid for something might have no bearing on the value of that item on eBay. Don't be tempted to sell something valuable for a low price or accept a lowball offer on an auction. You may have something really cool on your hands.

The *real value* of a product is what it is worth without any outside expectations from the customer. The *perceived value*, also known as its *intangible value*, is what a customer thinks the product is worth. Take frozen desserts such as Italian ice. This popular treat is made from water, sugar, and flavoring and costs pennies to make (its real value). So it is curious to see prices of $5, $6, and even $7 per pint for purportedly gourmet Italian ices in the freezer section of upscale grocery stores. But that's the perceived value, so shoppers will gladly pay it.

My company manufactures elegant gold and gemstone jewelry that we sell on eBay. All proceeds are used to feed low-income and homeless individuals in my community. I've seen other sellers set their jewelry on a table and snap a few photos. I'm sure they still made sales, but I guarantee you they left money on that table. Nicely presented on jewelry props, the same jewels sparkle more, attract more buyers, and command better prices.

It's human nature to question a low price: "If it looks too good to be true, it probably is!" We have all heard that so many times that we apply it to every situation, even if it's untrue. Certain items especially have ambiguous value, such as antiques, art, and collectibles, so a too-low price raises eyebrows and makes buyers wonder if it's real. Experiment with items that you've listed that gain lots of watchers but few bids, raise the price a little, and see what happens. A price increase may motivate the watchers to take action and buy now for fear the price could go up again.

You'll find spirited debates about this phenomenon on eBay's discussion boards (see Figure 11–9 on page 241).

Here are three recommendations for setting pricing:

1. Remind yourself that eBay is really big—much bigger than you may think. There's probably a buyer out there willing to pay a higher-than-average price from a reliable seller with a great feedback score.
2. Start new to eBay item auctions right where you want them to end up (often mine go much higher; I have many, many examples).
3. If you decide to use fixed price listings for items of intangible value such as antiques, art, and collectibles, set them at prices higher than you'd be willing to pay—you can always drop the price or accept lower offers at a later date.

My closing thought: don't cave in to pressure or worry that your item won't sell. There's always another customer around the corner, and another day to sell your item.

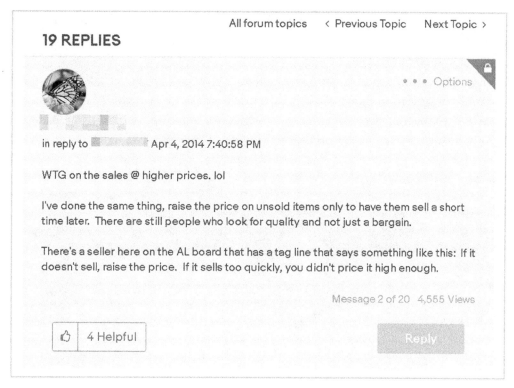

All forum topics    ‹ Previous Topic    Next Topic ›

**19 REPLIES**

••• Options

in reply to          Apr 4, 2014 7:40:58 PM

WTG on the sales @ higher prices. lol

I've done the same thing, raise the price on unsold items only to have them sell a short time later. There are still people who look for quality and not just a bargain.

There's a seller here on the AL board that has a tag line that says something like this: If it doesn't sell, raise the price. If it sells too quickly, you didn't price it high enough.

Message 2 of 20   4,555 Views

👍 | 4 Helpful

Reply

**FIGURE 11–9.** Here's a Community post in which an eBay seller explains the tactic of raising prices to catalyze sales.

## PIMP YOUR PRIDE

This seems truly obvious, but get out and broadcast yourself. Be vocal about what you're doing. Build a team of supporters with family, friends, and strangers. Be careful with social media because it can be a real time suck, so stay focused and use social media to promote your business as opposed to a distraction from it. I have had good success buying inexpensive YouTube ads, but I bid very low on them.

I discussed printing up business cards in Chapter 4. They don't need to be fancy, so design them yourself. A business card is just a way to rapidly convey to someone your name, number, email address, and eBay user ID. Consider adding a QR code that brings up your eBay listings or Store page ID, especially when meeting someone new.

I have other ideas, too, and while I write books to help people succeed in this business, I do want to keep a competitive advantage. I will say I've discovered a few wonderful groups on social media platforms where folks are literally giving valuable items away that have merit and can be sold on eBay. Use social media to start conversations and interact with others to help advertise and promote your business.

Paid ads can be expensive, but posting comments on other posts and within groups is a free way to gain views and interest. When using social media, be consistent, focus the message, and interact often.

My eBay Store consigns products and accepts donations on behalf of the local nonprofit organizations I help. To help publicize this fact, I have included it on my seller profile. You can find yours at https://www.ebay.com/usr/(your user ID). For example: https://www.ebay.com/usr/borntodeal (see Figure 11–10 below).

**FIGURE 11–10.** Click the Edit Profile button (indicated by the left-hand arrow) to change your profile. There are some pretty tight restrictions on what you can post on your profile, but you can mention, as I do, that you're open for new business opportunities (right arrow).

Here's what's allowed and what's not allowed on your eBay profile:

**Allowed:**
- Sharing information about yourself
- Showing off the items you're selling
- Featuring the feedback you've received
- Developing eBay collections of items you adore to show off to other eBayers
- Discussing your hobbies and interests

**Not allowed:**
- Trying to sell items outside of eBay
- Your contact details (you'll notice in Figure 11–10 above, I said "Message us . . ." but did not include contact information)
- Nudity or adult material

- Profanity or offensive stuff
- Irrelevant or rude comments about other users or listings
- Promoting products or services that are not allowed on eBay
- Violations of eBay's other listing policies

Take advantage of the opportunity to add branding to your profile by experimenting with graphics or having someone else help you make them. Then add these graphics and your promotional text to your profile by clicking the Edit Profile link, as shown in Figure 11–10 on page 242.

Here's a roundup of other ideas for promoting yourself and your business:

- Remember that everyone's a potential buyer and supplier to your business, so tell everyone what you do, when it is appropriate.
- Post a flier on bulletin boards anywhere you can find one. Remember that people use their phones to capture information, so don't waste time on those little tear-offs at the bottom, as we used to do in the days of horse-drawn wagons.
- Run loss leaders such as penny auctions to generate excitement and share the links with family, friends, colleagues, and even strangers, if appropriate.
- Whether or not you attend church, community churches as well as local nonprofits often need help selling donated items, and many will gladly turn over these items to you if you offer to sell them for a fee. One of my largest consignment accounts is the Kids' Community Dental Clinic in Burbank. The clinic receives thousands of donations of high-quality merchandise every year that we sell for them. Everyone wins!

## QUID PRO QUO

Quid pro quo is a Latin phrase meaning "a favor for a favor." In Japan, a keiretsu is a group of companies with interlocking business relationships. Big corporations around the world have a long history of robust cross-promotion; movie tie-ins are one great example.

You can start your very own keiretsu by cross-pollinating with other noncompeting eBay sellers. Let's say you sell clothes but not belts, and you know a really high-quality belt retailer on eBay. You can work out a link exchange with the other seller to refer business to each other. While it is against the rules to link off eBay, it is absolutely fine to link within eBay.

Forge alliances and build bridges. Work out deals with other eBay sellers to add links from your listings to their Stores if they do the same for your Store—and if their products are complementary but not competitive with yours.

If you run a website, promote your keiretsu friends using eBay Partner Network affiliate links so you can earn some extra money from the referral, and ask them to do the same for you. You can use email links, but you must apply for permission from the Partner Network before doing so.

What about purchasing? If you buy new goods, develop a regional cooperative to increase your buying power and score greater product discounts. This works best if your co-op partners don't sell on eBay and instead have a physical store or other online channels.

Scratching each other's backs should be simple, not complicated. Businesspeople routinely seek partners with complementary capabilities to gain access to new opportunities, reduce costs, and accelerate success. Test out partnerships, and be adventurous in the testing.

## RUNNING A BRANDED eBAY STORE

You'll notice some eBay sellers have a little blue door icon next to their feedback score in search results and on their profile page—this signals that they have an eBay Store (shown in Figure 11–11 on page 245). Stores provide a branded shopping experience, additional free listings, free packing supplies, and free business management tools.

Scan the QR code in Figure 11–12 on page 245 to see the latest Store selling fees, including the monthly subscription cost associated with each tier of eBay Store subscription and the final value fees for Store subscribers.

In my opinion, sellers should consider opening a Store when they can consistently maintain at least 100 listings at a time. The Store level that's right for you depends on your listed item volume. While a Starter Store supplies 250 zero insertion fee listings per month for either auction or fixed price formats, all other levels provide a mixed allocation of auction and fixed price listings at no additional cost. You can see details of the zero insertion fee listings by scanning the QR code. The allocations are use them or lose them. You have to use them up in the calendar month, and they do not roll over into the next month.

Just as you suspected, there's a catch. While the zero insertion fee fixed price listings are valid in any category, the complimentary auction listings are only valid in these categories:

- Antiques
- Art
- Clothing, Shoes, & Accessories
- Coins & Paper Money
- Collectibles
- Dolls & Bears

**FIGURE 11–11.** These search results show the eBay Store blue door icon. There are five levels of eBay Stores, in order from least expensive to highest: Starter, Basic, Premium, Anchor, and Enterprise. A higher monthly fee gets you more freebies and better discounts on final value fees.

**FIGURE 11–12.** Use this QR code to see eBay's monthly Store subscription and final value fees.

- Entertainment Memorabilia
- Health & Beauty
- Jewelry & Watches
- Pottery & Glass
- Sports Memorabilia, Fan Shop, & Sports Cards
- Stamps
- Toys & Hobbies

Follow these steps to launch a Store subscription:

1. Hover over My eBay at the top-right-hand corner of most eBay pages.
2. Click Summary.
3. Click Account.
4. Under the section Selling, click Subscriptions.
5. Click Choose a Store.
6. Click Select and Review under the desired Store subscription level.
7. Select either a yearly or monthly subscription option (I recommend starting with monthly until such time as you are ready to make a long-term commitment).

8. Enter your Store name.

9. Click Submit Order.

The eBay Store dashboard has all sorts of cool features. Follow these steps to navigate to your Store management page:

1. Hover over My eBay at the top-right-hand corner of most eBay pages.

2. Click Selling.

3. Scroll down to the Selling Tools pane.

4. Click Manage Store.

You're now at the Manage My Store page, where you can design, manage, and market your Store and promote your listings. From here you can do the following:

## Users and Permissions

Extend Store management permissions to trusted individuals (and revoke permissions at will). To grant access, click Permissions under the Store Summary subheading. Key in their name, email address, and permission level. There's also an activity log for transparency and accountability.

## Store Categories

Build Store categories as an additional way to organize and present merchandise within your Store. You can make up to 300, which don't have to mirror eBay's categories in any way. Assign the Store category at the time you list your item. If you don't create custom Store categories, your Store will use eBay's categories instead (see Figure 11–13 on page 247). Click the Store Categories link in the Store Design section of the left-hand menu. Assign up to two Store categories when you list items or add your new Store categories to existing listings by revising them.

## Branding Your eBay Store

Make it your own by branding your eBay Store. Starting from Manage My Store, click Edit Store. This is where you can edit your Store name and description, then upload branding. eBay supports custom billboards, just like social media profiles. Make a 1200-by-270-pixel billboard or hire someone to do it (I hire freelancers at Fiverr), and upload your logo. The logo should be at least 300 by 300 pixels; make sure it's square or it will look distorted.

## Featured Items

Extol the virtues of your best items by featuring up to four of them on your Store's landing page. Then sort and display the remainder of your listings any way you prefer. I

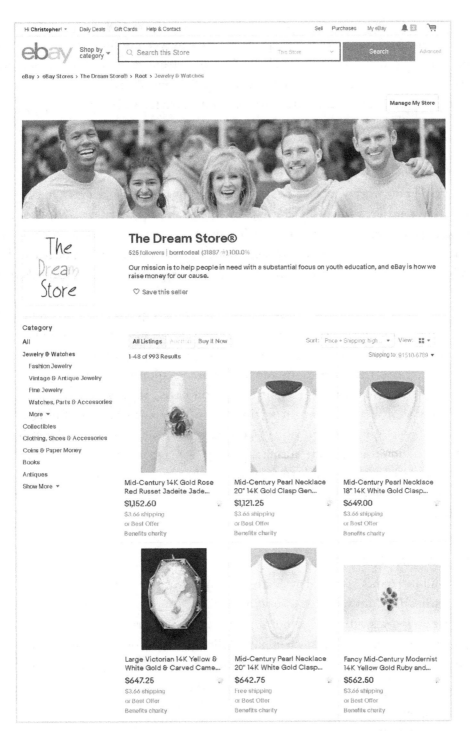

**FIGURE 11–13.** Here's the Dream Store®, an eBay Store I set up for a cause near and dear to me. You'll notice I do not use custom categories, so the standard eBay categories show up on the left-hand side of the Store.

like showing the big-ticket items upfront, and I believe a gallery of images puts my best foot forward. You can make changes to your Store in seconds. Sign in and go to your Store following the instructions on page 246 for getting to your Store management page. Click Edit Store in the section titled Set Up, Sell, and Track, and on the next page, click the "+" under the Featured Items section and search for and select listings you want to feature on your Store's homepage.

## Time Away and Automatic Response

Let people know when you're away by turning on the out of office message when you can't answer emails, such as on sick days or when you're on vacation. When someone messages you during this time, eBay will send an automatic response. Include your return date and, if desired, an emergency phone number where you can be reached. To configure this feature, hover over My eBay, click Messages, then click Change Settings (see Figure 11–14 on page 249).

From the next screen, you can tweak your inbox settings, add a signature, upload a Store logo to include on message replies (which is a smart branding idea), and then set up time away and automatic response (see Figure 11–15 on page 249).

You can use the time away and automatic response features separately or together. Click Time Away (see Figure 11–16 on page 250) if you're taking a break from selling for a sick day or on a trip that will prevent you from filling orders. Automatic response (see Figure 11–17 on page 250) can be used as a stand-alone feature to send an important automatic reply message, such as an explanation of how to find order help, a link to frequently asked questions, or a message telling customers how quickly you'll respond. Both features allow you to enter start and end dates.

## Promotions Manager

Deals and discounts attract new customers and create opportunities for cross-sells and upsells. Build up some inventory in your Store and then wow eBay buyers with some sizzling deals with the Promotions Manager. To get there, click My eBay at the top of the homepage or most eBay pages, click Selling, hover over Marketing, and then click Promotions. This simple tool provides you with five types of promotions:

1. Order discount
2. Shipping discount
3. Volume pricing
4. Codeless coupon
5. Sale event with a markdown

**FIGURE 11–14.** From eBay's Messages inbox, click Change Settings
to configure the time away and automatic response features.

**FIGURE 11–15.** Here's the Change Settings screen from your Messages inbox.
Click the Let's Go button to configure time away and automatic response.

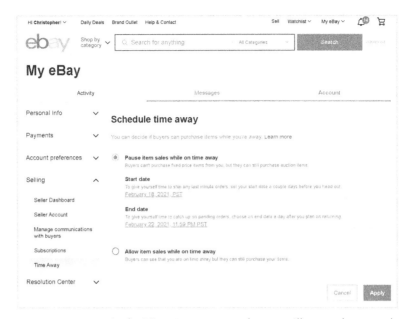

**FIGURE 11–16.** Here's the Time Away page, where you'll enter the start date and end date of your time off from selling. Time away won't prevent bids on your auctions, but you can opt to prevent buyers from purchasing your fixed price listings.

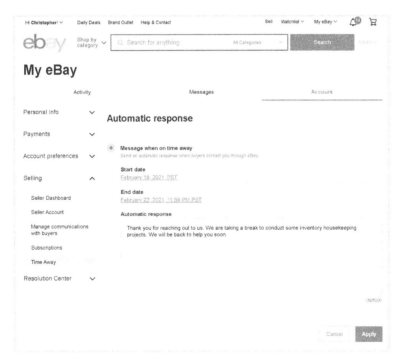

**FIGURE 11–17.** On the Automatic Response page, set the start date and end date and enter your automatic response message—or use eBay's default message, shown here.

## CHANGING HANDLING TIME

Instead of setting time away and choosing to prevent buyers from purchasing your fixed price listings, you can increase your handling time in bulk using the Mass Editor tool. This tool permits you to change multiple listings, even hundreds of them, quickly and easily. Here's how you access Mass Editor:

1. Hover over My eBay at the top-right-hand corner of most eBay pages.

2. Click Selling.

3. Click the Listings tab.

4. Apply the Active filter.

5. Either tick the check box next to the listings you'd like to edit, click the Edit button, and then click Edit Selected, or click Edit without selecting any listings and choose which group of listings you'd like to edit (up to 500 at a time).

6. Make the desired changes to your listings—handling time can be set to same day or up to 30 days after the order is placed.

7. Press Submit Changes to deploy the changes you made.

Remember to revert your handling time back to the usual number of days after your return to work. Changing the handling time won't apply to orders that were placed prior to editing active listings. Although you can remain a Top Rated Seller when you lengthen your handling time, a Top Rated Plus seal will only appear on listings with a handling time of same or one-business day. Be realistic with your handling time. It seems like you would really annoy customers if they had to wait for an extended period of time to receive their purchase. Long handling times would only make sense if you're selling something custom-made that warranted such a wait.

Use promotions to generate retail excitement by launching a sale event. Some people find sales simply irresistible!

You'll notice when adding a new listing that the volume pricing feature is available for that individual listing. The volume pricing option within the Promotions Manager, however, is applied to multiple listings based on your criteria. Choose items from your live inventory or set rules using categories and filters; the latter option will also include future listings that meet the same rules.

## Listing Frame

Brand each listing with the listing frame, a free optional section that can be placed below the item specifics area on your listings and that is only available to Store sellers. It's an all-or-nothing situation because the listing frame will be applied to all your listings.

The listing frame has a variety of options, but you should keep it clean and simple. Buyers should be focusing on the item, so you don't want to overload their visual senses and distract them. Tinker with the listing frame until it looks just right. Like cream and sugar in your coffee—not too much and not too little. Access the listing frame setup by clicking the Manage Promotions link under the heading Item Promotion.

## Email Marketing

This feature is available exclusively to eBay Store sellers, who can manage mailing lists consisting of attentive, interested buyers. We're not talking about spammy lists you buy from a broker; these are eBay users who specifically asked to receive your emails. Buyers are prompted to sign up for email newsletters when they save you as a seller. Building mailing lists is a cornerstone of every customer-centric business in the world. The free email allocation depends on your Store level (see Figure 11–18 on page 253), and there's a tiny cost beyond that.

There are a few rules and your emails can't include:

- Deals that occur outside of eBay
- Phone numbers or email addresses
- Links or images that divert business off eBay
- More than 100 HTML tags
- Active scripting, such as JavaScript

My first subscriber joined my mailing list in 2004 and has remained with me ever since—now that's loyalty! You can use eBay's turnkey templates or design your own layout.

You can also limit emails to buyers who have made purchases recently, while excluding the idle subscribers who haven't bought in a while. Access email marketing for Store sellers by clicking the Email Marketing link under the heading Store Marketing. Learn the ropes there and start sending!

| Store Type | Monthly Free Email Allocation | Additional Cost Per Recipient (over allocation) |
|:---:|:---:|:---:|
| Basic | 5,000 | 1 cent per email |
| Premium | 7,500 | 1 cent per email |
| Anchor | 10,000 | 1 cent per email |

**FIGURE 11–18.** You'll receive free emails with your Store that you can send to buyers who sign up for your Store mailing lists. You can create a master list or add sub-lists based on buying interests.

Here are some additional features you'll fall in love with that are included with Stores:

- Expanded and more sophisticated price research powered by Terapeak, eBay's product research tool that's provided at no additional cost
- Unlimited insertion fee credits for successful auctions
- Discounts of up to 50 percent off final value fees
- Free shipping supplies: $25 worth per quarter for Basic Store subscriptions, and $50 worth per quarter for Premium Store subscriptions
- Discounts on business services

Anchor Store subscribers (that's me) score these additional VIP luxuries:

- White-glove customer support
- Deeper insertion fee discounts
- $150 worth per quarter of free shipping supplies
- $25 worth per quarter of free Promoted Listings

Everyone who lists in volume should sign up for a Store—you'll save money on insertion fees and final value fees, and you will receive the red-carpet treatment in so many other ways. As an eBay VIP, your listings will be marketed to more buyers and you will see the result in your increased sales. Go for the month-to-month deal at first. You can always upgrade your subscription later, but downgrading or ending an annual Store contract involves early termination fees, so take it slow when you're just starting out.

# Chapter 12

# Organizing and Storing

Keeping track of a large inventory can be a daunting task, so you'll want to get an early start on inventory management. Don't wait until you grow. Your inventory will expand quickly because you'll see money coming in and you'll want to make more, right? When you're just getting started is the ideal moment to consider how you'll handle organizing and storing your inventory, not later on down the road when things become chaotic and items are hard to find. It is far easier to work with a well-thought-out system from the start.

I am very regimented and orderly when it comes to my inventory. Not just because I was in the Navy for eight joyous years, but because I'm terrified by chaos and the possibility that I'm going to misplace something and have to face a very unhappy or even hostile customer.

I think of space very three-dimensionally, and I use every cubic foot of my storage space. I also consider the fragility, mass, and sales velocity of items when storing merchandise (see Figure 12–1 below).

| What It Is | How I Store It |
| --- | --- |
| Small, durable, low-to-moderate-value items | Stored in bins, on shelves that are at eye level or at a height that doesn't require a lot of bending or reaching |
| Breakable | Wrapped in protective layers, such as bubble wrap, then boxed and sealed and stored on low shelves—an item that can't fall far won't break |
| Temperature- and moisture-sensitive items; e.g., comics, magazines, fragrances, vintage VHS tapes, leather goods, etc. | Kept in an HVAC-controlled space, with more delicate items stored in rigid containers, or, in the case of comics, specially made plastic storage containers, such as those made by BCW |
| Bulky but very light items; e.g., quilts, sleeping bags, etc. | Stored on top shelves, as long as injury isn't a possibility if the item falls on someone |
| Clothing | Stored folded, if folding won't hurt the garments; otherwise, use rolling racks and hangers—be sure to run a fan in the room to prevent moths from eating into wool fabrics (immediately use a room fogger if you ever see a moth, and use a fogger based on pyrethrins, which are safe enough—they are used in organic farming) |
| Shoes | These can go immediately into a Priority Mail shoebox, ready for shipping, with the SKU marked on the box; dress shoes should be protected from contacting each other, so bag them individually first |
| Electronics | Prepacked so it's ready to ship but won't be damaged sitting on a shelf; ideally stored at a level where bending or reaching isn't required |
| Everything else | Use common sense—protect, reinforce, and, when necessary, prepack to prevent even a tiny possibility of damage during storage |

FIGURE 12–1. This table explains my merchandise storage plan. Fast-moving products should be stored within easy reach; place slower-moving items on high or low shelves or tuck them into any available space. Make sure your stock isn't vulnerable to curious or careless roommates, family, friends, etc.

For the not-so-heavy stuff, I use Sterilite brand plastic shelving units, which are affordable and readily available. Major hardware stores have their own version of these, which come in five-shelf units. For heavier items, use a metal shelving unit. Commercial steel shelving is surprisingly affordable, easy to assemble, and holds hundreds of pounds per shelf.

I'm also a fan of Sterilite's plastic storage containers. They conveniently form a system with the shelving unit, with lidded containers that fit precisely on the shelves (see Figure 12–2 below).

**FIGURE 12–2.** Here's one shelf of a five-shelf Sterilite system in my warehouse. I use my Dymo label printer to generate bar code labels, which allow me to scan and rapidly update my management software. The bin numbers include the shelf number, so my team and I always know where we should return the bin once we're finished with it. Notice that the bins on the top shelf are spaced out a bit so I can sneak more items in between. We call this playing Tetris.

You can create a custom label in your item listing to help with inventory management, as I explained in Chapter 8 on pages 175 and 176. I enter two pieces of data for every item I list: the item location and the item SKU. Here is an example of one of my custom labels: 42/14225. The number "42" is the shelf number, and "14225" is the SKU. If the item is stored in a bin, I can also add the bin number to this label, like this: 42/1/14225, which indicates that the item with SKU 14225 is stored inside bin 1 on shelf 42. You can use any format you like: 42/1*14225, or maybe 14225-42-1, or anything else that suits your fancy. I use a sequential SKU numbering system because I mostly sell unique and one-off merchandise. Major retailers have spent a good deal of time developing their own methods, and in some cases the SKU includes information about the type of product, including color, gender, etc. For example, a clothing seller might use something like M-K-PUR-S-XL-001, which would indicate a men's (M) knit (K) purple (PUR) shirt (S) size (XL) and item number (001). Whatever works well for you is the best system—there are no hard-and-fast rules.

The SKU has a one-to-one relationship with a particular product. When I sell size large shirts in different colors, each color in size large has a unique SKU. A large red shirt would have a different SKU than a medium red shirt, and so forth. When I buy more inventory of those shirts, I use the same SKUs that match those colors/sizes so I can save time and just click the relist button.

## KEEPING OUT CRITTERS AND DUST BUNNIES

All items should be stored to avoid pests and dust—use trash bags for large items and plastic bags for smaller merchandise. Most of my inventory is stored in reusable, resealable Ziploc brand bags, ranging from sandwich size all the way up to two-gallon capacity. I discussed my reasons for using Ziploc in Chapter 8. If all you ever buy is store brand, that's OK, but try Ziploc and you will immediately see the difference. The plastic is thicker, and the closure seals better. Bags keep air, dust, and critters out of your stored merchandise.

A bug-free environment is hard to maintain. Even weatherstripping won't keep out every pest. I routinely use Hot Shot brand foggers in my warehouse and storage facilities, and the dead insects just litter the floor after each fumigation. I prefer Hot Shot foggers because they contain tetramethrin and cypermethrin, which are insecticides in the pyrethroid family—proven chemicals that, when used properly, are safe for humans. Hot Shot foggers are found online or in retail hardware stores. Do not use foggers in any space that is occupied by cats, even if you remove them while the foggers are being used. Pyrethroid insecticides are toxic to cats.

Expensive wool and natural fiber clothing is vulnerable to the larvae (caterpillars) of the clothing moth. They derive nourishment from clothing—wool in particular, but many other natural fibers as well. If you see even one clothing moth, you must fog immediately. A flying clothing moth means the larvae have already been dining on your inventory. A holey suit, while sounding very spiritual, has a substantially reduced value. Maintain expensive suits and pricey garments made from natural fibers in a well-controlled space. Use mothballs to prevent infestations and place thick, construction-grade trash bags over luxury garments—cutting a slit at the top to allow the hanger to poke through. Then tape up the top and twist and tie the bottom to keep unwanted visitors out.

If you're on a tight budget, reuse shopping bags and reclaimed twist ties to seal them up. Ask friends and neighbors to save unwanted bags for you as well. Psst! Ask those same folks to save clean packing peanuts and bubble wrap, too. Make sure they don't have holes by testing that they are airtight.

## ABATING THE ELEMENTS

Another important storage consideration is the sun. Make certain nothing you store near a window or expose to natural light is vulnerable to fading. I once foolishly placed a clothing rack next to a window, and within a very short time, I had a rack of worthless, sun-bleached garments. A loss of inventory due to negligence can be very costly, and as your inventory grows, consider strong and comprehensive measures to abate the elements. As you grow, you may hire experienced consultants to work with you on the issue, but in the meantime, use common sense and think through the elements' effects on your products.

Clothing can be stored in a warehouse without an HVAC system, because cold and heat generally don't cause problems there. Leather goods need a certain degree of humidity, or they'll dry out and become worthless. Excess humidity will also damage certain merchandise; for example, product labels peel off, mold and mildew form on the pages of books, the glue and finishes on wooden items degrade, and a plethora of other issues occur from too much moisture in the air. Fragrances must be kept within a temperature range set by the perfumer, so you must store them in a climate-controlled space. And certain goods, such as snow globes, must be protected from freezing.

The elements can rapidly transform valuable inventory into worthless inventory, so take good care to think these details through. However, merchandise generally does not need the same comfort as a human being. While it may be uncomfortable for you to work in an 85-degree warehouse, most of your items will be just fine at that temperature—but they won't do so well in a 110-degree space. The same is true of the cold. As long as the temperature is above freezing (32°F, 0°C), most products will handle the cold just fine.

Whether you're using a garage or a big warehouse for storage, think through the requirements of what you're selling and protect it from the elements.

## SECURITY AND INVENTORY CONTROL

This may come as a surprise to you, but not everyone is honest. Warehouse security is very important to your business. Even if your warehouse is a spare bedroom or a closet, when other people have access to the space, it's important to keep close control over your merchandise. Every environment is different, so there is no one-size-fits-all approach to protect your business from *shrinkage*—the loss of inventory through employee theft, administrative error, vendor fraud, damage, and, if you own a brick-and-mortar store, shoplifting.

People are also very curious. Virtually everything in my office is a project of some sort, and more often than not, if I have a visitor, they pick up something without asking. They might break it or walk out with it.

If it's breakable, pack it up. If it's valuable, lock it up. If you have a lot of uncontrolled foot traffic where you store goods (e.g., your home or a shared office), use locking cabinets or chests. For small, high-value items, buy a safe. I have two of them.

Ask yourself "What do I have to lose?" Do you need a $5,000 remote monitoring security system to protect your $500 plush inventory from a possible break-in? No. If your investment in your inventory is modest and you work at home, just tuck the merchandise away in a bin that you store out of sight somewhere—in your bedroom closet or under your bed. A large plastic footlocker is cheap and has holes for padlocks— buy one and lock it up. If you run a large warehouse, you probably already know how to protect inventory from shrinkage. Physical security is just as important in that case as electronic surveillance.

Inventory control should be fast, easy, and efficient. I've been using a computer to manage my inventory since 1988, when I started my first corporation, but whatever system works for you is the best system. I have seen people use card files to manage their inventory with great efficiency. If you are the only person handling inventory, and if you run a tightly organized system, you can forgo the inventory checks. If you have workers helping you, you should conduct periodic counts on a frequency of your choosing. Checking inventory against your list should be done by someone other than the worker who picks, packs, and ships. If you have 52 shelves of merchandise storage, then check one shelf per week; if you have 100, then check two each week, and so forth. Some companies conduct a full inventory every few months, which makes sense if you have the funds to pay for it and if you have high employee turnover or other factors that warrant the frequency.

I'll wrap up this chapter by saying that I didn't always give sufficient focus to organizing and storing my inventory. The numbers are staggering now, and as I write these words, there are over 20 thousand items in my warehouse. But thanks to my inventory management systems, it is extremely rare that an item goes missing. I only counted two items unaccounted for in one year, and that's pretty darn good.

# Chapter 13

# Pick, Pack, and Ship

discussed shipping options in Chapter 8 extensively. See Figure 8–30 on page 187 for a rundown on enabling the desired shipping service on the eBay listing form, but here's a quick list of key points that explain my shipping strategy service options.

- Offer local pickup for heavy or bulky products.

- Ship items under 1 pound by USPS First-Class Package.

- Ship items that weigh between 1 and 4 pounds by USPS Priority Mail.

- Items over 4 pounds should be shipped FedEx Ground or FedEx Home.

- Cross-border shipments up to 4 pounds should be sent via eBay international standard delivery or USPS First-Class Package International Service.
- Cross-border shipments of more than 4 pounds should be shipped USPS Priority Mail International or Priority Mail Express International.
- Request a trucking quote for pallets or really heavy items at Freightquote (https://www.freightquote.com).
- Add insurance to high-value items, and self-insure low-value items.

In this chapter, I'll walk you through more details on how to make smart shipping decisions that will get your products safely in the hands of your customers.

## SOURCING SHIPPING SUPPLIES

You can obtain free Priority Mail and Express Mail shipping boxes and envelopes of various sizes from the USPS for domestic and international parcels. Be sure to study the USPS flat-rate mailing program. You can score substantial savings on flat-rate shipments of up to 70 pounds. What you ship must fit in the flat-rate envelope or box. No weighing is required. FedEx and UPS also offer free packing materials for expedited services, but not for ground shipments.

Now that you own your own business and you must analyze every purchase to ensure you're getting the best possible price, be frugal. Find a reliable used postal scale on eBay or at a yard sale to avoid buying an expensive new one. Conduct diligent price research and shop around for supplies and equipment. Buying bubble wrap, tape, padded mailers, and shipping boxes on eBay may still be cheaper than buying them from a local packing supplies distributor. You should treat yourself to a nice tape dispenser because it will be in use for a very long time. I buy my bubble wrap on eBay but my cartons locally. I prefer to buy online if I can to save time and money. Pay vendors in cash if you get a substantial discount for it, and buy any items you use frequently in volume to get the best price possible. And remember: being frugal does not necessarily mean settling for a generic or inferior product.

Buying in bulk saves money, and you can purchase fewer sizes of boxes by using a box reducer (see Figure 13–1 on page 263) to rapidly adjust the depth of a box. This has two additional benefits: postage is sometimes lower, and less void fill is required.

Recycling saves you money and helps the earth, so give clean, reusable shipping cartons a second life. You can also reuse bubble wrap, foam peanuts,

> **TIP**
>
> eBay Store subscribers receive a supply of free eBay-branded shipping supplies (boxes, tape, etc.) based on their subscription level. Go to https://www.ebay.com/stores to learn more.

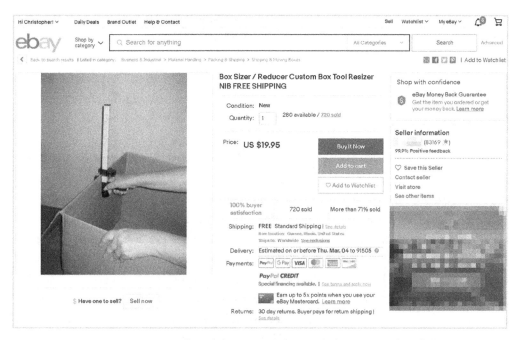

**FIGURE 13–1.** A box reducer is an essential shipping tool and can save you a tremendous amount of money over time.

and clean packing paper. A document shredder provides endless free void fill. Use construction-quality, heavy-duty plastic trash bags to wrap up delicate clothing or important area rugs. They save space, weigh virtually nothing, are waterproof, and resist cuts and tears. You can also sign up for the Buy Nothing Project, a hyper-local gift economy initiative, by visiting https://buynothingproject.org/find-a-group/, and ask members to save and give you packing supplies for your eBay business. The point to all this is to be creative and frugal in sourcing the shipping supplies you'll be using in your business.

## SELECTING THE RIGHT SHIPPING SERVICE

You can use any shipping carrier you choose as long as you promptly upload the tracking information. When you print a label from eBay, they retain the tracking number automatically. Tracking for eBay must include:

- A delivery status of "delivered"
- The date of delivery
- The recipient's address, which matches the one shown on the order details page
- Signature confirmation if an order has a total cost of $750 or more

Use USPS Registered Mail when sending valuable or irreplaceable items. It costs a bit more and requires a few minutes of extra paperwork, but is an excellent solution for jewelry, gold bullion, and priceless art. The additional security associated with Registered Mail means it's a tad slower than regular mail. FedEx, DHL, and UPS also offer international shipping, but I prefer eBay international standard delivery or USPS for international parcels. These methods are cheaper and the customs forms are less complex.

When shipping across borders, you must fill out a customs declaration form that describes and declares the value of the contents. Because this form goes outside the box, don't inform the world what's inside is an expensive watch or a high-end handbag—perhaps instead write "souvenir." Try terms like "used clothing," "grooming item," or "health and wellness product" rather than mentioning expensive brand names. But don't underreport the item's value so your buyer can save money on import fees and taxes. Remember: you are solely responsible for delivering the product in good condition. Lost, stolen, or crushed packages that are not fully insured will end up as a chargeback when the buyer opens a case. Making false and misleading statements on government forms, such as customs declaration documents, is illegal and could result in prosecution.

## THE BIG DEAL WITH MEDIA MAIL

If you sell media (books, music, movies, etc.), you should use USPS Media Mail, which is a highly discounted mailing service. Media Mail is limited to these goods:

- Books that have eight pages or more
- Blu-rays, DVDs, and CDs
- Other printed materials such as play scripts, book manuscripts, periodicals, and sheet music
- Computer software
- Guides or scripts prepared solely for use with computer software
- 16-millimeter and smaller films
- Test materials and scholastic test accessories
- Educational reference charts
- Medical information that's printed on loose-leaf pages and their binders, as long as they are distributed to doctors, hospitals, medical schools, and medical students

Media Mail is great when the product is cheap, but you should use a faster service for more expensive items because it is slow, and customer satisfaction is related to delivery speed. Use First-Class Mail for Blu-rays, DVDs, and CDs weighing four ounces or less for faster delivery.

There's another catch to Media Mail: the product can't contain advertising. Boxes could be opened for inspection, and if you're caught bending the rules, the package will either be delivered with postage due or returned to the sender. Either scenario would make for a very unhappy customer.

## INSURING YOUR SHIPMENTS

You may add a reasonable shipping and handling fee to cover packaging costs, freight, and optional insurance. Don't blindly buy insurance for every shipment. It's not always required, and on low-value items, it's not a good deal.

Consider this example: you ship 500 First-Class Mail or Media Mail parcels worth $25 each, and USPS charges $1.65 to insure each one, in addition to the cost of postage. That's $825 you've spent on insurance and passed the cost along to your customer. In my business, less than one in 500 shipments are lost or damaged. I add a very small handling fee that covers all refunds for these issues. Self-insuring 500 packages would save you $800, which you could retain as profit or pass back to your customers.

Priority Mail gives you $50 in automatic coverage, while UPS and FedEx cover $100 in losses on every parcel. And for Top Rated Sellers who ship at least 300 boxes a month, Priority Mail includes $100 in coverage when you print the label from your eBay account.

## RUSHING YOUR DELIVERY OPTIONS

Everyone expects everything to arrive yesterday. When I sell a diamond ring, I offer free overnight delivery because a proposal is usually imminent. Offering quick, free delivery is great for business.

You are required to indicate your handling time on the listing form. When you ship the day you're paid and upload tracking in a timely fashion, eBay registers an automatic five-star DSR for shipping time.

eBay displays a delivery estimate on every listing to inform buyers when they can expect to receive the product if they make a purchase. The estimate is calculated based on all other shipments traveling a similar distance using the same shipping method.

While most retailers are focusing on reducing the time it takes customers to receive their goodies, not all items have to get there yesterday. A smaller company such as yours doesn't benefit from the huge discounts the big guys enjoy. Savvy eBayers know that free shipping isn't free at all—you're just adding the freight cost into the price you charge. Some customers (e.g., collectibles buyers) don't want or need things fast; they're looking for a great deal on the things they love.

## HANDLING FRAGILE OR DELICATE ITEMS

Pack up delicate merchandise such as china, crystal, etc. immediately for shipping to avoid accidental damage. Don't allow employees to eat or drink while handling merchandise. Sooner or later, something will spill and ruin an expensive or rare item. I mentioned Sterilite products earlier, and they make very nice small plastic storage containers that I use to temporarily store fragile items until I pack them up for shipping.

Here are some more tips for packing delicate items for shipping:

- Wrap items separately, especially if they scratch easily. Direct contact of items within the parcel during shipment may cause unforeseen damage.
- Use enough packing and cushioning materials. Not too much, however. Big boxes cost more to send. All carriers have size limits, and some charge what's called dimensional weight (aka volumetric weight or DIM weight), which means you're billed for the size of the box as well as its weight.
- Double-box the fragile stuff and add cushioning around the inner box of at least 2 inches on all sides.
- Use strong boxes. If you like to reuse boxes, toss any that are beat up.
- Cover or cross off previous labels.
- Buy quality clear shipping tape. Cheap tape will come undone in warm or wet weather.
- Place a packing slip or invoice inside the box in case the outer shipping label falls off to prevent it from being lost.

However, we all eventually suffer a broken Baccarat or a mashed Fender Stratocaster. What do you do when an item gets lost or arrives damaged?

## COPING WITH LOSS AND DAMAGE

You'll occasionally have to deal with losses, whether a parcel goes completely missing or the contents are damaged. Expert packing will avert most disasters plus you should assume that every shipment will be tossed about and handled roughly (Figure 13–2 on page 267). There are two very important facts to remember:

1. eBay will always resolve a dispute relating to a missing or damaged package in favor of the buyer, which is what is promised by the Money Back Guarantee.
2. The buyer can leave unfavorable feedback in connection with the transaction that will result in lost sales if other prospective buyers are discouraged from purchasing through you.

eBay customer service reps don't necessarily have experience selling on eBay and their experience with shipping carriers and claims may not be extensive. eBay support

**FIGURE 13–2.** This image was provided by a customer of mine who opened an eBay Money Back Guarantee case. I have no idea how USPS managed to mangle this package that contained a vintage music CD. The contents were destroyed. I self-insured it and refunded the customer promptly. I sent the image to the USPS district manager.

will respond to a loss or damage Money Back Guarantee case by issuing your customer a refund and collecting that money from you.

Here are my tips for how to deal with these unfortunate situations:

- Be prepared because at some point you will cope with a missing or damaged shipment and you'll want to understand how each carrier handles those situations.
- Engage with your customer the moment they open a case or you discover that something's wrong. Put yourself in their shoes and imagine how you would want to be treated. Offer an apology even if the issue is beyond your control, for example if they are the victim of mailbox or porch theft.

■ Remain professional and calm while offering solutions. If you have more of the same item and if you consider the value low, then offer to ship a replacement.

■ If an item arrives damaged, ask for photos for proof and then issue a prompt refund. Do not wait until you are reimbursed by insurance to do so. That will upset most people. You are the person who deals with filing and handling a loss or damage insurance claim.

■ When you've made a mistake, such as packing poorly, you may just have to take a loss. Look at the long-term, bigger picture; your reputation as a seller is more important than one transaction.

## PROTECTING YOURSELF FROM BUYER DISPUTES

If a dishonest buyer falsely claims the product was not as described and opens a case, eBay will reimburse you up to $6 per return shipping label if you report them. eBay is the judge and jury in these situations, so have proof such as video or photos to back up your position. If eBay decides in your favor, it will remove negative and neutral feedback, defects, and open cases in your profile metrics when these dishonest people pop up.

Any item used or damaged by a customer that is then returned also requires some backup proof. You can deduct up to 50 percent from the refund to cover the lost value of the item before you open a case, or eBay will work directly with the buyer to resolve any issues relating to the return and mend any nasty feedback you suffered when the buyer wronged you.

I consider scams the virtual version of shoplifting. If you're on eBay long enough, someone will try to scam you. It's the reality of owning a business. Return fraud affects all mail-order businesses, and with an internet-only business, at least you don't have to cope with shoplifters. When this happens, eBay will usually help you. The most common shipping-related scam is for the buyer to claim they never received the item, which is why you must have tracking, unless the item cost is so low you can simply send another one. As far as eBay is concerned, if you can prove delivery, you will win.

Report buyers to eBay in the following circumstances:

■ If they demand something not offered in the original listing

■ If they make false claims, such as stating the product didn't arrive when it did or claiming it wasn't as described in order to return the item when the seller isn't offering free returns

■ If they misuse returns, such as sending back a different item, using or damaging and then returning the product, or falsely claiming it was not as described

■ If they bid for any reason other than to buy the product, such as bidding up the price to prevent others from bidding and then later retracting their bids

■ If they open excessive eBay Money Back Guarantee requests or abuse the eBay feedback system to harass a seller

Report problem buyers by following these steps:

1. Click Help & Contact at the top of the homepage or most eBay pages.
2. Type "report" into the search box.
3. Select the link entitled *Report an issue with a buyer*.
4. Review the eBay recommendations for when to report a buyer.
5. If you are confident that the buyer has engaged in prohibited behavior, click "Report a buyer" and follow the instructions.

## PREVENTING SHIPPING ERRORS AND MISHAPS

When it occurred, you didn't give it a second thought. You were so excited to sell your mint 1989 Sony Walkman that you didn't question the buyer asking you to change the shipping address—after all, $1,200 is a lot of money. You packed well and agreed to the signature waiver. "I'm traveling and will be out enjoying my vacation, so could you waive the signature since I'm not at my vacation home most of the day?" he wrote.

Then it happened. The dreaded case was opened. The account was taken over by a fraudster who just fleeced you. Had you followed the rules and shipped to the address on the order confirmation page, with a signature required (on orders $750 and higher), you would have been covered by eBay's seller protections.

Follow the rules. Ship only to the address on the order. If a customer makes an error on the shipping address and it's a $5 pack of temporary tattoos, then sure, send it out to the new address. If you can't eat the loss, then inform the buyer you'll cancel the order and relist it so they can buy it again and enter the correct address. If they balk, they very well could be a scammer and you should ask eBay for an opinion before proceeding. If you sold something tangible (not digital or downloadable), and you shipped to the address on the order details page (and got a signature if required), you'll be covered in the event of a dispute. Never use a buyer-supplied shipping label. You must be able to provide valid proof of shipping and delivery if a case is opened later.

# Chapter 14

# The Back Office

Dealing with all the behind the curtain operations of a business may not be fun for everyone. I am used to all the back-office requirements of my eBay business because I've been coping with it since 1999. It's like all chores, you get accustomed to doing them and resign yourself. No one would listen to me complain anyway! In this chapter, I'll cover some of the most important back-office topics, including business legal structures, managing the paperwork, and tax considerations.

## SELECTING YOUR LEGAL STRUCTURE

Remember that I am neither an attorney nor a tax professional, so verify all legal and tax decisions with a licensed professional. Let's take a look at various legal structures that businesspeople use to operate a company. If your aunt is a CPA or your brother-in-law is a tax attorney, you can skip this section and bend their ear over lunch. (Just be sure to pick up the tab.) Otherwise, please read on.

- *Sole proprietorship.* This is the most common business structure for someone starting in business. You'll be considered a sole proprietorship if you don't register any other form of business entity. You can use your existing bank account, and eBay will move your sales proceeds via ACH into your personal bank account. If you're just an itty-bitty homebased casual eBay seller, you'll be a sole proprietorship.
- *Partnership.* This is the simplest way for two or more people to own a business together. Partnerships are a good way to manage a business when you aren't the only owner and you'd like to test things out before advancing to a more formal business structure.
- *Limited liability company (LLC).* This protects you from liability in most situations in the event of lawsuits or business failures. LLCs are not very common in eBay businesses.
- *Corporation.* This is a legal entity that is separate from its owners. Most corporations issue stock, are taxed separately, and can be held legally liable for the corporation's actions while shielding the stockholders and management from lawsuits in most situations. There are different flavors of corporations. For example, I run an S corporation, which is a special type of legal structure that avoids double taxation because all income flows to me personally while still affording me legal protections. Consider another book from Entrepreneur Press, *Ultimate Guide to Incorporating in Any State.*

## MANAGING THE PAPERWORK

As with all business endeavors, making eBay deals requires that thing most of us dread—paperwork. I stay on top of my eBay business through planning and organizing. Many people have told me I'm the most organized person they know, but that wasn't always the case. Here's a quick rundown on the records I suggest you keep:

- *Customer and eBay emails.* Hold on to these until the returns grace period expires. If you're working out some issue with a customer, then keep them for 90 days after you resolve that issue. While an IRS auditor might one day come knocking on your door, what you need to know from the income side of things is stored safely on eBay's servers. However, eBay doesn't track your cost of goods or expenses, so you must keep those records yourself (see the next section for more on that).

- *Shipping records and proof of insurance.* Keep these until you receive positive buyer feedback or until sufficient time has passed that it is unlikely anything went awry. Once positive feedback is received, I shred these records immediately. If no feedback arrives, I keep them for 90 days before disposing of them.
- *Purchase records.* Just how much record keeping you'll need to maintain in fulfilling your eBay sales depends on whether you are a casual seller, a hobbyist, or a business seller. Ask your tax professional for guidance. Keep purchase records for items you resell because the profit is the difference between what you sold it for and what you paid. Losses are deductible against your profits. You may not think it matters much now, but once your income starts to rise, you'll want to claim every deduction you can. So save your purchase receipts, because deductions are the best cure for big tax bills.

## PREPARING FOR TAX DAY

You're not always on the hook for taxes when selling things online. Here's what the IRS says, "Income resulting from auctions akin to an occasional garage or yard sale is generally not required to be reported. However . . . [if] an online garage sale turns into a business with recurring sales and purchasing of items for resale, it may be considered an online auction business." While I wasn't able to find a magic number that the tax collector uses to define the transition from virtual yard sale to a taxable business, eBay will formally report all eBay sales in excess of $20,000 if you had more than 200 payment transactions within the year.

But once you make your eBay fortune, it's time to pay Uncle Sam. For the little guy, I recommend using a simple accounting system. If you are still using a checking account, try a One-Write system. This accounting tool allows you to combine check writing and record keeping in one step. If you pay all your bills online, you can lean on Excel to organize your finances and transition to accounting software, such as Quicken or QuickBooks, when you and your accountant feel the time is right. Keep your business and personal finances separate from each other so that when tax time arrives, your CPA

> **TIP**
>
> Uncle Sam generally doesn't require a physical receipt for deductible business expenses under $75. But you must still keep good records of these expenses, which could be as simple as maintaining a spreadsheet. I use my phone to snap pictures of these receipts, upload them into Google Drive, and have subfolders for each year.

isn't hiring an army of bookkeepers to clean everything up. I recommend separate bank accounts even when you're operating a sole proprietorship and you're running a business, as opposed to occasional eBay selling.

For most businesses, even sole proprietorships, it pays to computerize. Get your accounting organized early or suffer extreme pain later. Trust me: I've made plenty of rookie accounting mistakes. The IRS requires a unique tax return form for each business entity type mentioned above. Sole proprietors use Form 1040-C. For other legal structures, an entirely separate return is required in addition to your personal return. Our tax system is honor-based, and while your friends might boast about not reporting cash tips or pocketing all their garage sale loot, every dollar of business profit is reportable. The IRS offers free tax advice: call (800) 829-1040 for individuals and (800) 829-4933 for businesses.

If eBay is your only business, tracking income is a breeze. Simply keep a separate bank account for your business and use gross receipts to determine income. If you don't deduct all legitimate business expenses (postage, packing supplies, rent, utilities, office supplies, etc.), you'll end up paying taxes on all your income. That would be unnecessary—you can deduct business expenses and the cost of what you sold (known as COGS, or the cost of goods sold).

I use QuickBooks to organize my business and personal finances. Some misguided accountants encourage their clients to track endless expense categories, but it doesn't need to be that complicated. Go to the Expenses section of your IRS business tax form and work backward from there. There's a surprisingly small number of expense categories to keep tabs on, and QuickBooks or any other good accounting software will have the same expense categories on the chart of accounts. Track your income and expenses in real time to avoid stress at tax time.

If you're a business newbie, these are the most frequent rookie accounting mistakes:

- Overthinking and overcomplicating income and expense tracking
- Hiring expensive lawyers and tax professionals to provide advice the government gives out freely
- Over-reporting or underreporting income

> **TIP**
>
> While eBay is legally required to collect state and local sales taxes in many jurisdictions, some sellers must still collect and remit sales tax on their own. Check with eBay and the appropriate agency in your state to see what's required. Ask a tax professional to point you in the right direction. I believe eBay will soon be collecting 100 percent of sales taxes across the U.S. as more local governments realize it's easier if eBay does the bean counting.

- Failing to separate business and personal expenses
- Missing out on deductions
- Treating an employee as an independent contractor
- Filing and paying taxes late (ask your accountant or the IRS about quarterly estimated tax payments)

By this point in my life, I have filed quite a few tax returns. You may not fully appreciate the time savings of preparing quarterly or monthly P&L statements, but start looking at this now. A well-organized plan means you can hand your tax preparer your P&Ls, and they shouldn't require much more than that to get going.

## PAYING STATE TAXES

Some states do not charge residents a personal income tax—unfortunately, my home state of California is not one of them. Tax preparation software is so good that it can accurately and rapidly generate federal and state returns simultaneously, but when my taxes are high enough to cause sleepless nights, I ask for a second opinion.

Figure 14–1 below will launch eBay's page that explains claiming tax-exempt status.

**FIGURE 14–1.** Scan this QR code to access eBay's page on tax exemption. You can fill out and upload the forms found there to claim tax-exempt status when making purchases for resale.

While a 1099-K sounds like a vitamin shot, it's the important tax form that eBay sends to you and the IRS every year to report your total eBay income if your annual gross payments exceeded $20,000 and you had more than 200 transactions. All business income needs to be reported, but eBay only notifies the IRS if you meet these requirements. Accidentally threw away the 1099-K form thinking it was junk mail? You can always secure a copy from the IRS. Request one by visiting https://www.irs.gov/individuals/get-transcript.

I'd like to close this chapter by reminding you to enjoy life—including your business life—by using the KISS principle ("keep it simple, stupid"). Question everything you do and eliminate everything you don't need to do—that goes especially for the back office. KISS the needless work goodbye so you can focus on making money, not generating endless accounting reports.

# Chapter 15

# Scaling It Up

There is a pot of gold at the end of the eBay rainbow. My eBay business has generated millions of dollars and continues to reap consistent rewards. Entrepreneur Press never publishes get rich quick books—and I never evangelize overnight success. Success is the product of smart, hard work and requires persistence and stick-to-itiveness. Let's use this final chapter to explore how you can scale things up to big time status.

## GROWING BEYOND THE BEDROOM OR BASEMENT

How do you handle growing pains? Proceed with extreme caution. Expand too quickly, and your eBay business will collapse on itself because you'll be unable to manage the growth. Maintain a high standard for your customers' experiences. At the same time, if you grow too carefully, you may be missing out on valuable opportunities. Keep your focus on the customer and work backward. If trends tell you that a product is selling at a steady clip and the future looks bright, go deep on inventory. Test endlessly and keep adding steady winners. Dump zombie products as quickly as you acquire good ones.

Before adding storage space or a warehouse, look at scalable rental space. When your business is still small, working out of a garage or home office and using an à la carte warehouse or a 3PL vendor will lessen the anxiety of setting up your own facility as you expand. Flexible warehouse and personal storage allow for a long engagement before you get married to a particular location. Contact the local chamber of commerce or look online for business locations that offer complete turnkey warehouse solutions. If you can delegate the pick, pack, and ship process, all the better. This works well at scale but not so well for unique items such as antiques.

I have always advised businesspeople to live and work in the same community. Time is our most precious commodity and a long daily commute is foolish, yet millions of people keep making this mistake. Don't be one of them. When exploring business locations (warehouse, office, etc.), keep these five points at the top of your mind:

1. Stay as close to home as possible.
2. Make sure the space will meet your needs for at least the next three to five years.
3. Confirm easy access to shipping carriers.
4. Make certain there are workers nearby who are eager to work for the wage rates that your business can offer.
5. Scrutinize startup and ongoing costs such as leasehold improvements, utilities, and maintenance.

Temporary and scalable contract storage is probably ideal until your sales are steady and predictable. Setting up your own shop is expensive, and the initial outlay may include:

- Security deposit and first and possibly last month's rent, if you're leasing
- Business formation costs such as incorporation fees
- Licensing fees
- Exterior building signage
- Furniture and fixtures
- Office supplies
- Warehouse equipment such as shelving, bins, forklift, etc.
- Insurance
- Website setup

- Computers and software or cloud licenses
- Marketing
- Payroll to cover launch and continued operations until you become profitable
- Inventory

Here's another tip: be easy to work with. A prospective property owner will feel at ease when you enrich their day by smiling and being positive. A first impression happens in a flash, but the memory of it lasts forever. Your friendly nature will score you better lease terms and favorable opportunities with building owners, improvement contractors, vendors, and customers. As your eBay business expands, your smile will improve every relationship, and opportunity will float to the top like cream.

## EXPANDING YOUR TEAM AS YOUR BUSINESS GROWS

A business owner is a superhero. You're juggling daily life, family duties, chores at home, social obligations, and, of course, your company—possibly even a day job. Initially, you're wearing every hat. But as your business grows, like Superman, eventually you'll need to venture out of the Fortress of Solitude and become an employer.

Before you post that first help wanted ad, take a close look at your workday. Do you engage in tasks that provide zero value to your business? Take a week, a month, or even longer to scrutinize your routines and eliminate unnecessary work immediately. Are you printing extra copies of your orders and keeping them in a file to collect dust? Do you have your phone set up to alert you when you get messages on your personal social media accounts? Are you answering personal calls during work hours? Are you surfing the web endlessly, lured in by headlines and ads? Are you piling papers instead of shredding them? Are you stymied by indecision (yes, decision-making is a task)? Online advice columnist Brandy Jensen claims that 20 minutes is the perfect amount of time to spend on any task—"the Goldilocks number when it comes to doing things." I agree with her.

A-players put their professional lives first and focus on what matters most. Once you have stopped updating your social media status multiple times a day and eliminated unnecessary tasks, often your business will take off. But if you've become a model of efficiency and laser focus but still see signs that you need help, then it's time to start growing your team.

You need to hire help when:

- Customer messages are receiving slow responses or no replies at all.
- Your feedback is taking hits because customer service problems are not being handled quickly enough.
- Order shipping is delayed, and you're struggling to meet order handling times.

- It takes you weeks or months to list the backlog of inventory you've purchased.
- Your family and friends complain you're spending too much time working.
- You've lost the joy and inspiration that brought you to self-employment in the first place.
- You're seriously contemplating quitting even though sales are great.
- You can't recall if you've completed an important task or met a critical deadline.

For many people, the thought of hiring an employee seems daunting. The mere mention of payroll taxes and all that legal stuff is enough to discourage them. But don't stress because it isn't that hard to hire.

So how do you get the word out that you're hiring? Mastering the hiring process takes practice. It's critical to keep an eye out for talented people everywhere you go. Selling on eBay is not difficult, and a sharp learner will pick it up quickly. Spread the word to family and friends. Consider new job seekers—that is, applicants without prior job experience. Avoid job hoppers—something that's easy to spot on resumes. Also avoid workers with long gaps of unemployment as well as short employment sprints.

You can post ads on job sites, promote your jobs on social media, and post notices on community bulletin boards. Mention your job openings at every opportunity. Everyone knows someone who is looking for a job. Students and seniors are both great candidates, because they are more likely to be interested in part-time positions, which is great for eBay work. What makes your job more attractive than most is that it's completely flexible. As long as the work gets done, you can do it at any time of the day. Students appreciate evening jobs, and you'll be more than happy to accommodate flexibility in working hours and days. Seniors also often want to work and stay active while bringing years of experience and wisdom to the job. You'll also find that shorter, more intense work shifts are far more attractive to employees than long, boring ones.

## CREATING A DREAM TEAM

If you work entirely by yourself, having another person around who is an asset to your business will brighten your day, relieve the pressure on you, and help you grow profits. A poorly screened, hastily selected worker won't. A demanding, drama-filled, unreliable employee is worse than having no employee at all. If you employ multiple people, one bad employee can drag down the entire team. Lazy people inspire laziness and spark resentment in others. High standards are contagious, just as low standards spread faster than a wildfire.

Your business must focus on outstanding customer service delivered with extreme alacrity. Employees must align with your goals, be vigilant, and maintain a steady sense of urgency. No one can give 100 percent every single day, but a dream team achieves stellar results, which is only possible when your team really clicks.

If you expect everyone to be a clone of you—forget it. That's never going to happen. Compelling team purpose requires a straightforward vision, clear responsibilities, and a positive team culture. Magic happens when employees enjoy their work, expectations are realistic, and they feel heard and supported. People complain about their bosses when they feel alienated or unheard. Here are some things all successful bosses do:

- Keep communication flowing
- Avoid the big boss attitude
- Develop a sense of teamwork and camaraderie
- Praise good work
- Provide honest feedback that never attacks the person
- Allow independent thought
- Give more responsibility
- Avoid being too rigid
- Allow for regular two-way feedback
- Promptly address employee complaints
- Pay people fairly and on time
- Never threaten someone with firing or use money to bend people to your will

As a successful leader, you recognize that people are independent human beings with emotions and personal lives. When you take these into consideration and show true care for your employees, not only will work relations improve, but your employees will also feel better about themselves and their work.

## WHAT TO DELEGATE

Avoid delegating anything that is boring, an emergency, vaguely defined, highly confidential, or in need of boatloads of planning. Delegating mindless tasks in particular is a surefire way to get your best and brightest employees heading out the door. Sellers of commodity items find it easy to hire employees to type up listings. Antique dealers find it very difficult to delegate this task because it requires specialized knowledge, but it's possible and easier to teach someone how to pack fragile valuables.

Presentation matters a lot in online retail. Dirty items and dark photos raise eyebrows and generate doubt in buyers, who wonder if it's dirt or damage. While it makes sense to delegate routine tasks such as cleaning and prepping merchandise, you should also offer your workers interesting tasks that they might enjoy and outsource jobs someone else might do better. Use the local tailor to mend a suit or the cobbler to shine up cowboy boots.

Let's circle back to the task of typing up listings. Adding users to your eBay account is a snap. Here are the steps to follow to add an authorized user:

1. Hover over My eBay at the top-right-hand corner of most eBay pages.
2. Click Summary.
3. Click Account.
4. Under the section Account Preferences, click Permissions.
5. Click Add User.
6. Enter the person's name and email.
7. Check the appropriate Permissions box(es) (Figure 15–1 below).
8. Click Add User.

Workers can create and edit drafts, which is the minimum permission you'd need for a person helping you list items. You can allow experienced workers who fully understand eBay's listing policies and restrictions the authority to publish and revise listings. With so much at stake for your business, newbies should be limited to creating and editing drafts that you later review and approve to ensure they comply with eBay

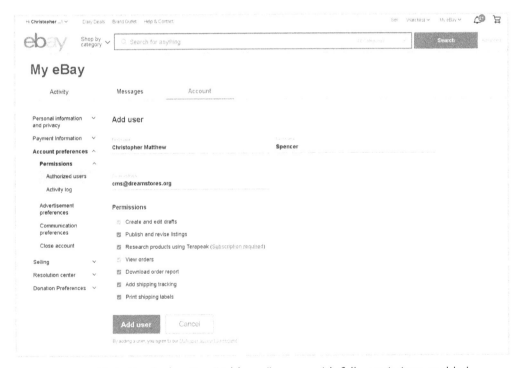

**FIGURE 15–1.** Here's the eBay "Add user" screen with full permissions enabled.

policies. As your helpers sharpen their skills, trusted workers can be allowed to go all the way and post items.

You can view the Activity Log on the Permissions page to see what your workers are doing. Instantly remove users when they should no longer have access.

Here are some jobs eBay sellers can delegate to employees:

- Merchandise sorting, cleaning, prepping
- Photography
- Item research*
- Listing*
- Customer service (answering emails or calls and handling issues that arise)*
- Packing and shipping
- Processing and restocking returns
- Bookkeeping*
- Marketing (promoting the business, making offers to watchers, launching eBay promotional campaigns, social media marketing, etc.)*

*These jobs can also be managed remotely by virtual assistants, who are independent contractors, without having to set up a payroll service.

## INDEPENDENCE DAY

You made it! It's Independence Day—for you. eBay is an idea whose time has come, and so has yours. eBay is a time-tested online marketplace that has propelled millions of entrepreneurs forward and helped so many people become millionaires. Now you have all the tools you need to leverage eBay to the fullest, whether you're sourcing, selling, or both. You can now achieve the success you've always wanted. You can realize the financial independence you've been dreaming of while you help other people. An eBay business involves creative, varied, exciting work on the very cutting edge of the internet and new technologies—what could be better? You can do it. I'm so certain of it that I'd like you to email me at borntodeal@gmail.com with your personal success story. I want to hear it, and maybe you'll see it in the next edition of this book—by that time, you'll be an old hand at all of this!

# About the Author

Christopher Matthew Spencer is a Burbank, California-based businessperson, author, and public speaker. He owns wholesale, retail, hospitality, real estate, and publishing companies. Experienced in the consulting field, he has worked for and advised businesses of different sizes, from startups to Fortune 100 companies. Christopher is an eight-year veteran of the U.S. Navy. He volunteers at least 10 percent of his time and donates at least 10 percent of his income to nonprofit causes and takes immense pride in helping entrepreneurs achieve their dreams and score big in business.

# Index

CPSIA information can be obtained
at www.ICGtesting.com
Printed in the USA
JSHW030018170921
18760JS00006B/8